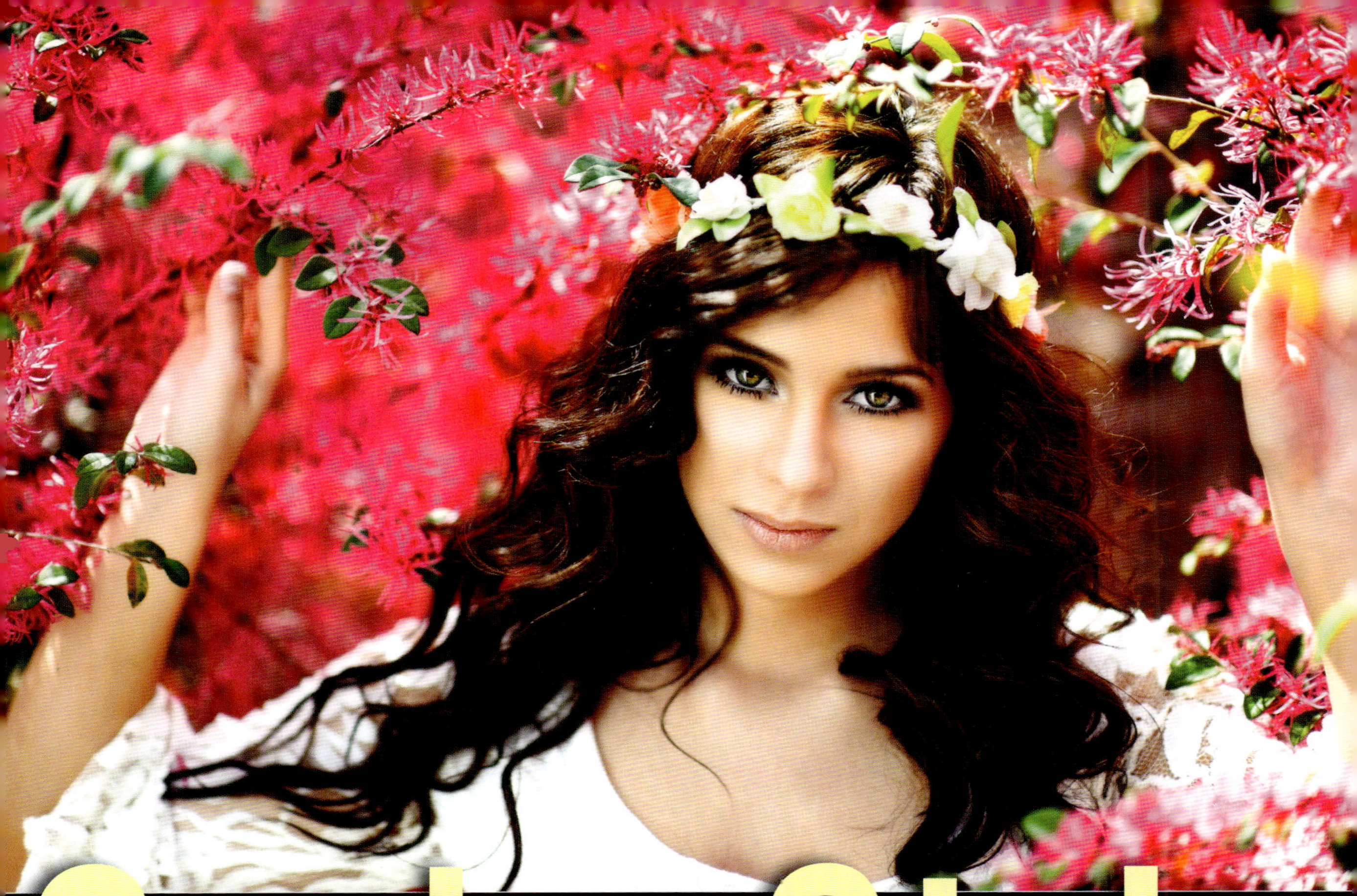

Senior Style

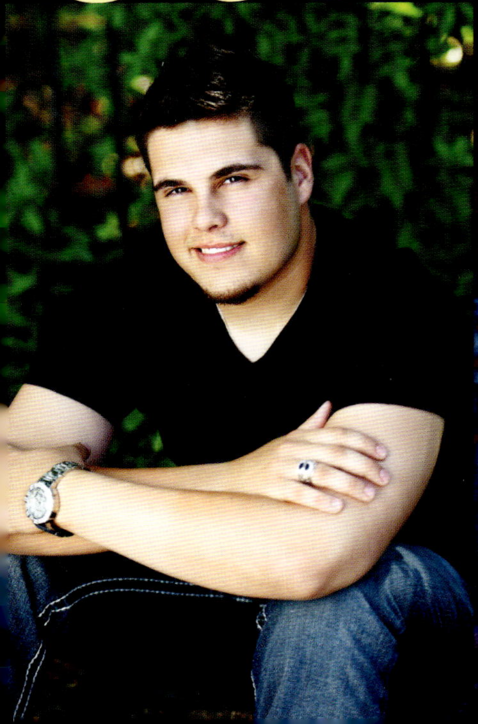

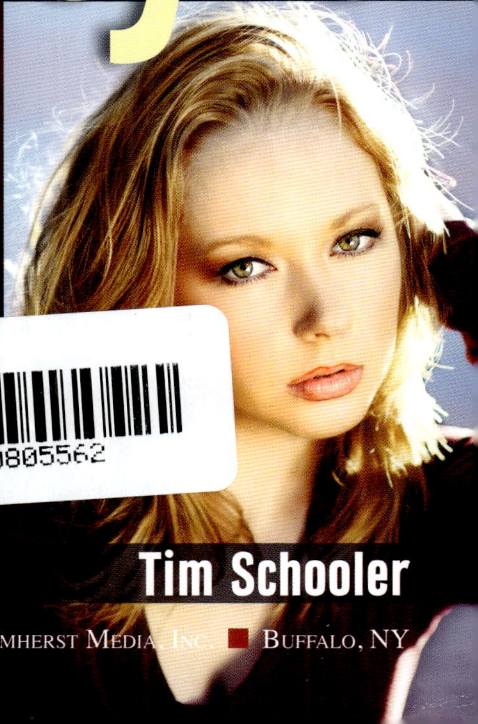

Tim Schooler

Amherst Media, Inc. ■ Buffalo, NY

About the Author

Tim Schooler is an award-winning, internationally published photographer specializing in senior, family and children, and maternity portraits. His images and techniques have been featured in *Rangefinder* and *Professional Photographer* magazines, as well as in numerous books, including *The Best of Senior Portrait Photography, 2nd Edition,* by Bill Hurter and *500 Poses for Photographing High School Seniors,* by Michelle Perkins. To learn more about Tim, visit www.timschooler.com.

Acknowledgments

Learning photography has been less a destination than a journey—from a hobby I was very passionate about to a full-time career. In that time, I have been inspired by many great photographers (Dean Collins, Monte Zucker, and Don Blair to name just a few). I studied their work and tried to learn as much as I could about what they did. I would like to personally thank a few people who helped me more than they know: Jonny, for letting me tag along on weddings, critiquing my work, and taking me with him to local guild meetings; and Stanton, who really taught me how to "see" light all around us. And definitely not least, I need to thank my wife for countless hours spent helping with the book and Michelle Perkins of Amherst Media. This book would not have happened without them. In an industry that is constantly changing and evolving, I still find myself learning new things and hope I never lose the desire to grow in my knowledge of the craft. If this book can in any small way help others who have the same love of photography, then I will consider it a success.

Published by:
Amherst Media, Inc.
P.O. Box 538
Buffalo, N.Y. 14213
www.AmherstMedia.com

Publisher: Craig Alesse
Senior Editor/Production Manager: Michelle Perkins
Associate Editor: Barbara A. Lynch-Johnt
Associate Publisher: Kate Neaverth
Assistant Editors: Beth Alesse, Harvey Goldstein
Editorial Assistance from: Sally Jarzab, Carey A. Miller
Business Manager: Adam Richards
Warehouse and Fulfillment Manager: Roger Singo

ISBN-13: 978-1-68203-020-2
Library of Congress Control Number: 2015953683
10 9 8 7 6 5 4 3 2 1

Contents

SECTION 1

Background and Basics

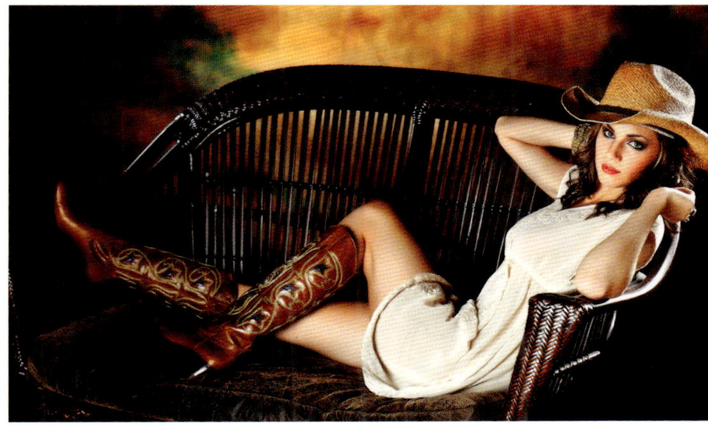

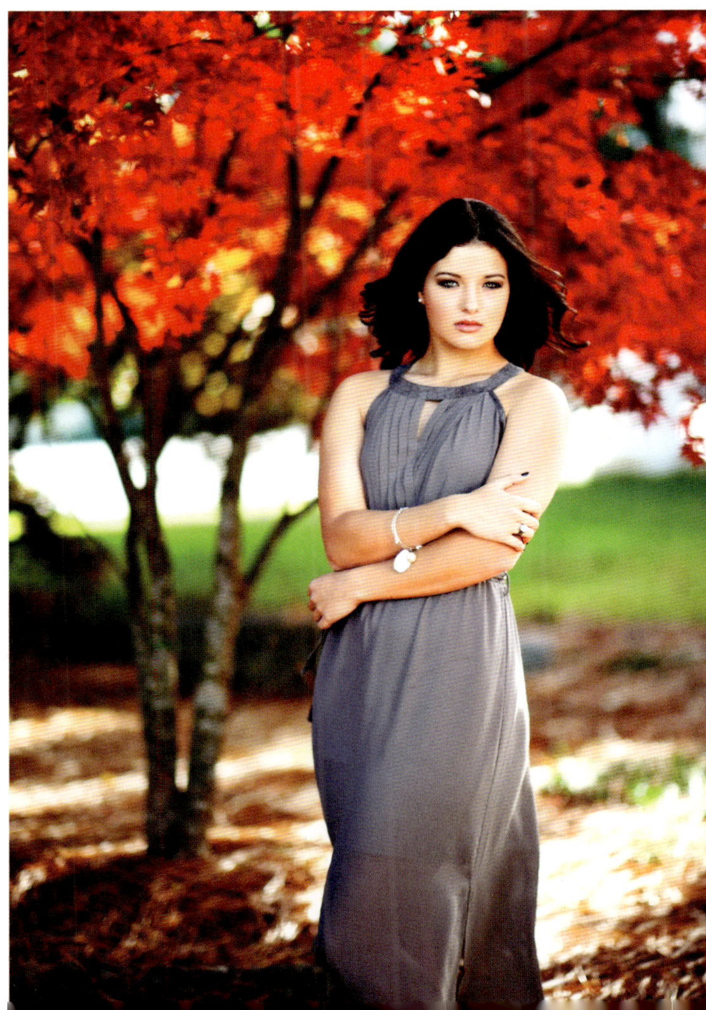

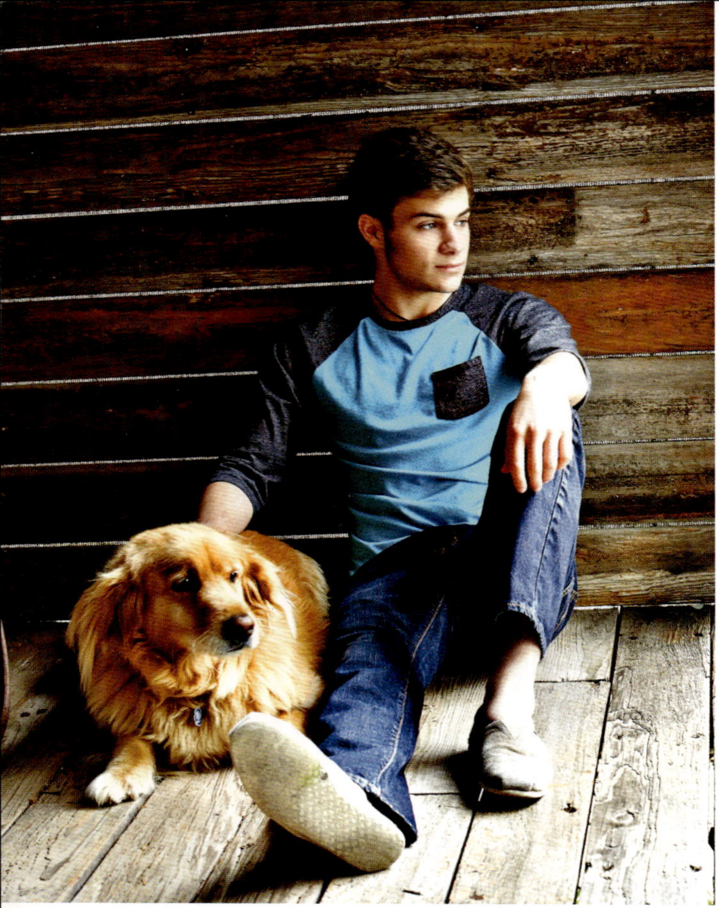

SECTION 2
Location Photography

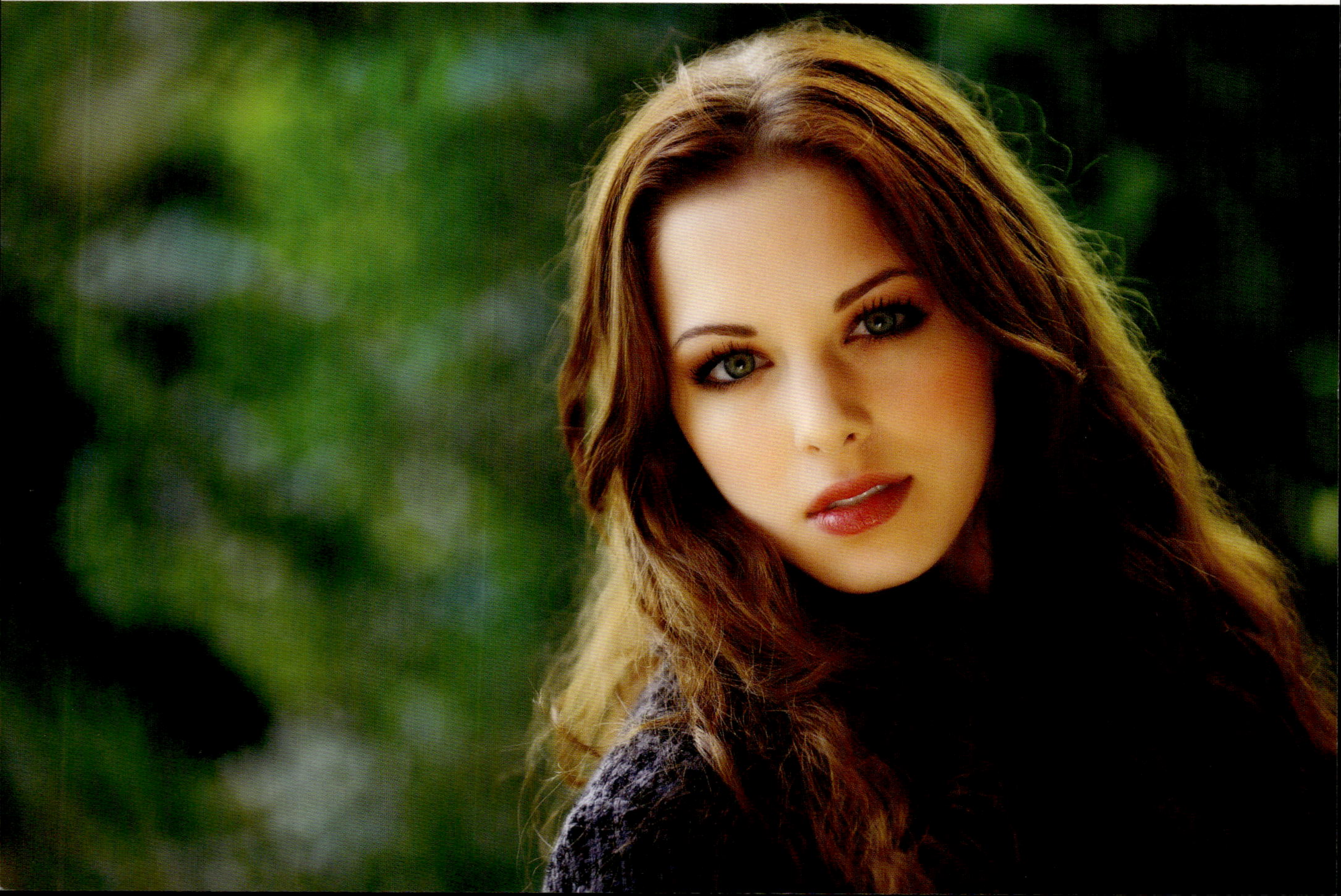

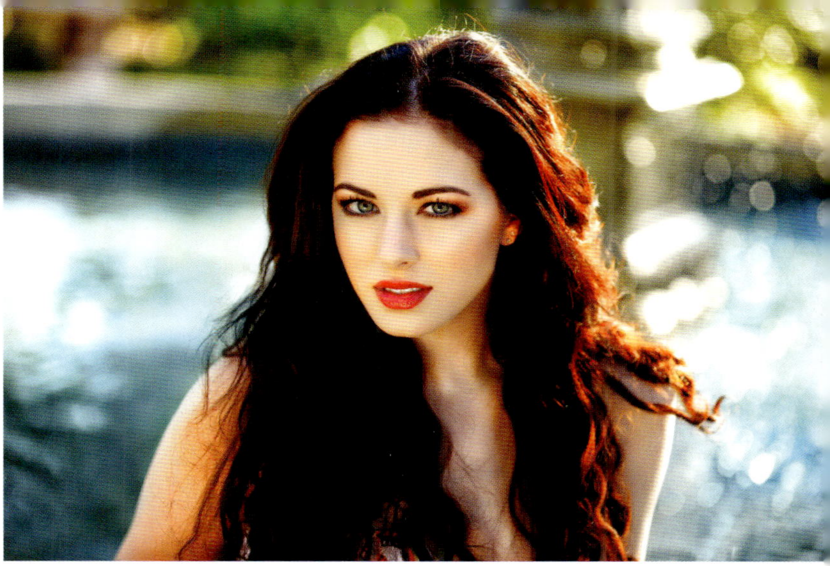

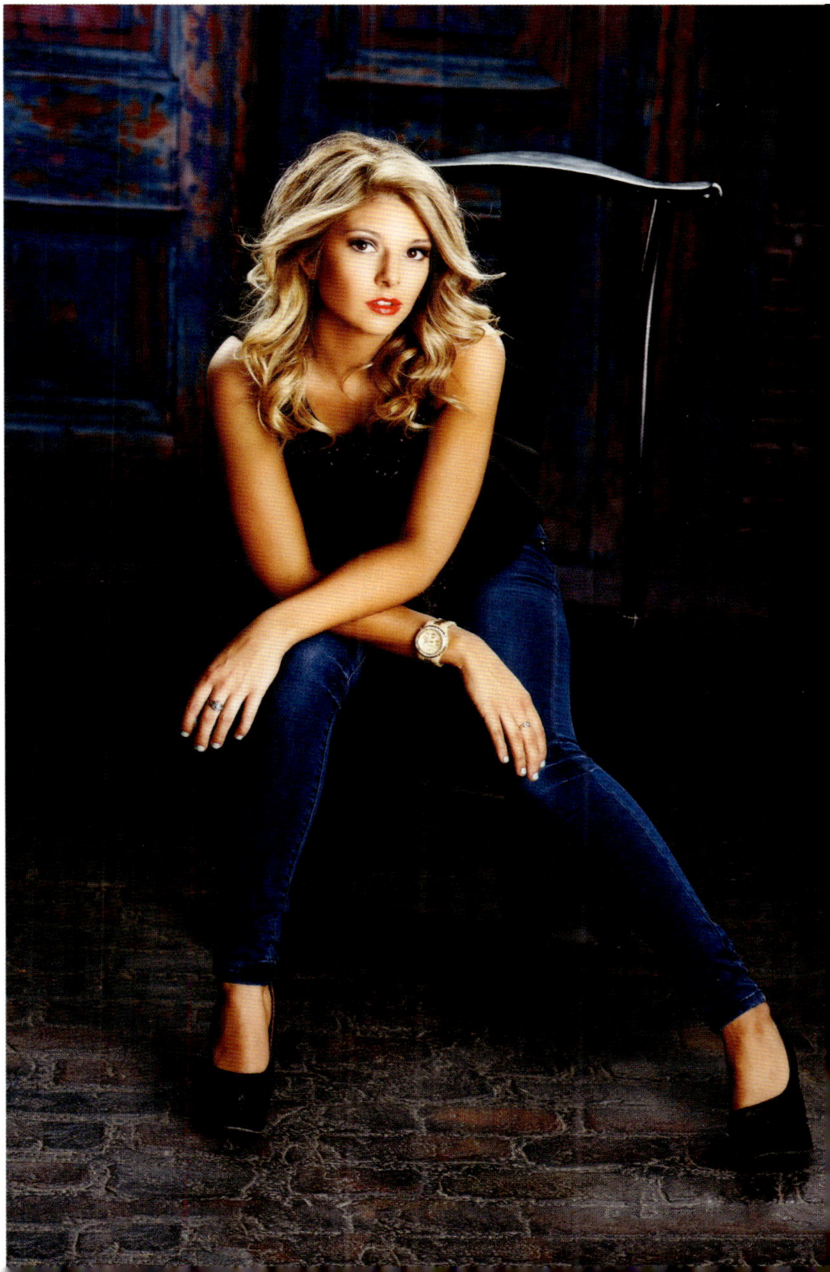

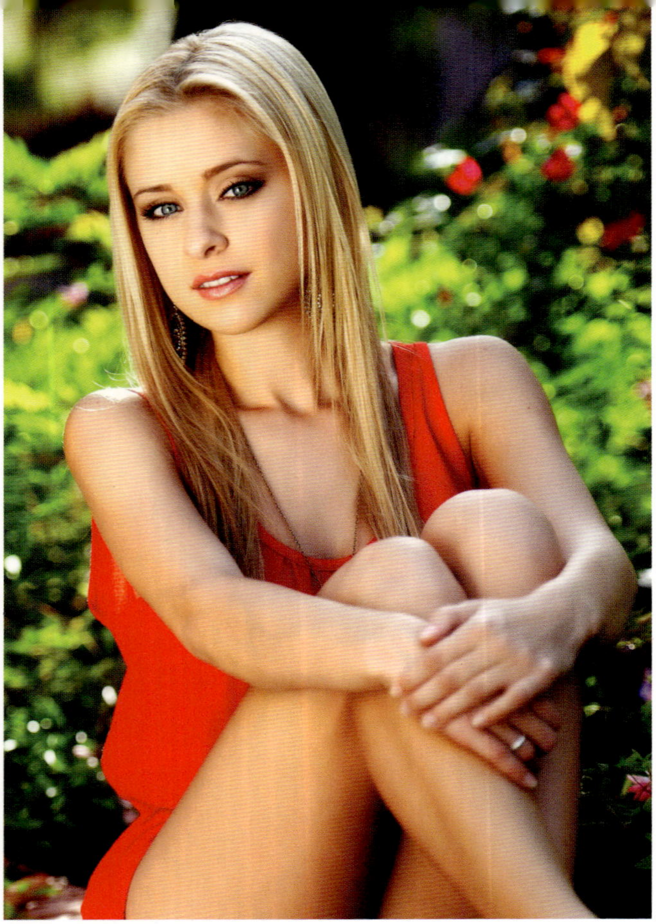

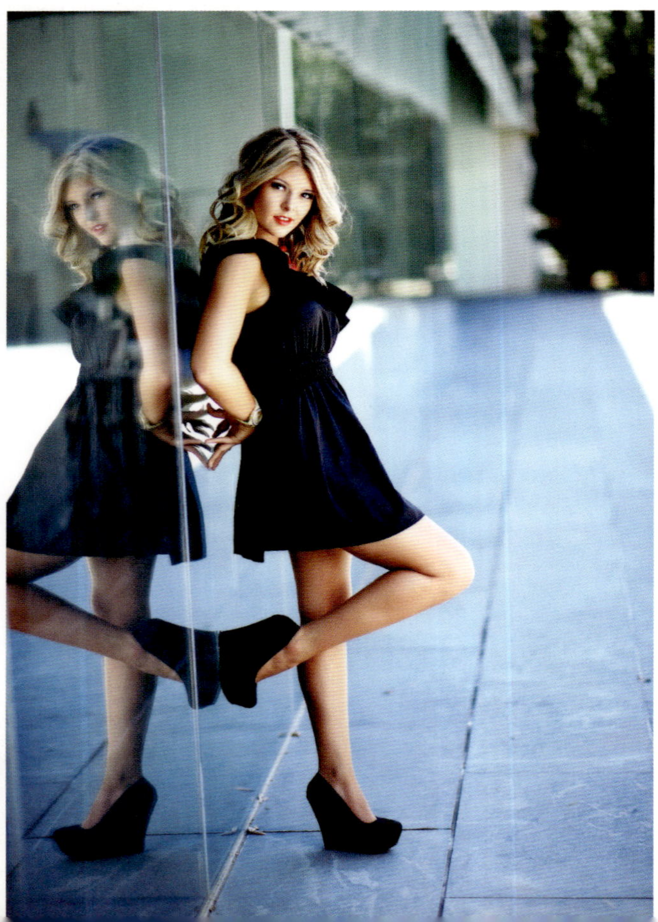

SECTION 3

Studio Photography

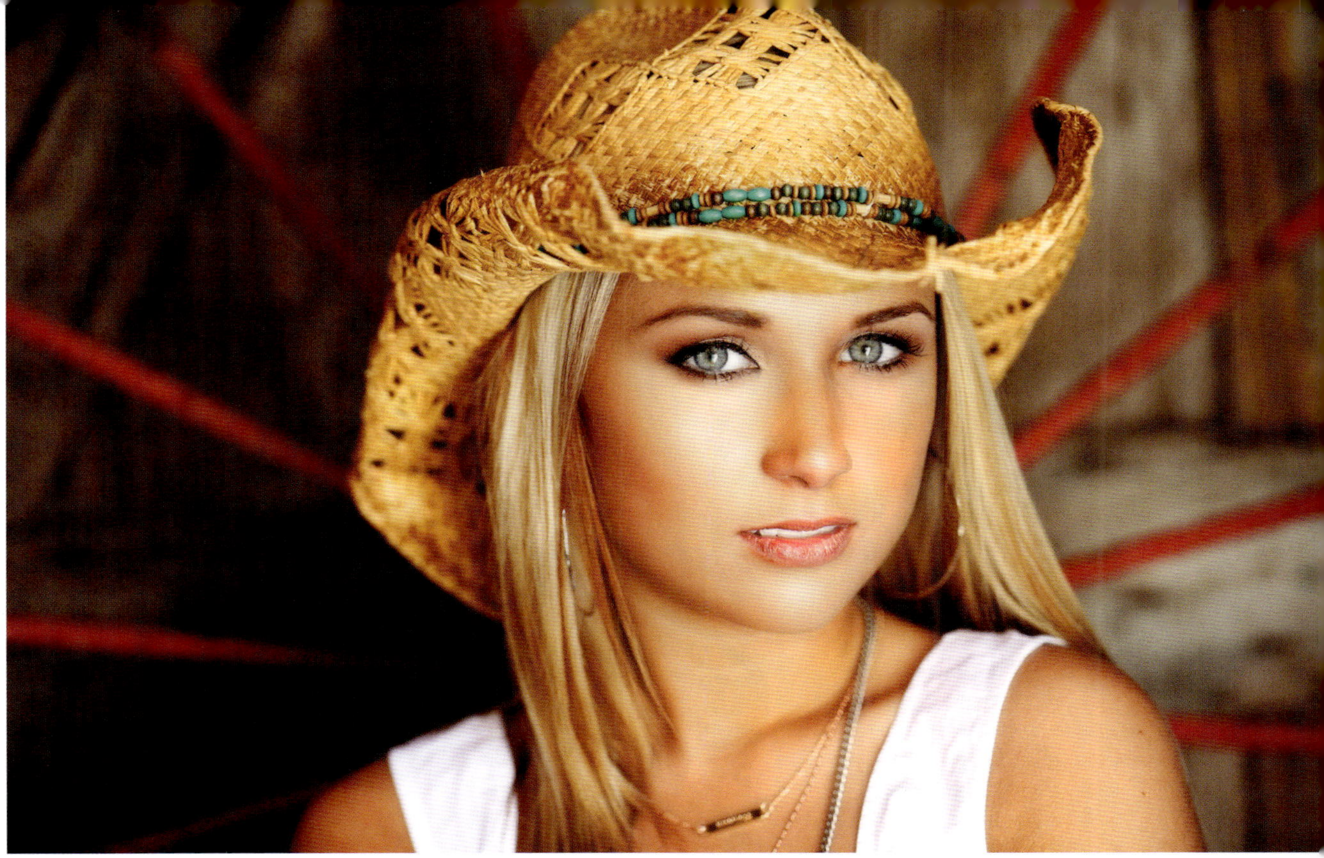

SECTION 4

After the Session

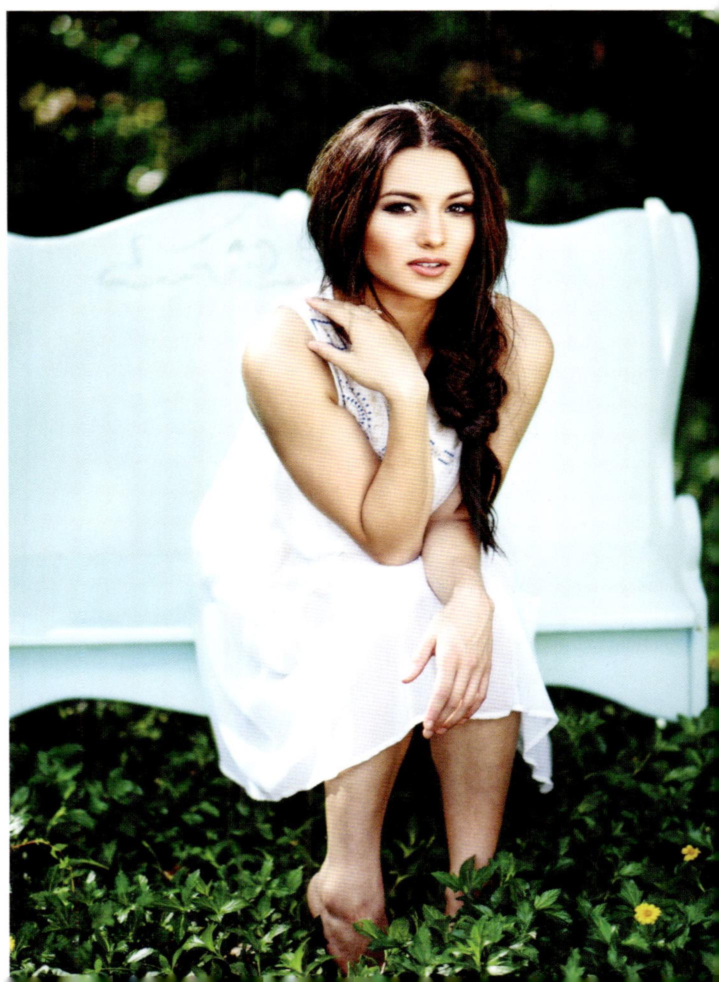

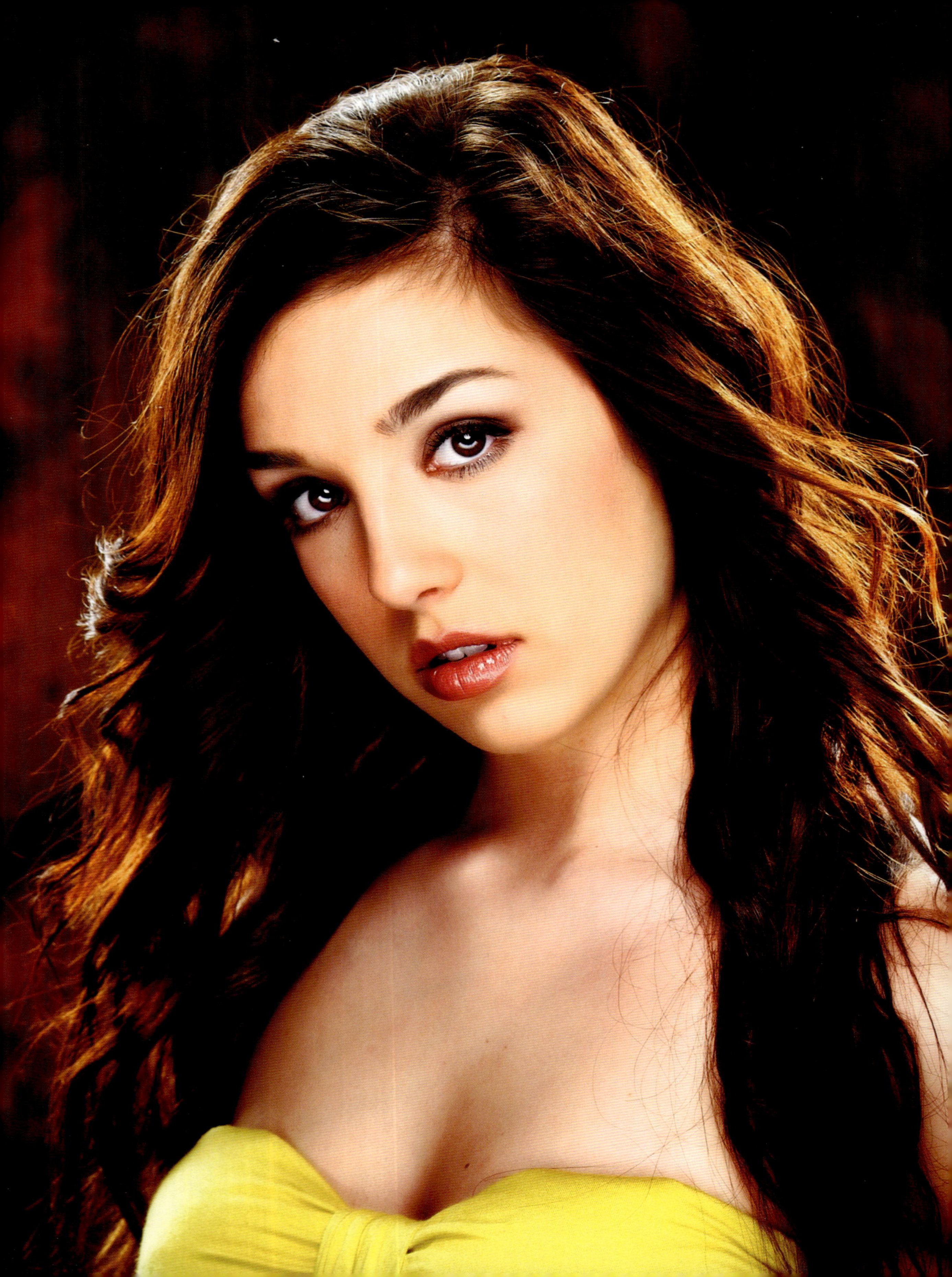

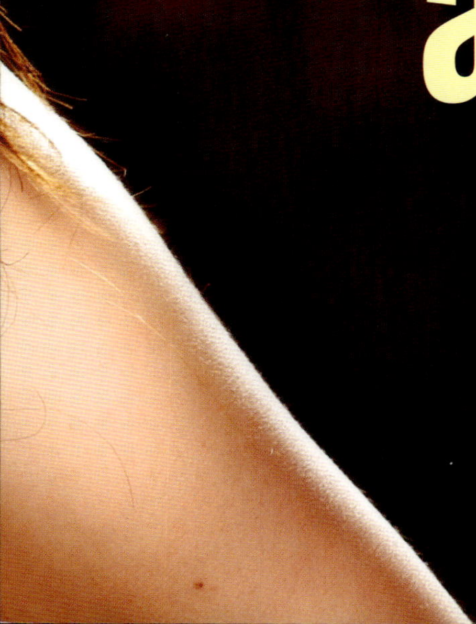

Background and Basics

Fundamental skills for creative and financial success in an ever-evolving industry—and how to set the stage for great images at each session.

1. Specialization or Diversification?

The Beginning

As I child, I always had an interest in photography. When I was ten, I got my first camera—a Polaroid black & white, and I loved taking pictures of all kinds of stuff.

Throughout the years, I continued doing photography as a hobby and made some modest forays into professional jobs by photographing a few sports teams. When I married and my own kids eventually started playing sports, I kept photographing, taking action shots of my kids and their teammates. Before long, people started asking for images of their kids—and I started to see how my hobby could actually grow into a profession.

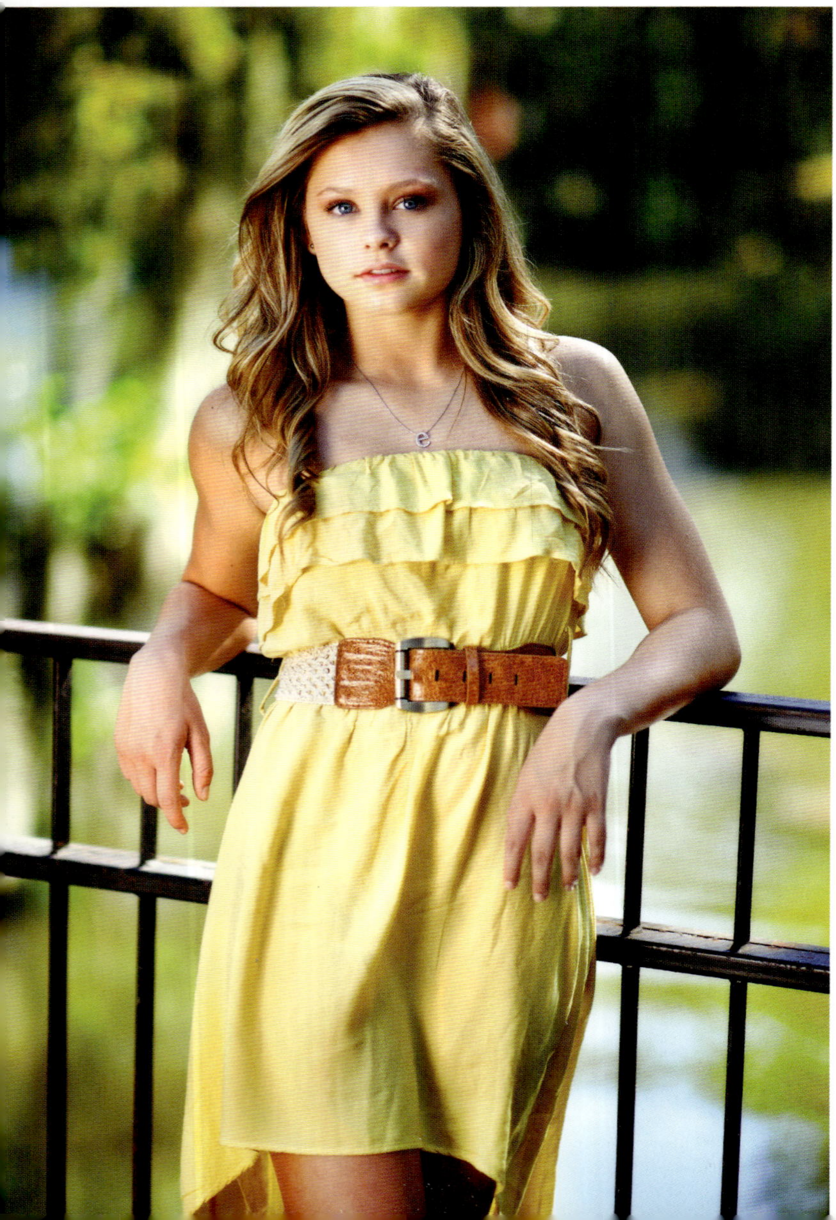

Learning

As I kept shooting for teams and families, I started educating myself—reading books, going to photo guild meetings, and absorbing everything I could about natural light, reflectors, and posing. (Keep in mind, this was before the Internet became what it is today—so I couldn't just go to YouTube!)

Specializing in Seniors

Through word of mouth, my business started growing. For three or four years, I enjoyed photographing weddings, as well as children and some families. In the 1990s, however, I started gravitating toward senior portraits. Photographing kids was wonderful—but, in those days of more posed images (as opposed to today's more relaxed lifestyle portraits), it was also very taxing. Seniors

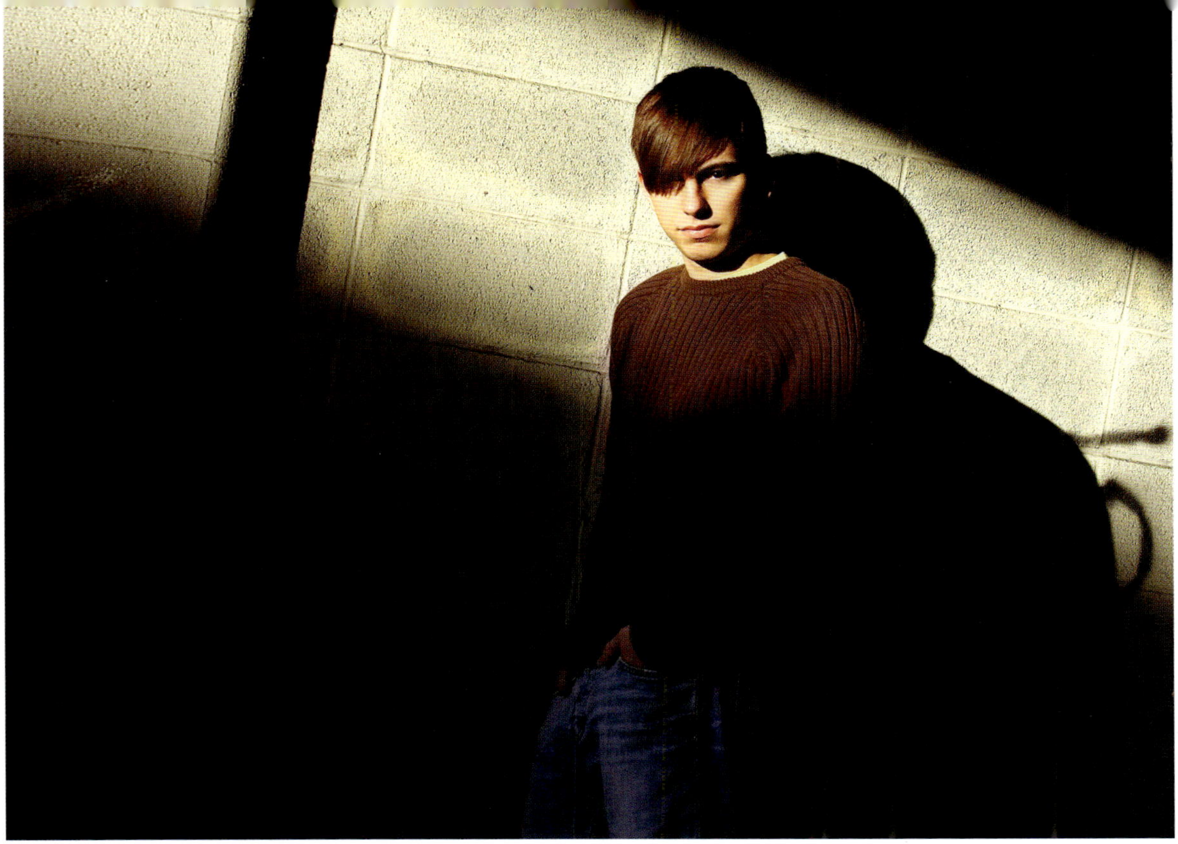

were just as fun and energetic to photograph—and *they wanted to be there!*

It wasn't long before I had a waiting list of seniors every year. I became almost exclusively a senior portrait photographer; the demand for those bookings squeezed everything else out.

Times Are Changing: Diversification

It's been quite a few years since then—and the world has changed. Now that my wife and I have seven grandchildren, photographing them has made me realize it's a segment of photography I have missed and actually enjoy. Additionally, digital cameras have made it easier to enter the industry on a part-time basis and diversification certainly does not hurt. Specialization is still an option, but in order to remain busy I think it's more important than ever to work on improving skills and being creative. Accordingly, I'm now headed back to photographing a more diverse clientele. I'm changing up my web site to show non-senior work (still keeping a prominent senior section) so prospective clients will know that, yes, I do more than senior portraits. Basically, I'm cycling back to what I started out doing: a little bit of everything.

In this book, however, I'm going to focus exclusively on senior portraits, which remain a strong and creative sector of the professional photography market. As you'll see, the lessons learned in this genre will also translate nicely to other areas of portraiture.

> "Senior portraits remain a strong and creative sector of the professional photography market."

2. Space and Staffing

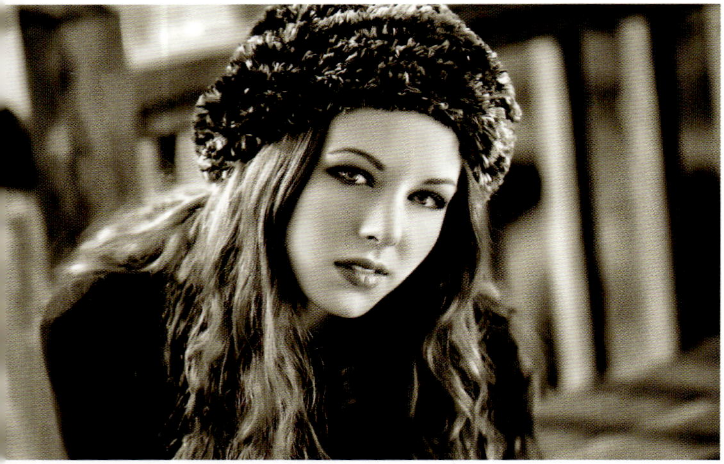

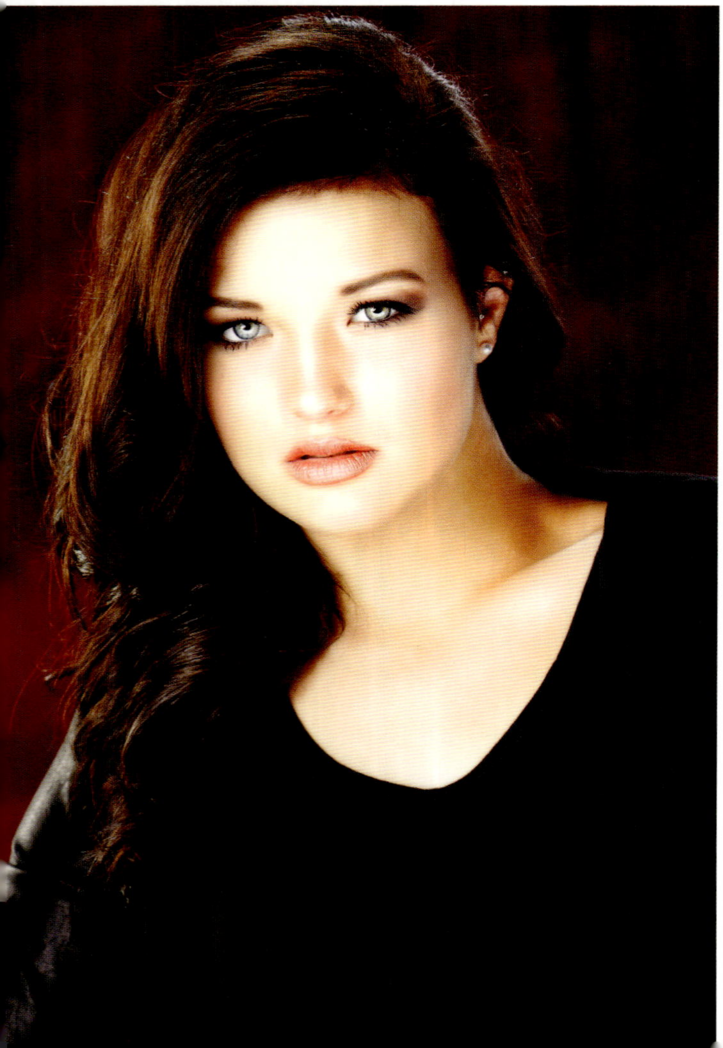

A Commercial Space

While many photographers today operate without a commercial space, we own a studio in downtown Lafayette, Louisiana—and we're planning to stay there. The studio gives us a professional place to meet with clients to plan their session, review their images, and take their orders (more on this in section 53).

Additionally, some types of photography simply lend themselves to studio shots. Most of our seniors arrive saying they only want outdoor images—and I love doing those; they're my specialty!—but there are things we can do in the studio that we can't do outside. As often as not, when seniors *do* opt for some studio images, those are among their favorites from the day.

Another reason that a studio space is important for us is that weather is a big issue in southern Louisiana; we get a lot of rain. It's nice to have a backup location—and we've installed a few areas behind the studio where we can do outdoor looks even on rainy days. Combined with a few nearby locations that offer shelter from bad weather, this lets us proceed (in most cases) without rescheduling the client's session.

Staff

Most of the year, the studio staff consists of myself and my wife. During peak senior-portrait season, I sometimes bring on a part-time employee to assist with scheduling and running the preview sessions with our clients.

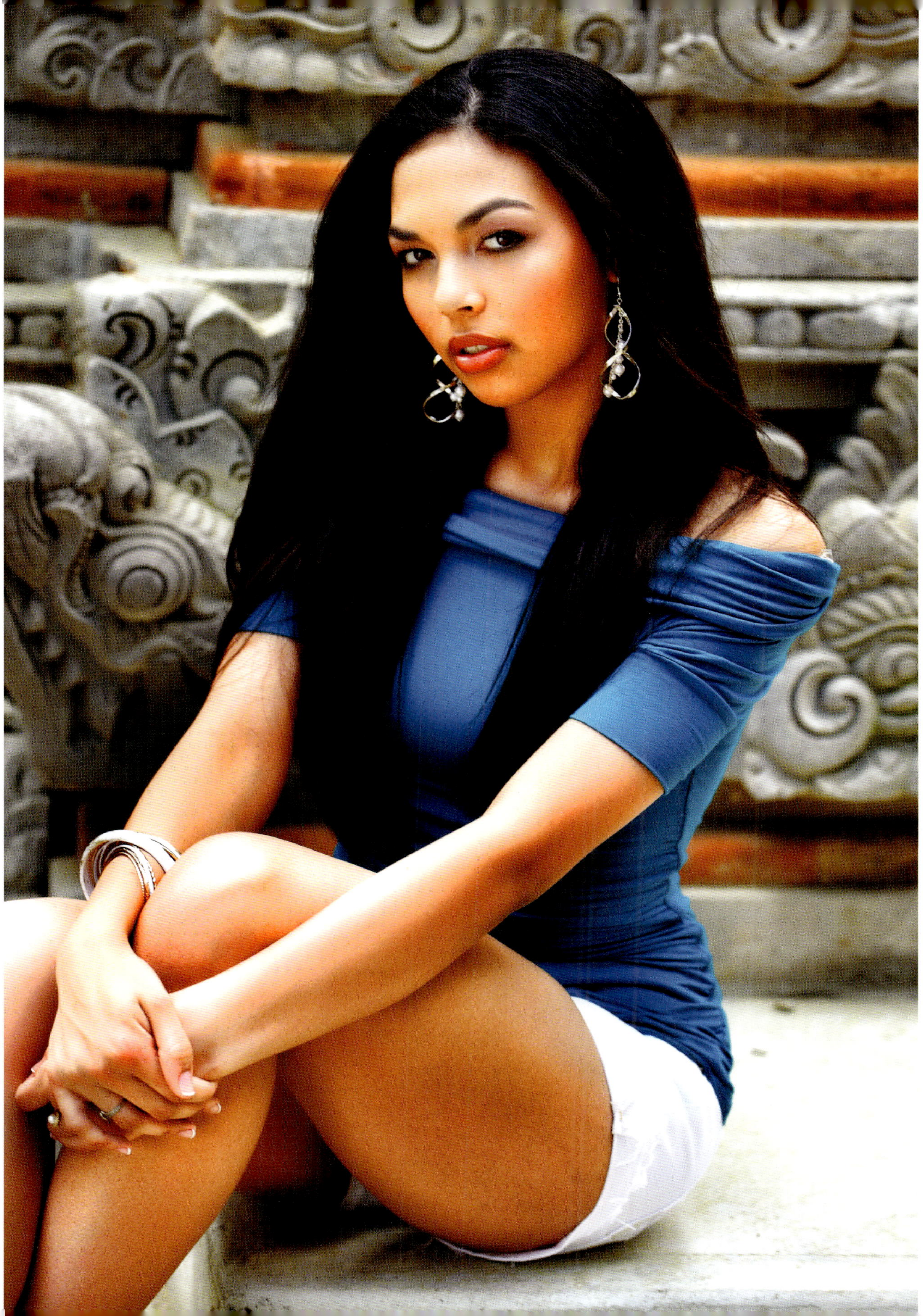

3. Attracting Clients

Word of Mouth

All of my clients come to me via word of mouth, my web site, and social media. I don't do any additional advertising or marketing.

Social Media

Social media has, in particular, been huge for us; I don't know where we'd be without it. We were fortunate to get on-board early. In 2004, before I even knew what social media was, a senior asked me if the studio had a MySpace page. When I looked into it and saw lots of kids posting photos, I knew that's where I needed to be. I hired a high-school student to help get us started—and before long we had thousands of friends and our business exploded because no one else in our market was reaching kids through this portal. Over the years, that networking has translated into success on Facebook and now Twitter and Instagram.

Social media has been great for us because it's where the young people are. However, it's a double-edged sword, because it's been great for everyone else, too. It makes every photographer look legit, even if they have no physical address. If they have a cell phone, they can book clients.

Recent Trends

Most recently, we've been finding that more and more clients are simply finding us through a Google or Yahoo search. That means we need to stay on top of our search-engine optimization (SEO) and ensure we are on the first page of results when people search for photographers in our area. The rules for this are always changing, so it's a challenge.

Another change in recent years is that it tends to be parents who are finding us on social media and Internet search engines. For many years, we had primarily kids reaching out (then we'd follow up with the parents).

In short, the ways we reach and interact with clients are always evolving. We keep looking for fresh approaches.

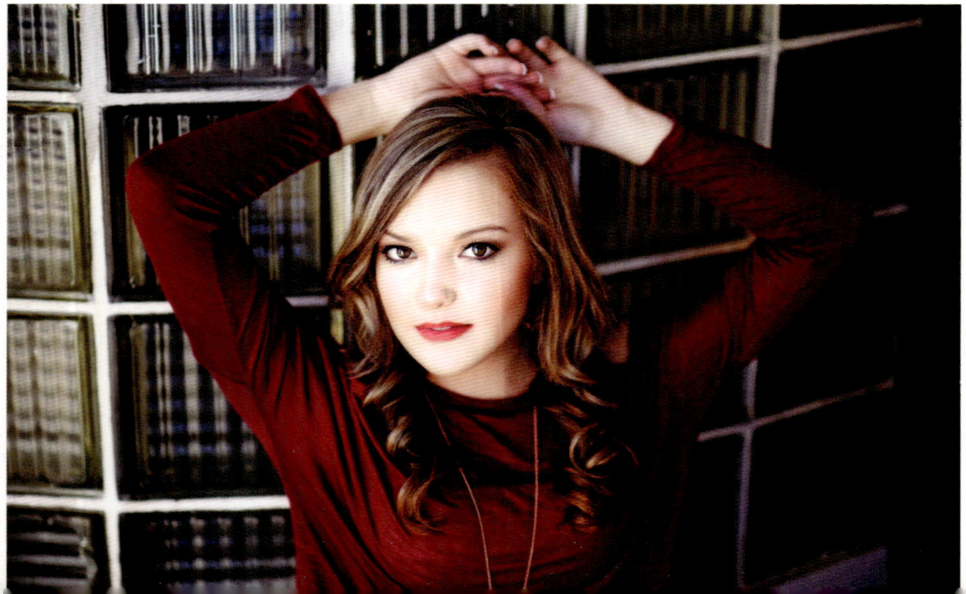

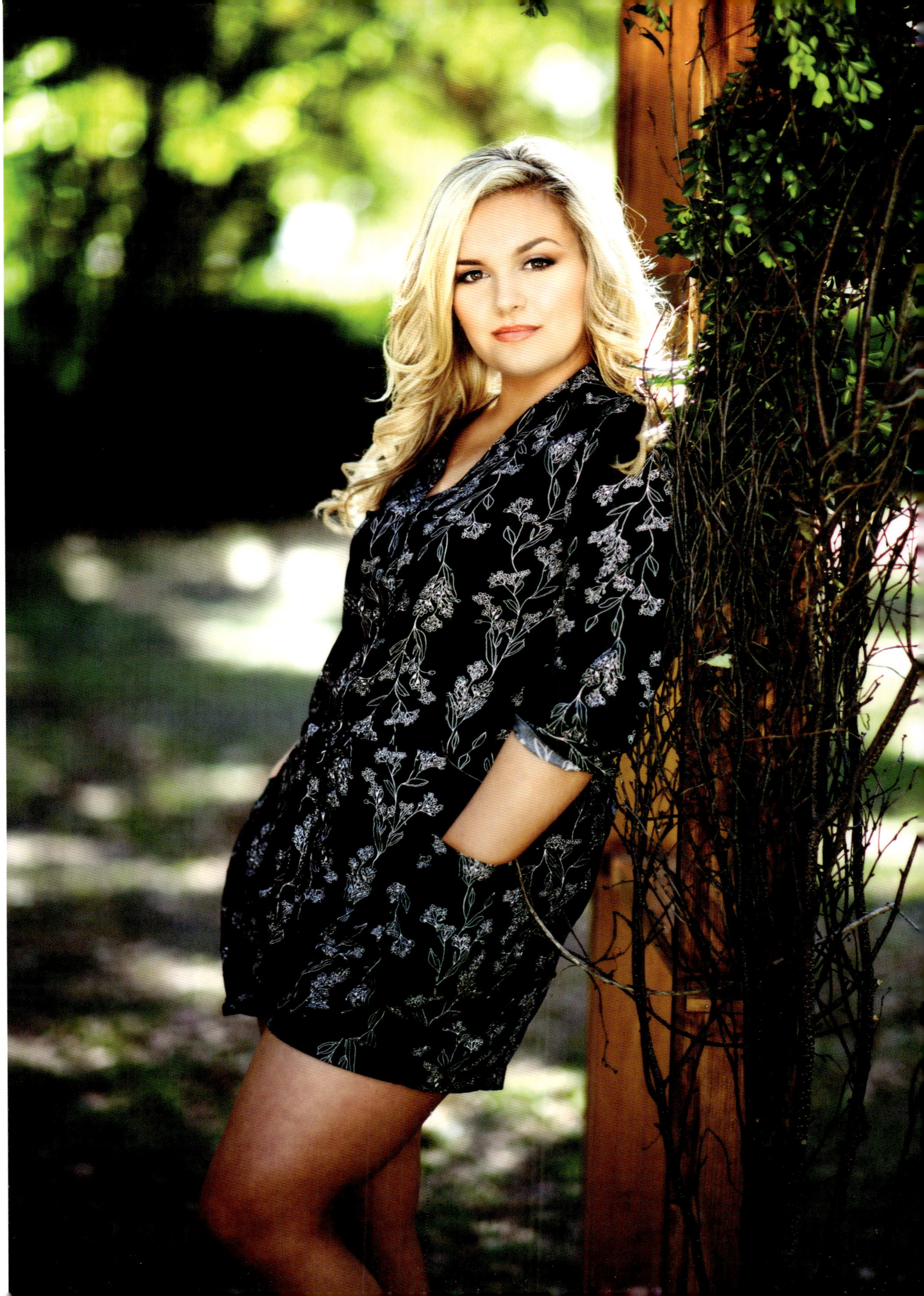

4. Booking the Session

Our First Contact

In most cases, people make their first contact with the studio via e-mail, using a link on our web site. As soon as we hear from them, we respond with a quick note. In this, we answer any specific questions they posed in their inquiry and ask if it would be okay to call them. I make it clear that this won't be a pushy "sales" conversation. I tend to say something like, "I'd love to explain everything to you—no pressure. Can I call to tell you about what we do?"

Packages and Pricing

A conversation is especially helpful when it comes to communicating with clients about our pricing. While we have "packages," they are designed to offer clients much more of an *à la carte* experience than most studios provide.

At each price level, clients receive a certain number of poses and a specified value of "gift prints." They can choose a lot of smaller prints or a smaller number of larger prints—as long as they don't exceed the total allocation, it's up to them to decide what works best for their needs. If they need more prints than a certain package allows, they can upgrade at any time. They can also upgrade to choose a package that includes more poses.

I learned from Denis Reggie the importance of understanding that people tend to buy from the middle of the offerings. The example he cited was Wendy's. The fast food chain sold

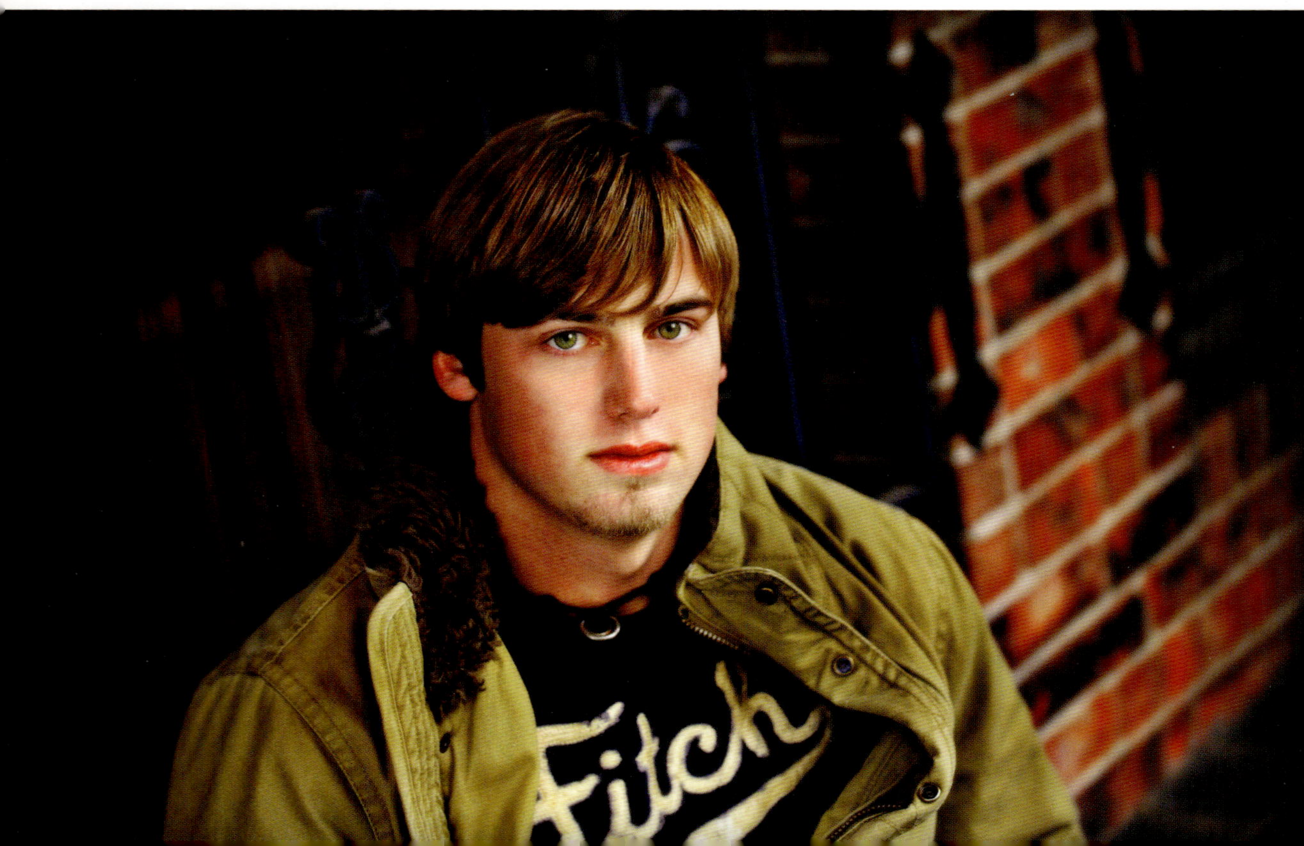

lots of single-patty burgers, but they wanted to sell more double-patty burgers. They accomplished this by adding a *triple*-patty burger. Not many people were actually going to purchase a three-patty sandwich, but its presence on the menu tended to pull people up toward the middle; for a few cents more, they'd order a double instead of a single.

The same thing works when selling photography. Our base package is a good value with three poses and a good number of prints—but for just $100 more, we give clients *double* the prints, which makes it hard to resist. We have four total levels, with each upgrade offering more prints and more poses.

Clients don't have to decide at the outset what they're going to spend; we treat everyone the same. All of our sessions include multiple locations and four to five clothing changes. That way, when clients get their photos, there's a lot to choose from. We don't have to try to upsell them, because they're going to be reluctant to completely cut a location—or, with teenagers, a special outfit they spent hours picking out at the mall!

As a result, we rarely sell just that three-pose base package—and sometimes the nine poses in the top package aren't even enough, so we go totally *à la carte* from there.

A Session Fee

Part of what makes this work is charging a session fee up front. This is a modest fee, but it helps cover the time we invest in shooting each client's session. It's important to acknowledge that, just as in other professions, our time is worth something. And, like doctors and mechanics, we have fixed costs that need to be covered. Not being compensated for your time is a recipe for a short career!

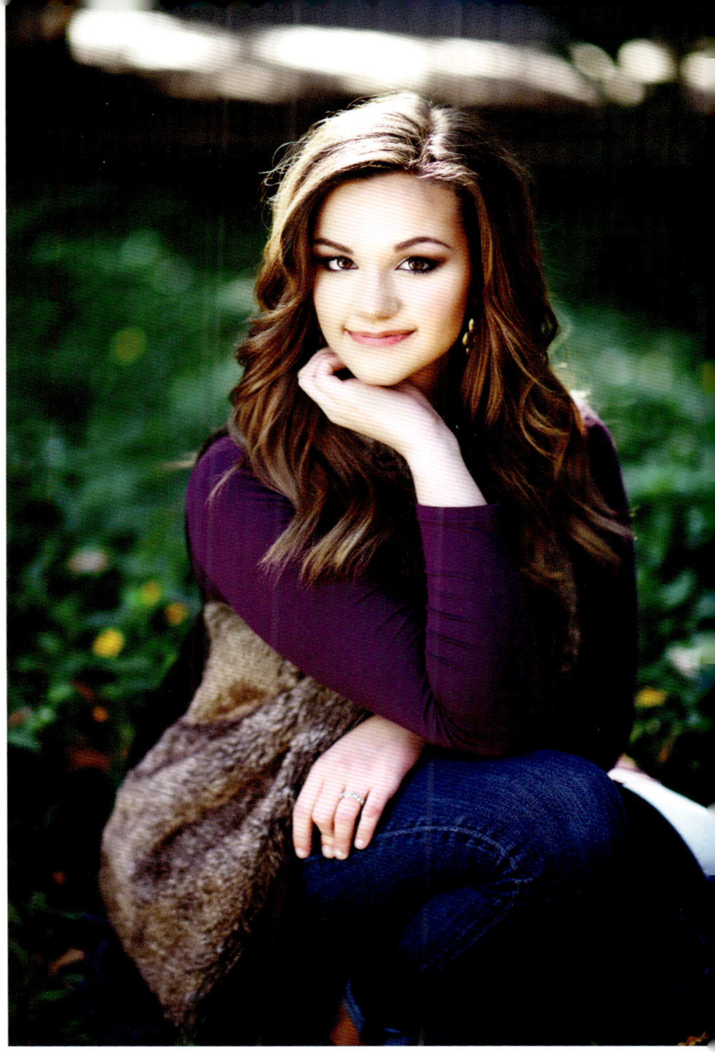

"We don't have to try to upsell them, because they're going to be reluctant to completely cut a location — or, with teenagers, a special outfit they spent hours picking out at the mall!"

5. The Consultation

Advantages

For local clients, I always encourage a visit to the studio for an in-person consultation. This is a great way to set the stage for success on the day of the portrait session—and for a good sale down the road. This is because the *experience* of the whole process is critical, and a face-to-face meeting is the best way to break the ice and make everyone feel comfortable and relaxed.

Even if I'm with another client, I make sure to pop in during every consultation so they see *my* face and know that I've seen *them*. One thing that can make subjects nervous about their session is concern about their personal appearance. If they have acne, a little extra weight, or some other "issue," they may worry about how the photographer will react. Getting that interaction out of the way during a consultation means no surprises to worry about at the session!

During the consultation, I like to joke with my clients and set the mood for a fun, relaxed session. Most of my business is with young women, and I grew up with sisters so I can relate to them well. I always show respect and try to put them at ease.

What to Cover

At my consultations, I emphasize the fact that each client's session is personalized for *them*. That means I need to know about them—about their personality, hobbies, personal style, tastes, etc. I also provide them with guidelines for what we advise in terms of clothing selection, hairstyling, and makeup (more on this in sections 4–6). Additionally, we cover what props they might want to bring to the session—sporting gear, musical instruments, etc. This is another way to personalize their images (see sections 33, 35, and 46).

When a Meeting Isn't Possible

About half of my clients live two or more hours from my studio. Some of them will plan a day trip to Lafayette to do some shopping and have their photo consultation. If that's not feasible, we'll send them a PDF listing all the most important points and follow up with a phone call to make sure everything is clear. (*Note:* This same PDF also works well as a script for our employees when doing in-person consultations, ensuring nothing is missed in the discussion.)

"The experience of the whole process is critical, and a face-to-face meeting is the best way to break the ice and make everyone feel comfortable and relaxed."

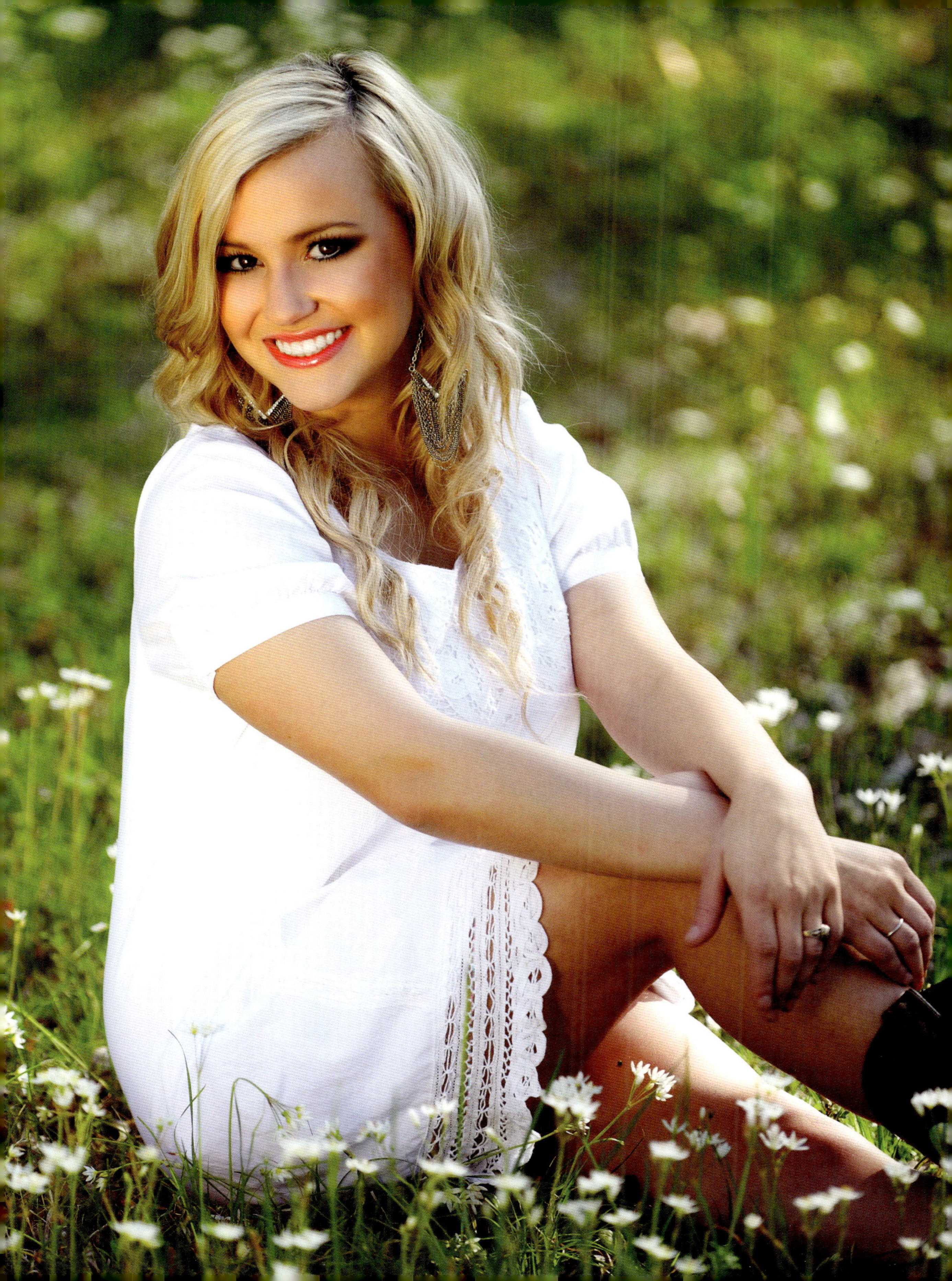

6. **Clothing Selection**, Part 1

Advice, Not Rules

It's part of the job of professional photographers to give our clients the benefit of our experience and help them make informed decisions when selecting the outfits they'll bring to the sessions. That said, I don't dictate "rules" to my clients; I just give them my advice.

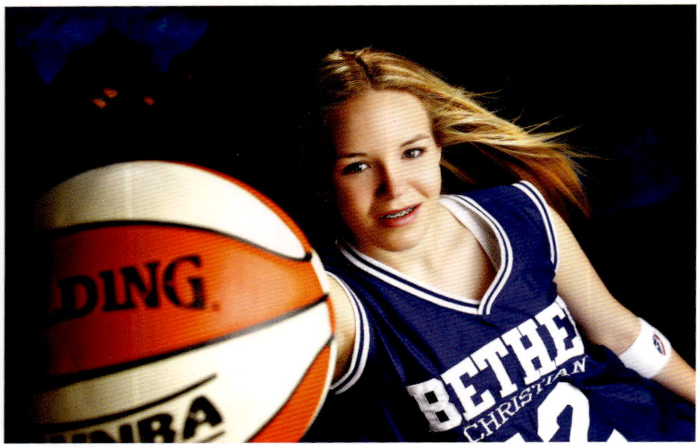

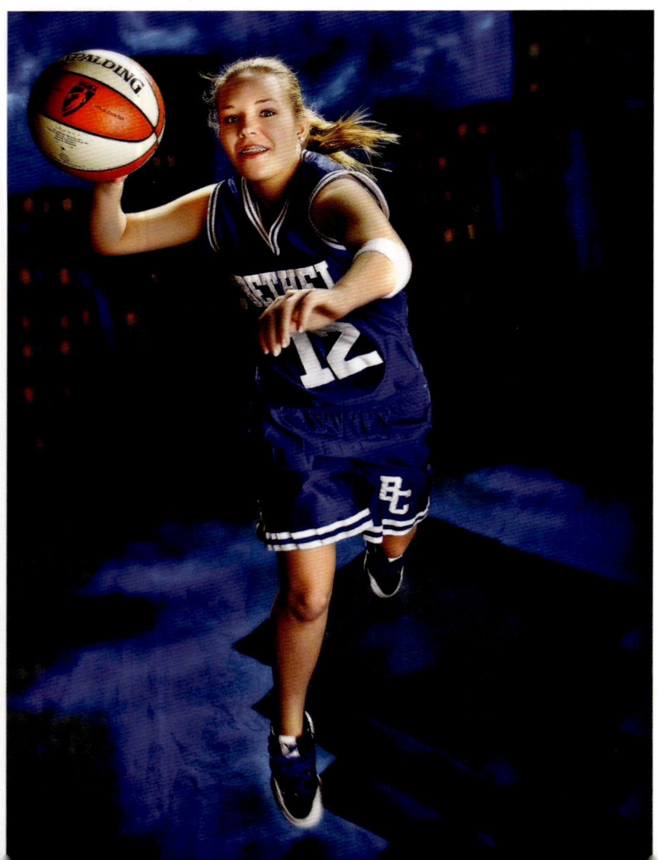

First and foremost, I want them to look carefully at the clothing and think about how it will look in the portrait. Clients are spending a lot of money on their portraits and we don't want any surprises. They should also make sure it's something they will really *like* and, hopefully, enjoy for years to come. This makes classic styles a better choice than trendy ones.

General Guidelines

It's best to avoid "wow" colors, as well as stripes, plaids, and other bold patterns. These types of clothing tend to pull the attention away from the face—and the face is the number one thing we want to see in a portrait. While these colors/patterns look fine in everyday life, they rarely look good in a static image. A better choice is clothing in solid, darker colors—but, again, we'll work with whatever they bring.

Cropping bare arms can result in awkward looks, so I recommend that clients opt for styles with long sleeves. Given the current styles and the warm climate where I live, this is a suggestion that is often ignored—but it produces a nice look for clients who opt for covered arms.

It's also nice for clients to bring clothes in a range of styles. This could include relaxed looks (what they wear to hang out with friends), casual styles (what they wear to

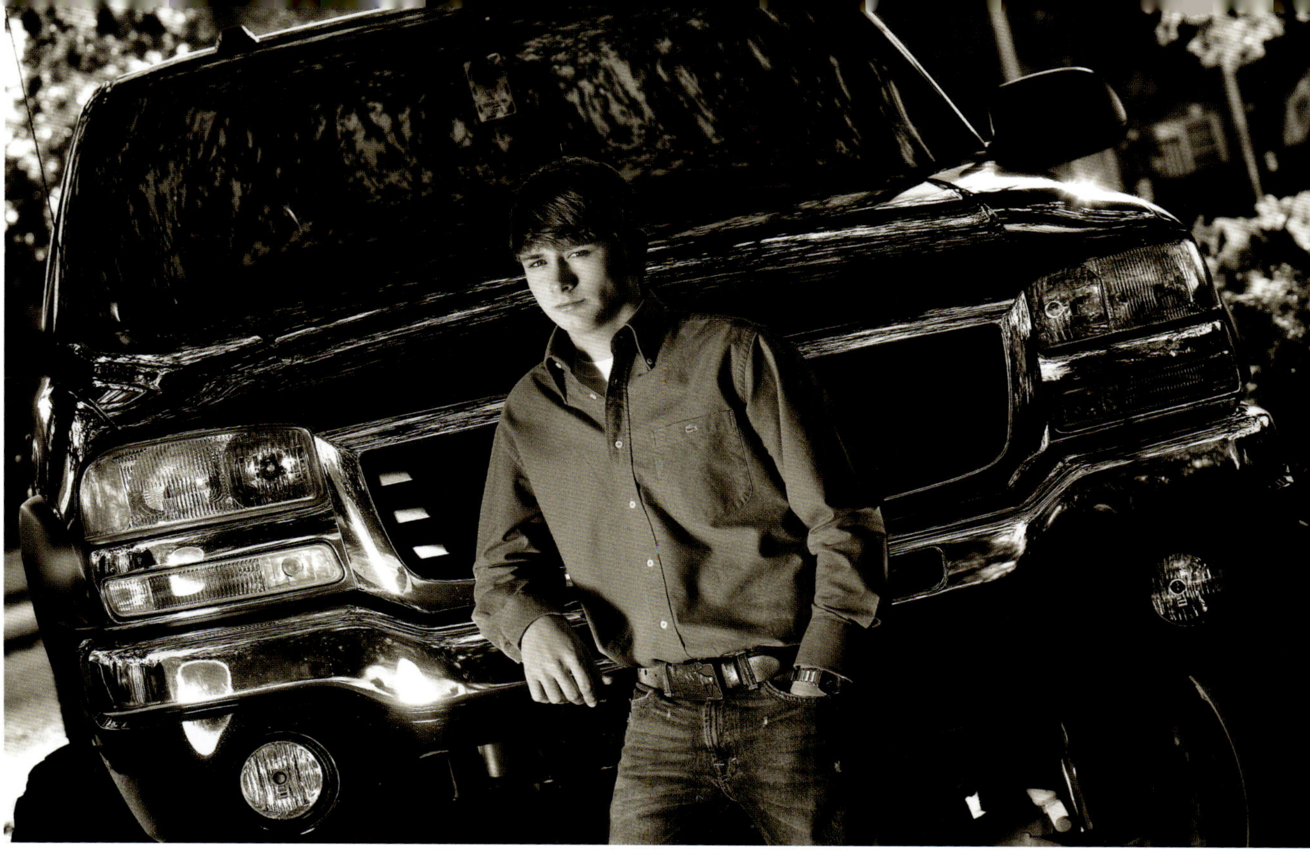

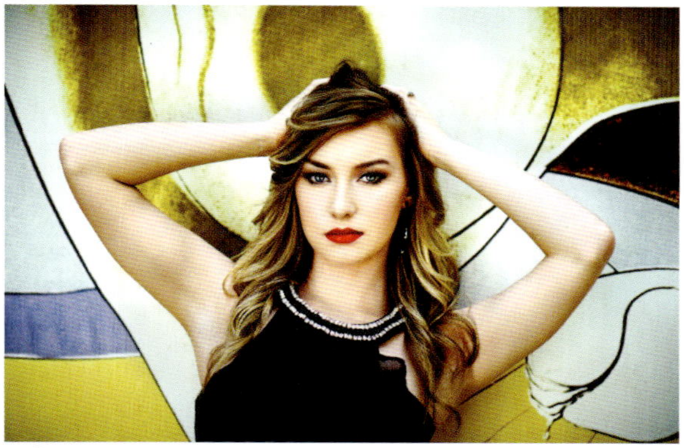

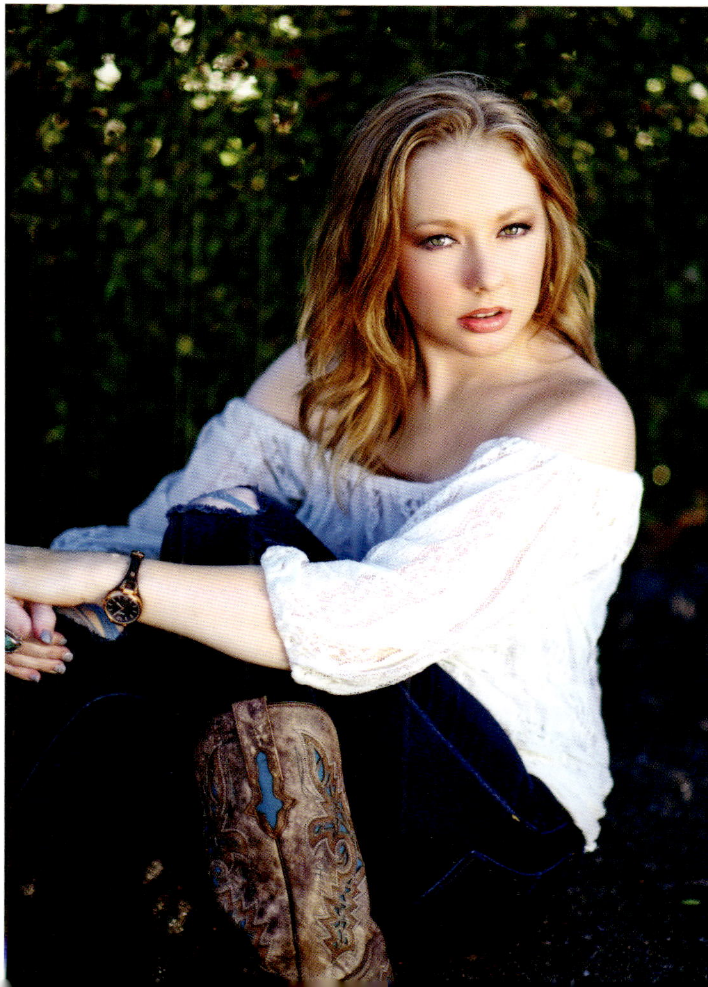

school), and something a bit more fancy (what they'd wear to a concert or a night out). For senior portraits, what Mom wants to see her child wearing is also an important consideration. Additionally, if they have one, I like to have them bring a performance outfit—whether it's a band uniform, cheerleading outfit, or sports uniform. Basically, their portraits should say, "This is who I was at seventeen years old."

7. **Clothing Selection**, Part 2

Girls' Clothes

If there's a common issue we face when photographing teenage girls, it's that they may want to look a little too sexy—especially for Mom's taste. The things that communicate sexiness in a portrait are the clothes, the expression, and the pose. My rule is that no more than two of those three qualities can have a seductive look. If the subject opts for a sexier outfit, that will be toned down by choosing poses and/or expressions that are more G-rated.

Guys' Clothes

Guys tend to bring fewer outfits to their sessions—but that's changing as men become increasingly fashion-conscious. Every year, we see a bit more variety. That's good news, because moms and girlfriends all like special portraits of their guys. Moms especially love nice images of their sons; when we have a great session with a senior guy, we almost always get a great order.

Hairstyles

We caution both men and women against getting a haircut the day before the session—especially if it's a new style that they might not end up liking. For guys, facial hair is fine (as long as, for senior portraits, Mom is okay with it).

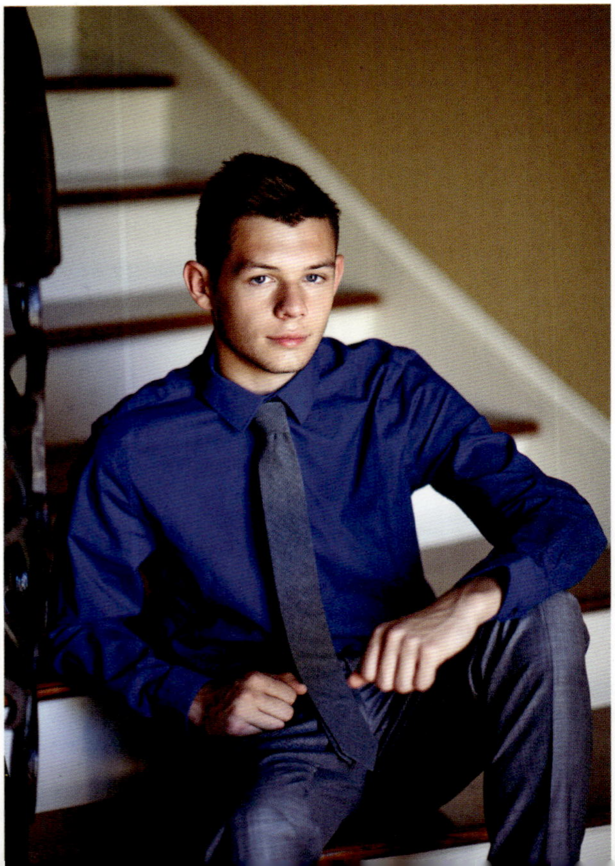

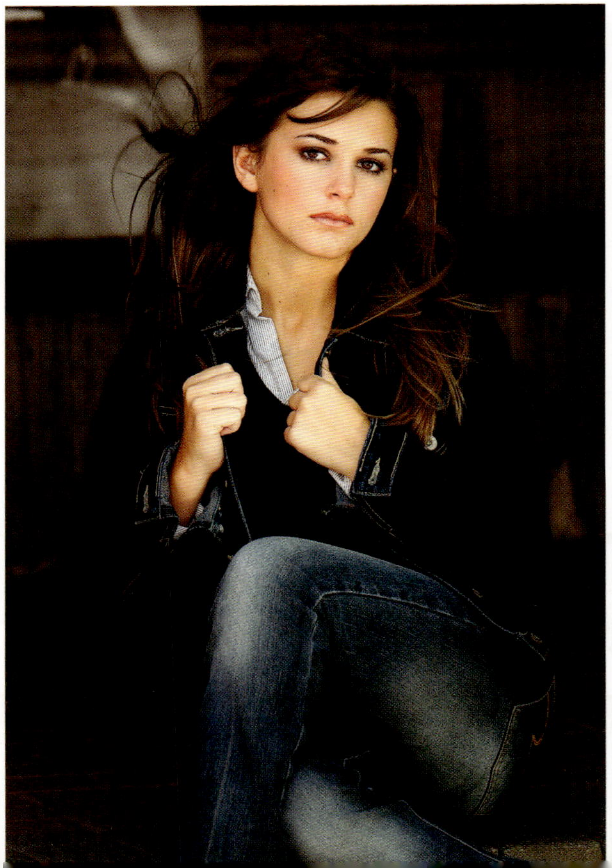

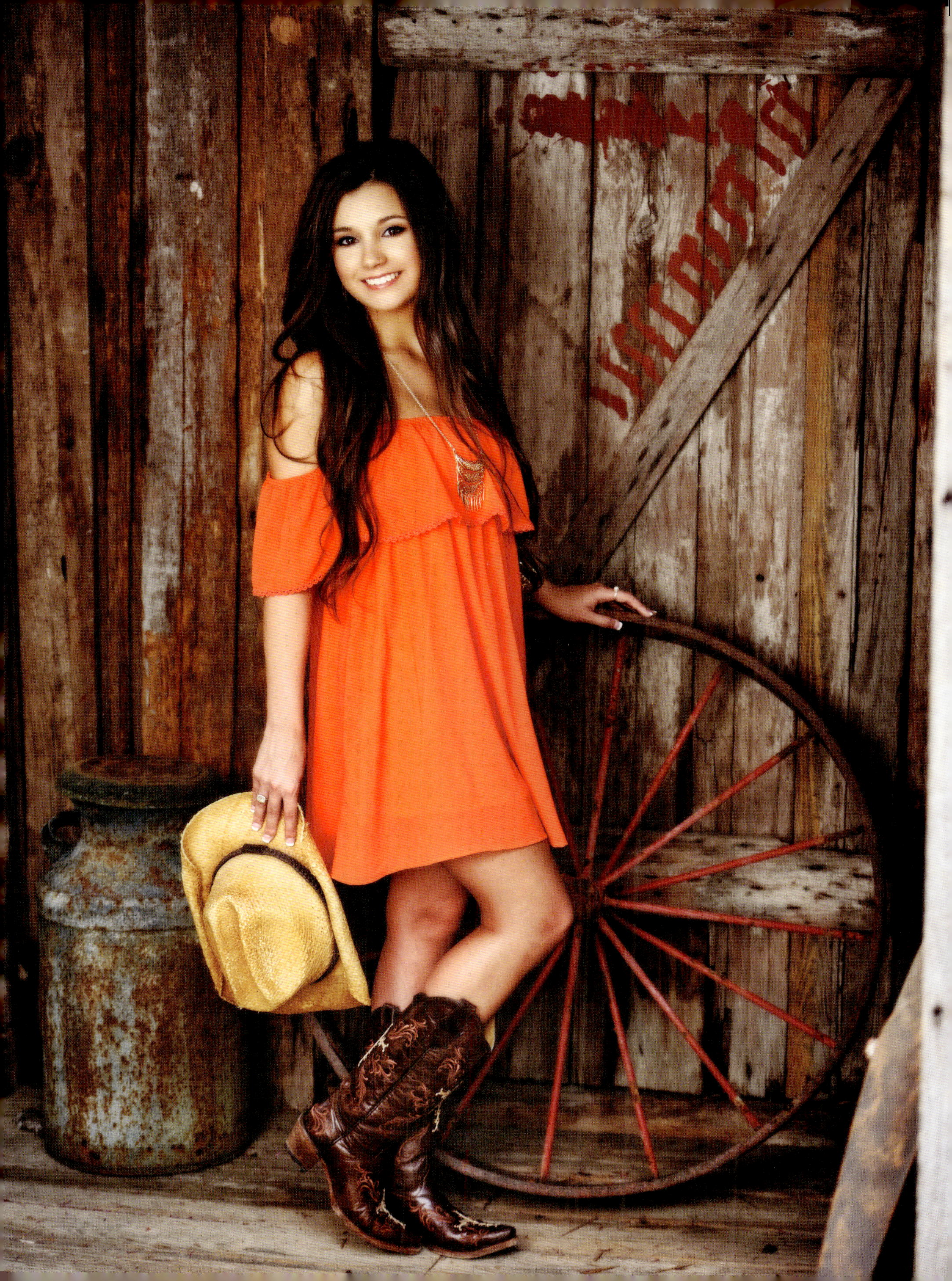

8. Getting the Session Started

Session Times and Days

Currently, we photograph portrait sessions only on weekdays, and generally around 1:00PM. Of course, this is not exactly the best time of day for lighting if the subject's session is to include location portraits—but no client wants to get up at 5:00AM for their portrait session, and I don't want to spend all my evenings shooting (that's a recipe for burnout!). Therefore, I've found places to shoot and approaches for light modification that let me get nice location looks at a time of day that makes sense for everyone involved.

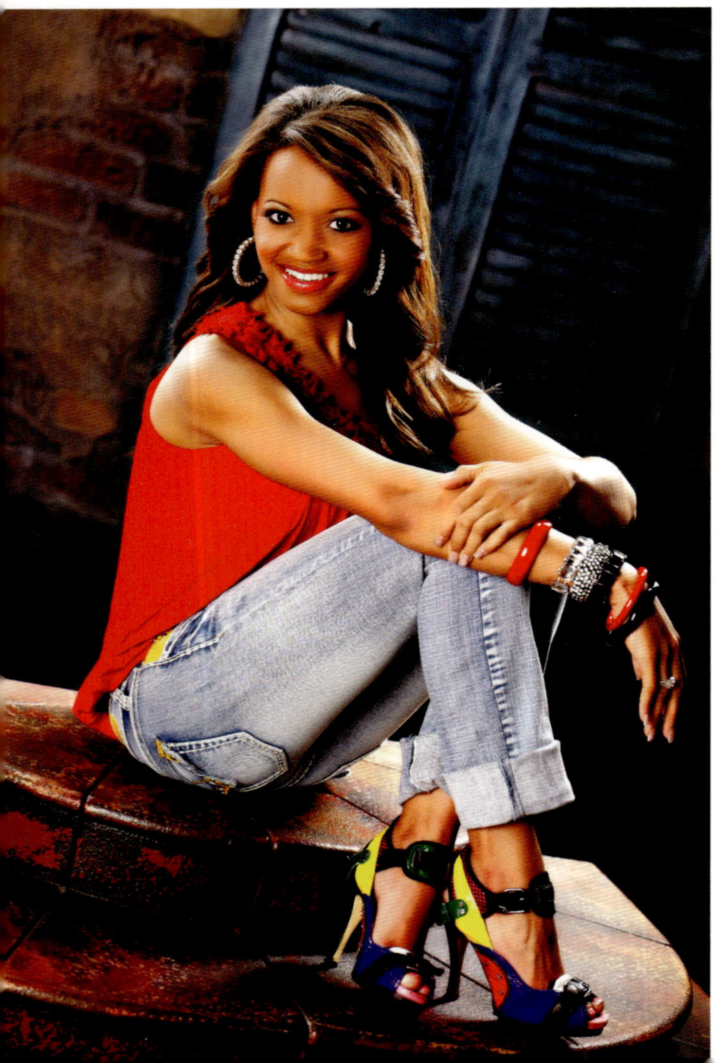

We allow about two hours for our portrait sessions. By that point, my subjects are usually tired and ready to wrap up the shoot. Especially because the weather tends to be hot here, pushing it beyond that duration tends not to be fun or productive.

Arrival and Styling Choices

Whether we'll be shooting location portraits, studio images, or a mix of both, we meet up with clients at the studio to start the session. If the weather is great, we can venture out from there to any locations chosen for the session—but if it's not a great day for outdoor shooting, we can work in the studio or at some nearby sheltered areas that offer outdoor looks.

Additionally, I have a makeup/hair artist who can come to the studio and meet up with the client to do their styling a couple hours before the session. This is a great option, since their look is completely fresh when we start shooting. For clients who opt to use their own stylist, we ask them to arrive at the studio 20 minutes before the start time of their session.

Before we start, I look through the clothing that the client has selected for their shoot and help them pick the outfits that will work best at the locations they have selected (more on that in section 16). I like to guide the process by saying things like, "This is going to look

“I like to guide the process by saying things like, ‘This is going to look great, don’t you think?’ This helps me nudge the decision in the best direction while still making them feel involved.”

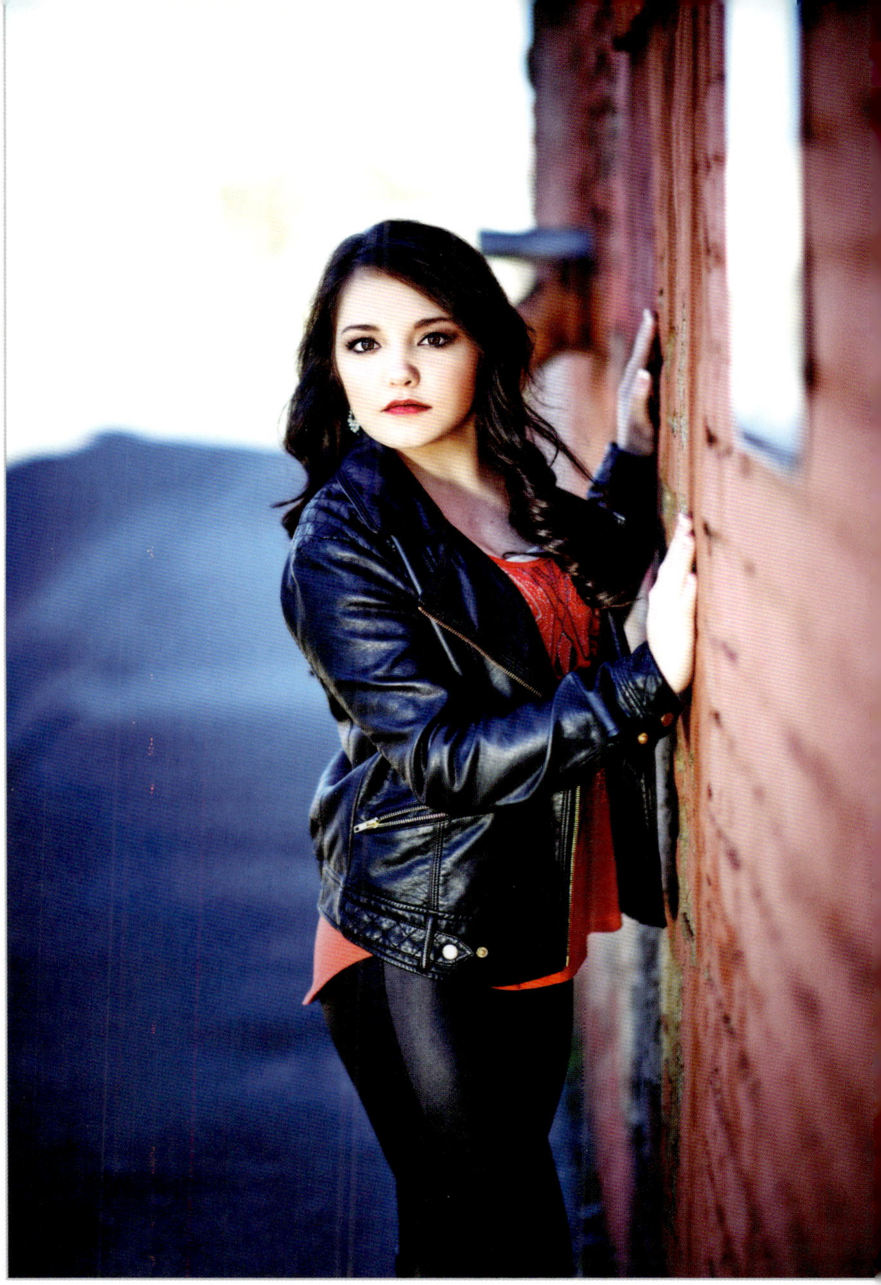

great, don’t you think?” This helps me nudge the decision in the best direction while still making them feel involved.

As we move from location to location, it’s great to have a variety of clothing available in case our initial selection doesn’t work as well as anticipated—or in case we encounter a location where an unexpected clothing choice turns out to be perfect. Always encourage clients to bring more clothes than they think they’ll need!

We emphasize that we have a finite amount of time, so it’s important to be on time. If an appointment is scheduled at 1:00PM, that means we will start shooting a 1:00PM.

Keep It Fun

Above all, it’s important to have fun—especially as we kick off the session and work on getting them relaxed. This is even more true for guys, who usually arrive convinced that the shoot is going to be boring. I like to keep my subjects constantly involved in the process. I show them the LCD for encouragement. It always helps to get them excited when they see how great they look.

9. My Gear

Make Smart Choices

When I was getting started in photography, I had "equipment fever," like most new photographers do. I was so enamored of hardware, hoping that better gear would translate into better images. Of course, that's not the case. Having the *wrong* gear (bad lenses, cameras with no manual exposure settings, etc.) can certainly mess up your images—but beyond some basic minimum functions, the brand or model of gear isn't going to make your images better or worse.

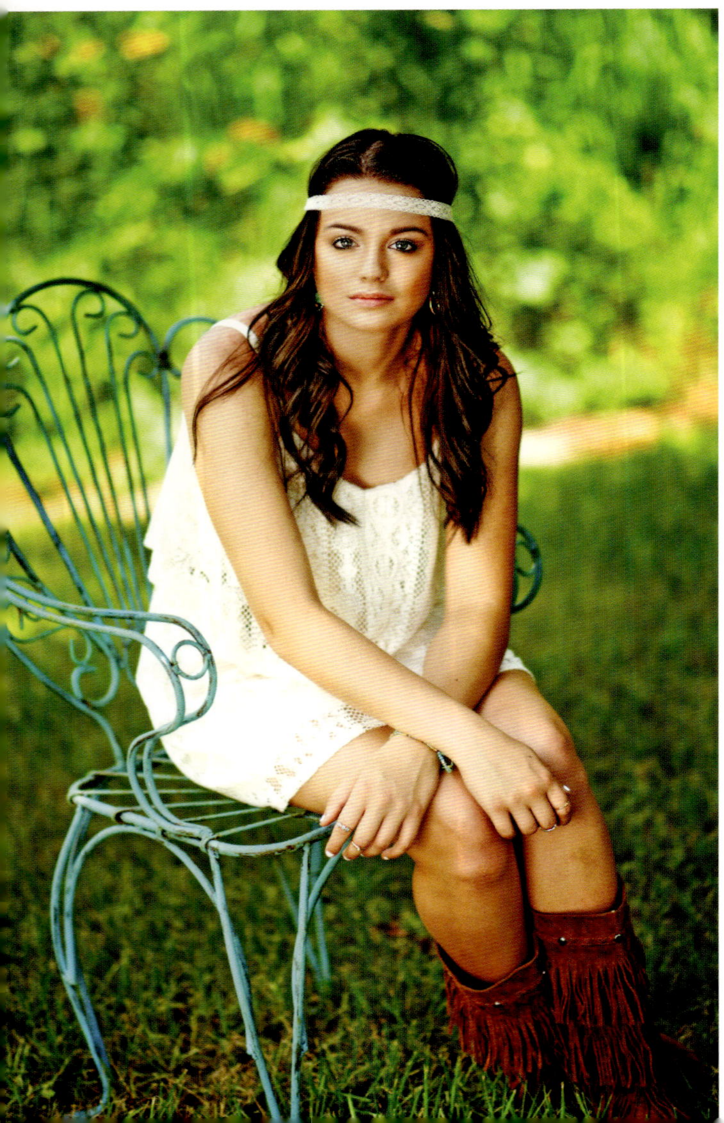

Today, when people ask me what kind of camera I use, I often reply, "A black one." I have changed brands and models over the years based on what I need the gear to do. When I do, I look for the device that offers the best version of the features I need for the job—and the most versatility. For example, a 12MP camera is plenty big enough for shooting senior portraits. If that's all I shot, that would be all I needed to own. Because I also photograph families and commercial work, however, I also use a 34MP camera.

I'm including a list of what I shoot with as of this writing. These are the products that meet my current needs. Some of them might work for you—or your gear might be totally different. Decide what you want to do, then pick the tools you need to get it done.

Organization

I store my camera gear in a Pelican 1519 case, so it's always ready to go. As I shoot, I take out one thing at a time and make sure my kit is all back together at the end of the session. Here's what's currently in the case:

Cameras
Nikon D700

Nikon D750
Nikon D810
Spare batteries for each camera

Lenses
Nikon 14–24mm f/2.8 G
Nikon 50mm f/1.4 G
Nikon 85mm f/1.4 G
Nikon 70–200mm f/2.8 G

Small Flash
Nikon SB-700 flash
Justrite camera rotator bracket
Manfrotto quick release adapters

Other
Shutter release cables
Sandisk 8G CF cards (multiple)
Sandisk 32G SD cards (multiple)
Lens cleaning kits
Pocket Wizard Plus III
Pocket Wizard Plus X (2)

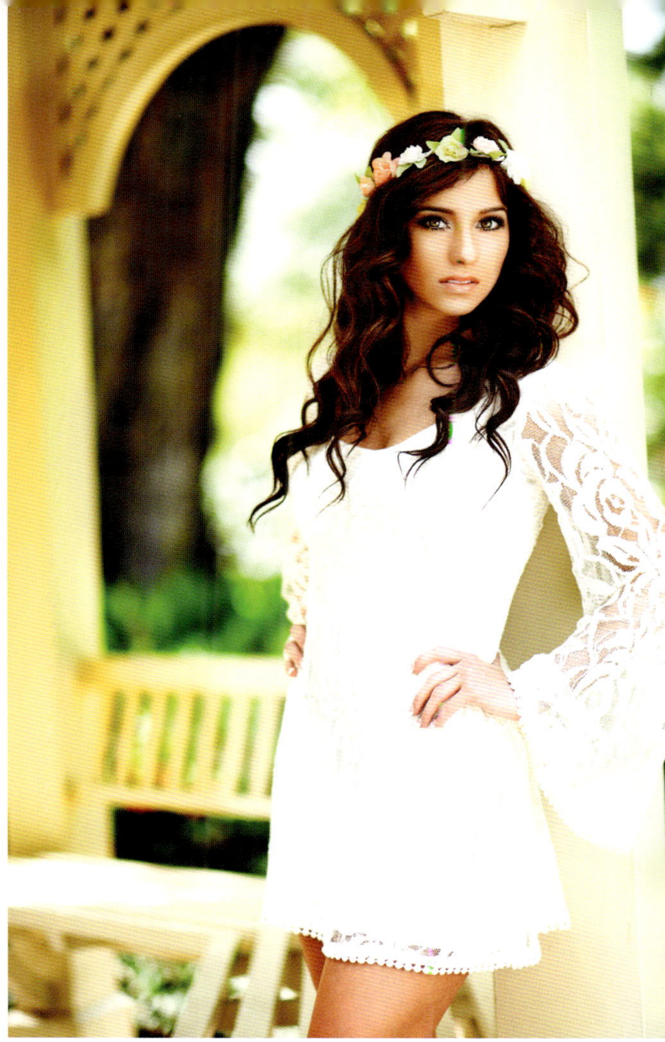

I keep my lighting kit separate from my camera kit. If I unpacked it, here's what you'd find:

Lights, Meters, and Modifiers
White Lighting X 3200 moonlight
White Lightning Einstein monolight with integral Pocket Wizard receiver
Paul Buff Mini Lithium batteries (2)
Pocket Wizard Plus X transceivers (2)
Sync cables (various)
monolight reflectors
Sekonic L-358 light meter
Paul Buff 47-inch folding Octabox
Umbrellas (assorted)

Stands and Supports
Light stands (2)
Gitzo G1327 Mk2 carbon fiber tripod
Manfrotto ball head with quick release
Manfrotto carbon fiber monopod

Reflectors
Photoflex 74-inch white/silver reflector
Photoflex 74-inch translucent scrim
Photoflex 74-inch black/black gobo
Photoflex 52-inch soft gold/white reflector
Photoflex 52-inch white/silver reflector
Lastolite LL LR3631 33-inch TriGrip Reflector (white/silver or silver/soft gold)

10. **A Great Experience**, Part 1

Better Photos, Better Sales

Here's a simple fact: if your subject is comfortable and enjoys the session, the pictures will be better, they will buy more, and they'll tell their friends about you. People like buying from people they *like*—and they return to them. So how do you make clients feel happy and relaxed? It's a process that must be woven through every aspect of their interaction with you and your business.

Set the Stage

I have a nice studio in an old building that appeals to clients right away. We decorated the dressing room with antiques to build on this vintage feel and let clients know they are someplace special. From the moment they walk through the door, we're working to help them relax by presenting, in ourselves, a comfortable and welcoming demeanor.

Choose the Right Words

I also like to offer a genuine compliment on the subject's appearance when they arrive. Saying something like, "You look pretty today," or "Your makeup looks really nice," works quite well. The key, throughout the process, is to be genuine; you should never fawn

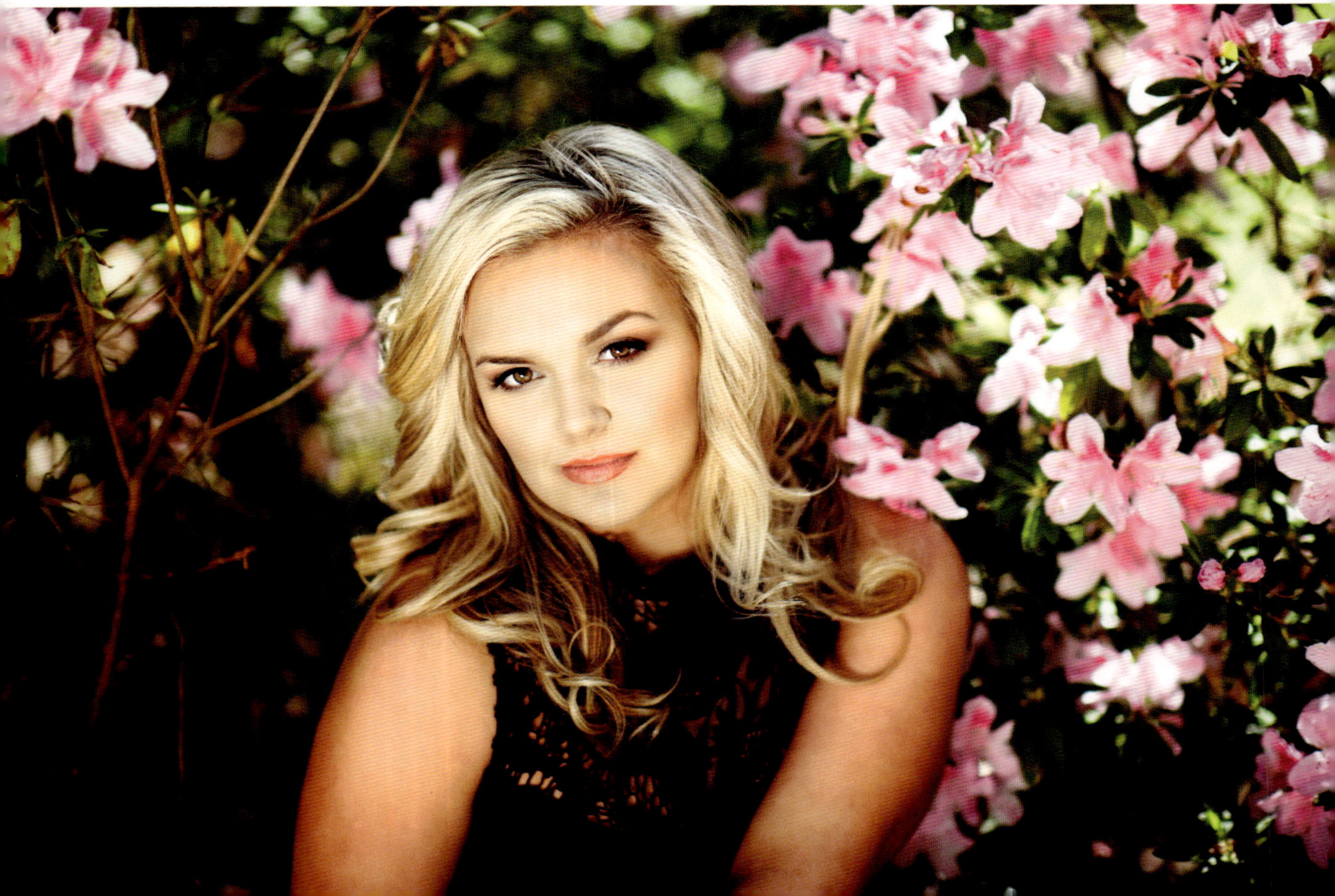

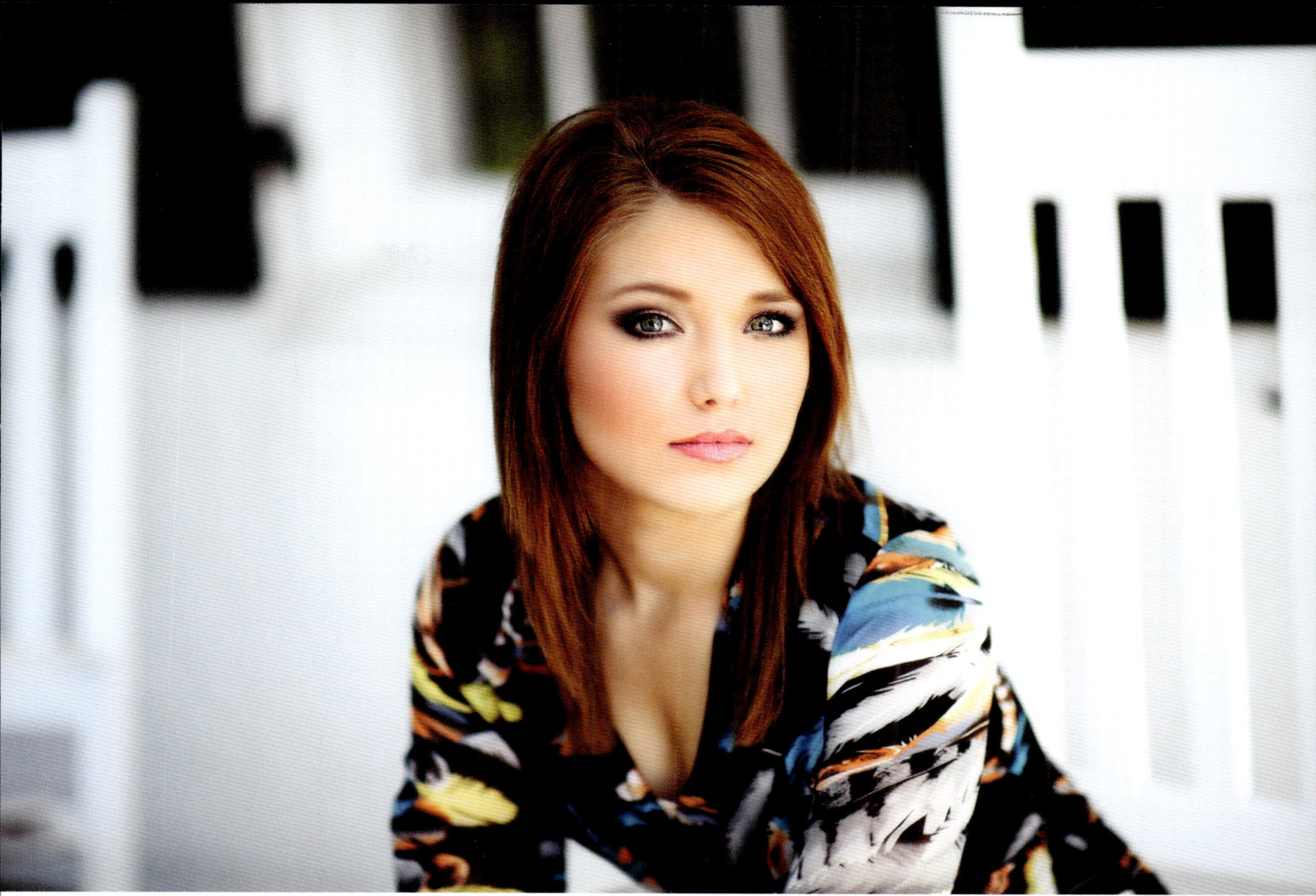

over the client or say anything that could be misconstrued as inappropriate.

Choosing the right words is something that helps clients feel at ease throughout the session. For example, I would never ask a girl to "look sexy" (I have daughters myself, after all!) Instead, if I want a more intense expression, I'll ask her to look "serious." Likewise, if a girl's bra strap is showing, I'll point out that her "undergarment" is peeking out at her shoulder and ask Mom to help adjust her top.

The key is always to speak in a way that is complimentary and doesn't make them feel awkward or self-conscious. Here's another example: girls sometimes opt to wear short skirts or low-cut tops. In some poses, this can reveal too much of their bodies. Instead of saying, "Your undergarments are showing" or "I can see too much cleavage," simply tell the model how you need her to adjust her pose—"turn a little to your left," or "move your feet closer together." This lets you *solve* the problem without *explaining* the issue and making her feel embarrassed.

"From the moment they walk through the door, we're working to help them relax by presenting a welcoming demeanor."

11. **A Great Experience**, Part 2

Make It Feel Like a Collaboration

When subjects are having a good time at their session they'll want to stay longer and they'll get more invested.

Part of making the shoot fun is simply telling them that it's *going to be fun* and that it's going to be about *them*—that it's not just about you taking a bunch of pictures. I always make it clear that I am open to their ideas. I ask for their opinions and don't try to limit their ideas. Then, I use that input to guide them to what I think will work best and what we can accomplish in the allotted time.

For example, we usually shoot five or six outfits, but I request that subjects bring more than that. When we're looking through them, I'll ask, "Which are your favorites? Which do you really love?" If I don't agree, or if know one outfit will look great at a selected location, I'll steer them in the better direction.

Throughout the process, we take our time and customize the session for the client. This interaction is an important way of building the perceived value of our product and the experience of working with us.

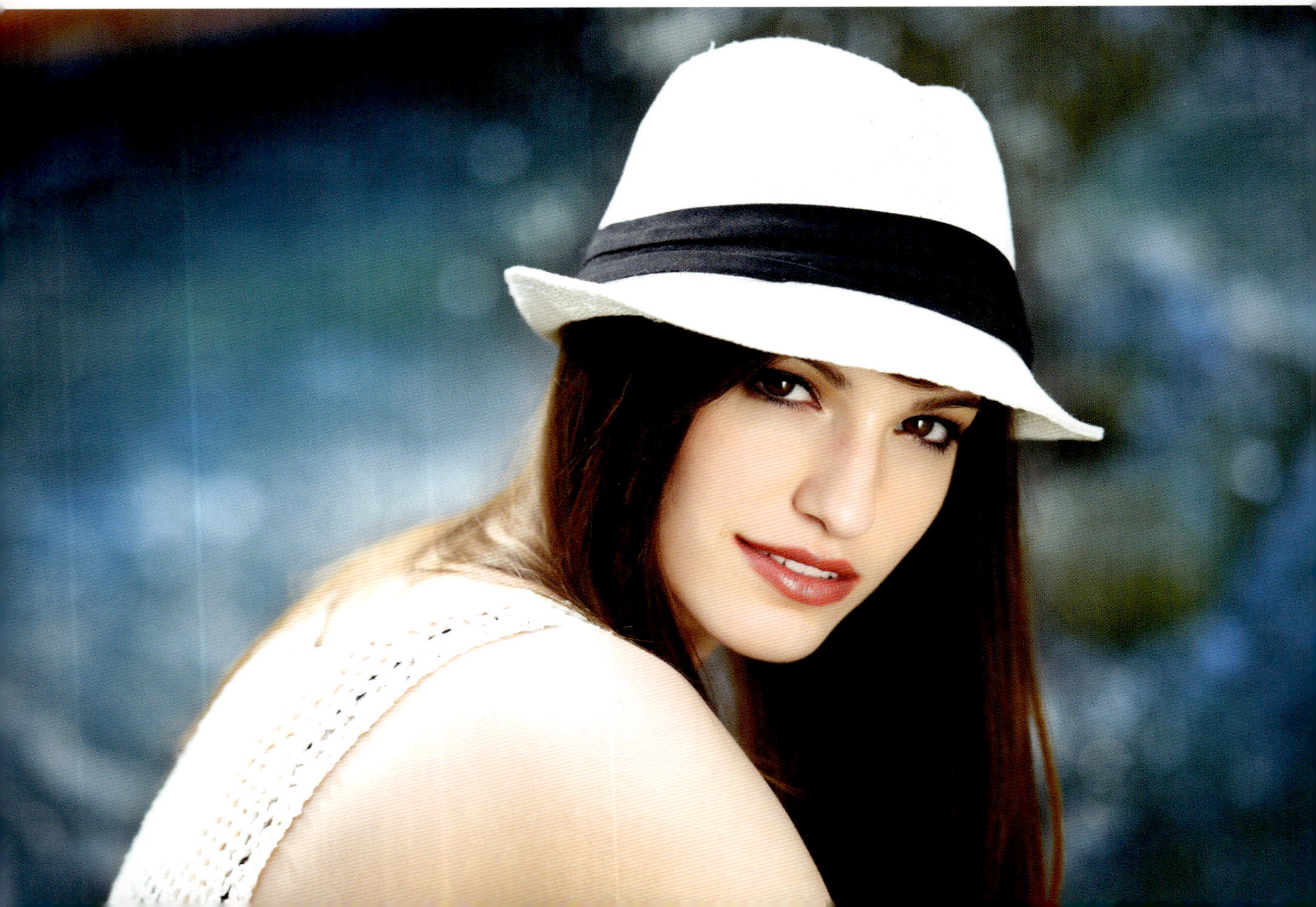

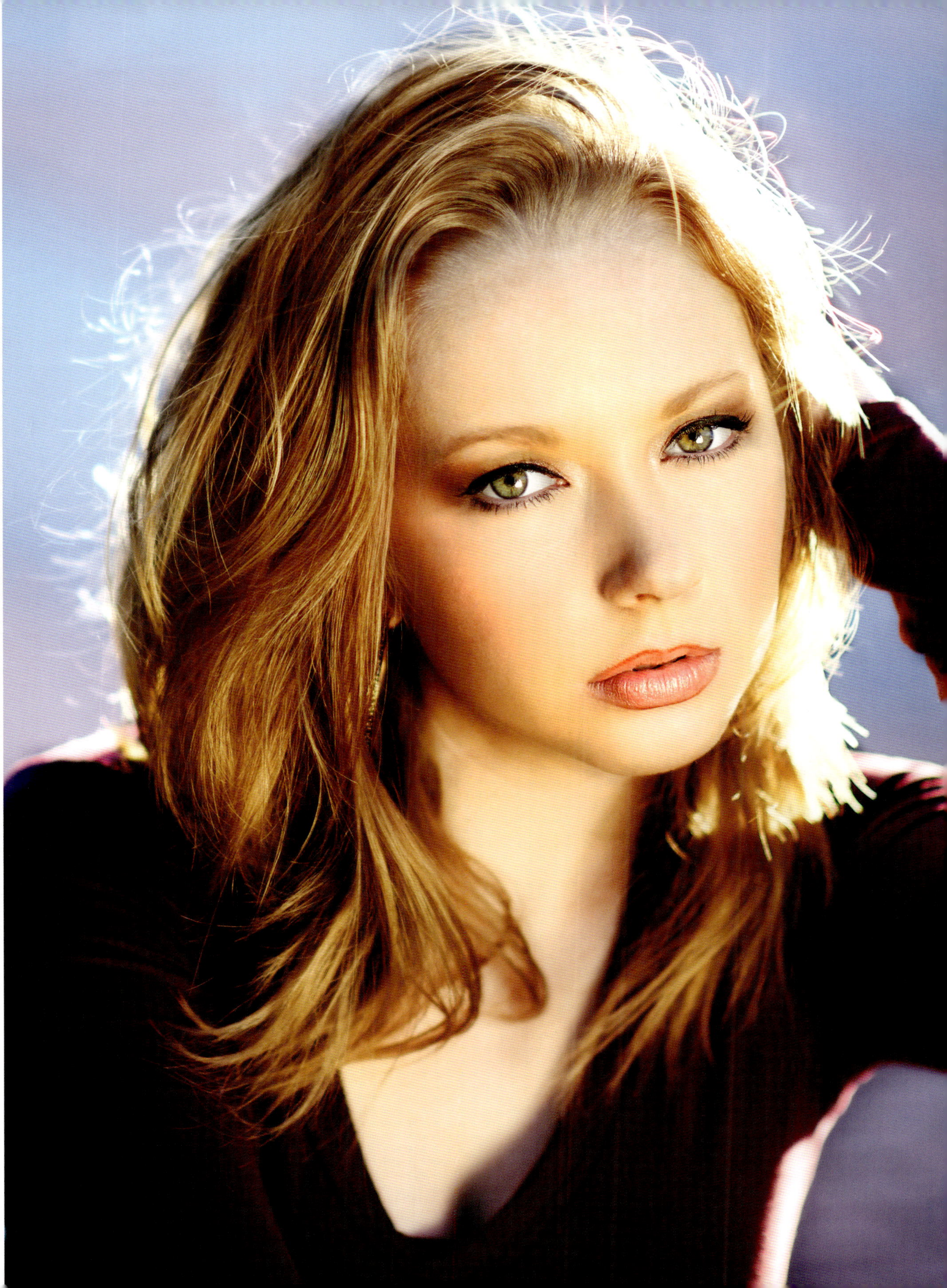

12. **A Great Experience**, Part 3

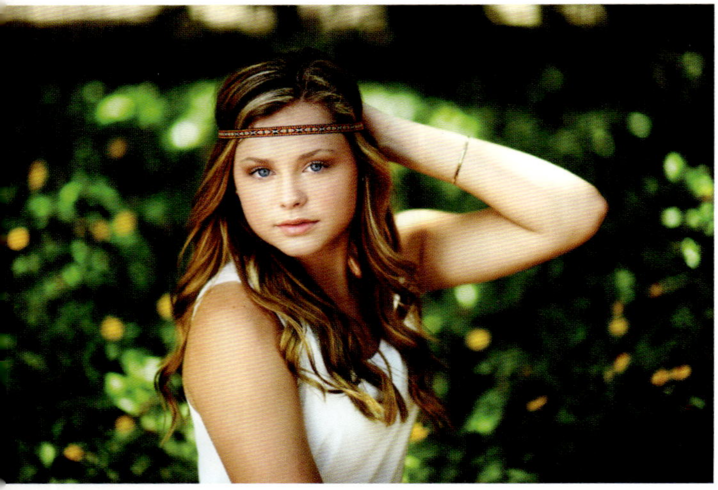

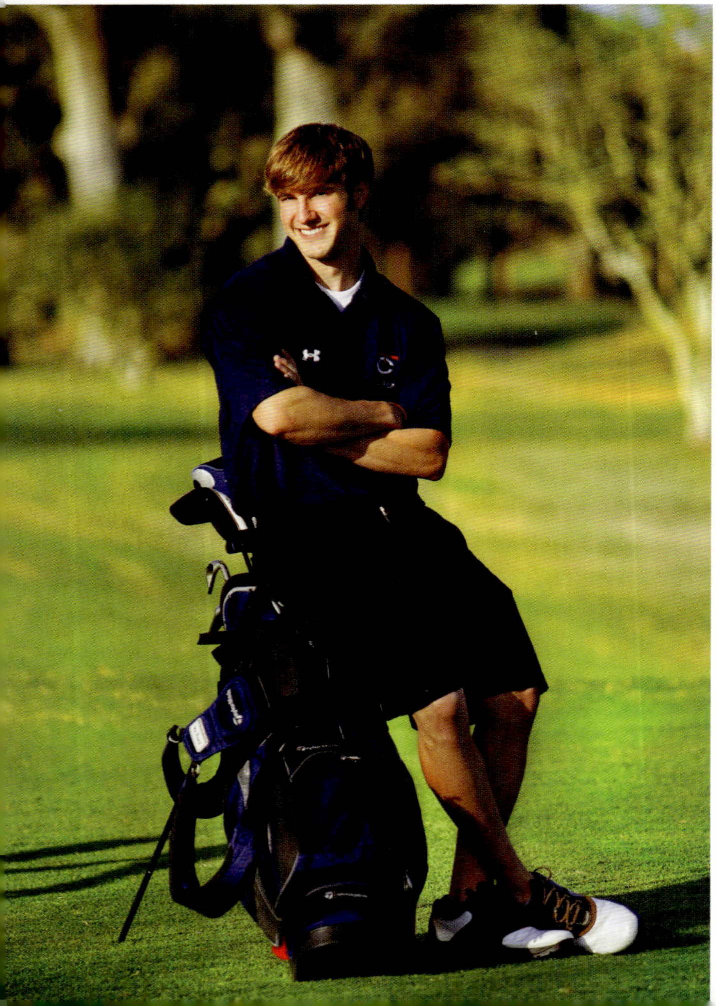

Make It Feel Important

We also let clients know that we regard their images as important—and they should, too. Senior portraits might feel a little frivolous to some, but this is actually the first of only two or three big events in most people's lives that get professionally photographed: the senior portrait, their wedding photos, and portraits with their first child. Documenting who they are at this age, as they enter adulthood, is an important milestone.

Learn to Read People

All your sessions will feel more relaxed if you can learn to read people well. Some people will always surprise you, of course, but often you can get a good sense of your subject's

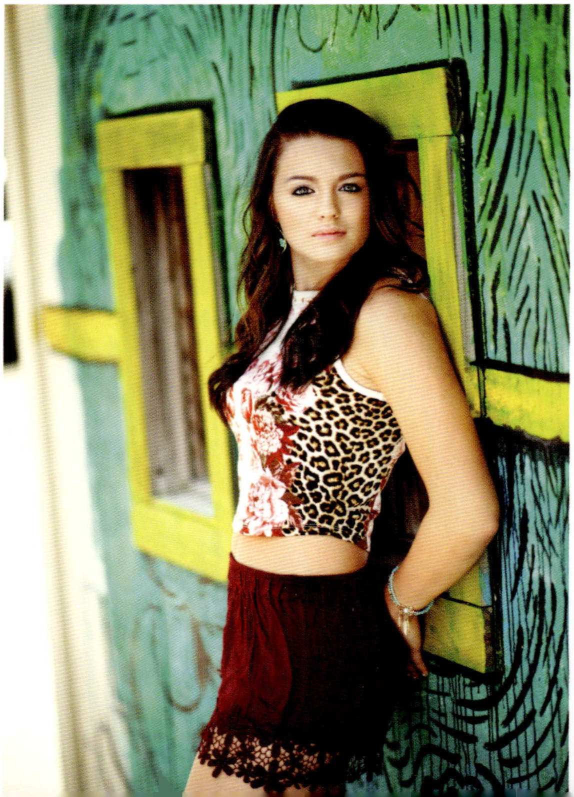

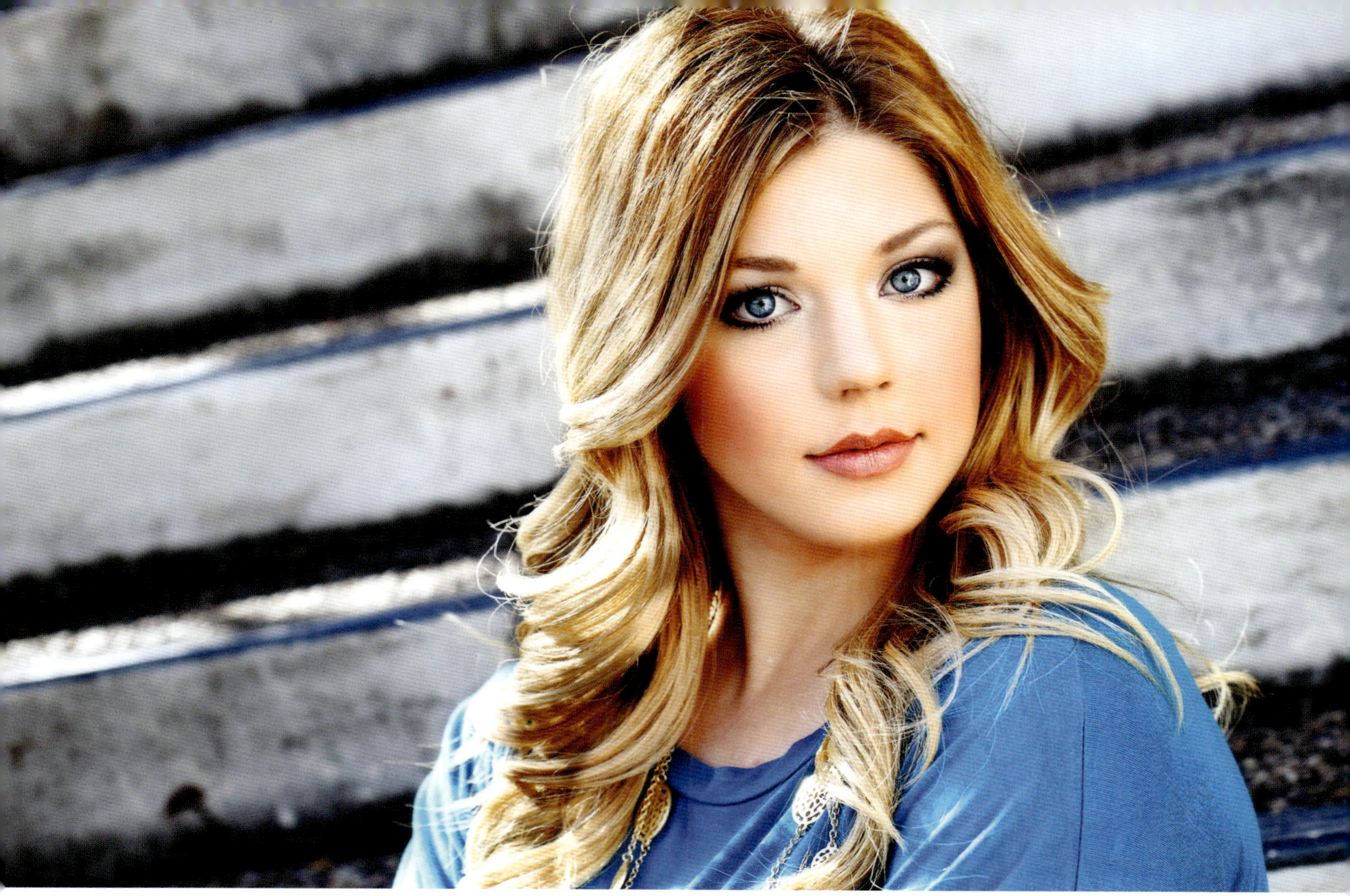

personality by the way they dress. Trendy clothing tells you one thing; a peasant top tells you something else. Some subjects are really outgoing and like to cut up during their session; others are more nervous and reserved. Understanding their personality can help you tailor your approach to ensure great images and a positive experience.

Find Their Beauty

Most people have concerns about how their finished portraits will look. It's your job to find the beauty in everyone and allay those fears. Sometimes, you'll have to coax it out of them. Showing them a great photo on the back of your camera is a solid way to convince them they look terrific. For particularly shy subjects, you may want to show them previews on the LCD throughout the session. When you hear a subject say, "Wow! I didn't know I could look like that!" you know you've won them over!

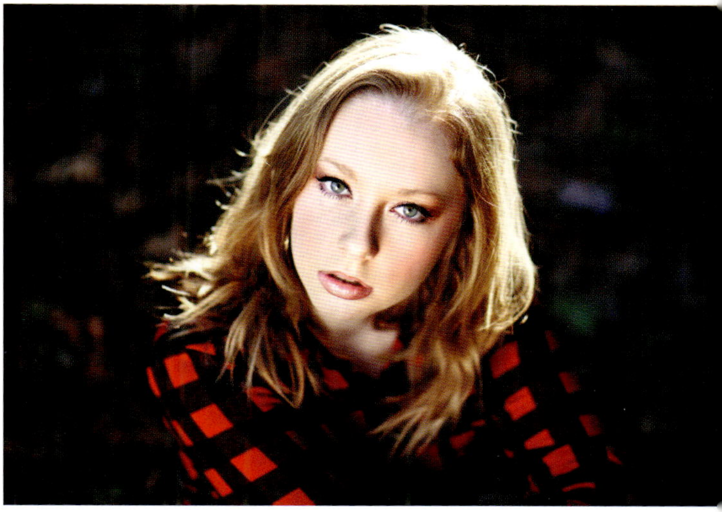

13. **Posing**, Part 1

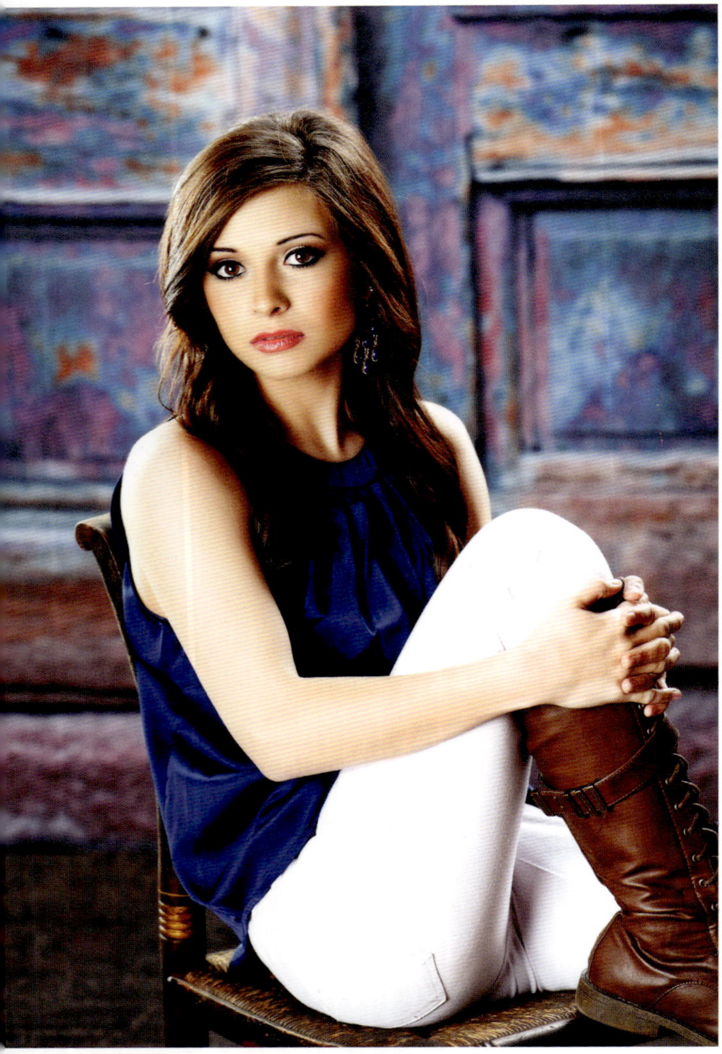

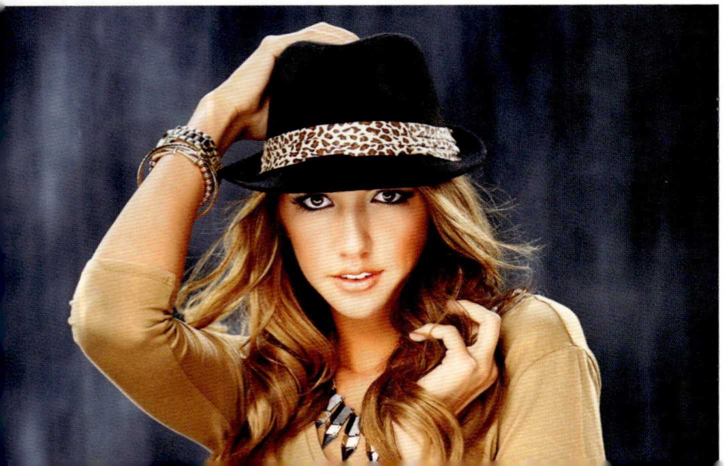

Why Posing Matters

Yes, we all want our or portraits to look natural, not stiff or forced. However, clients do need to be posed if we really want them to look their best.

No matter how good everything else is, if the pose looks awkward, the image won't work. While "lifestyle" photography, with people just standing around, has its proponents, I find that my clients really need posing. They don't understand what will look good and what won't—or that what "feels right" doesn't always looks good when frozen in a still image.

Professional photographers should be trying to create an exceptional, flattering image—and good posing is one of the things we can use to help us achieve that goal. Otherwise, they could just have Mom take the photo!

Master the Fundamentals

When it comes to posing, my biggest influences have been Don Blair, who was the king of posing, and Monte Zucker. A lot of photographers struggle with posing because they need to learn the traditional rules of flattering the human form, rules that photographers like Blair and Zucker totally mastered. Then, it's okay to go and do something different—to do funky stuff, try different things, and break the rules. But you have to remember that those traditional rules were created for a reason: they reliably produce flattering results.

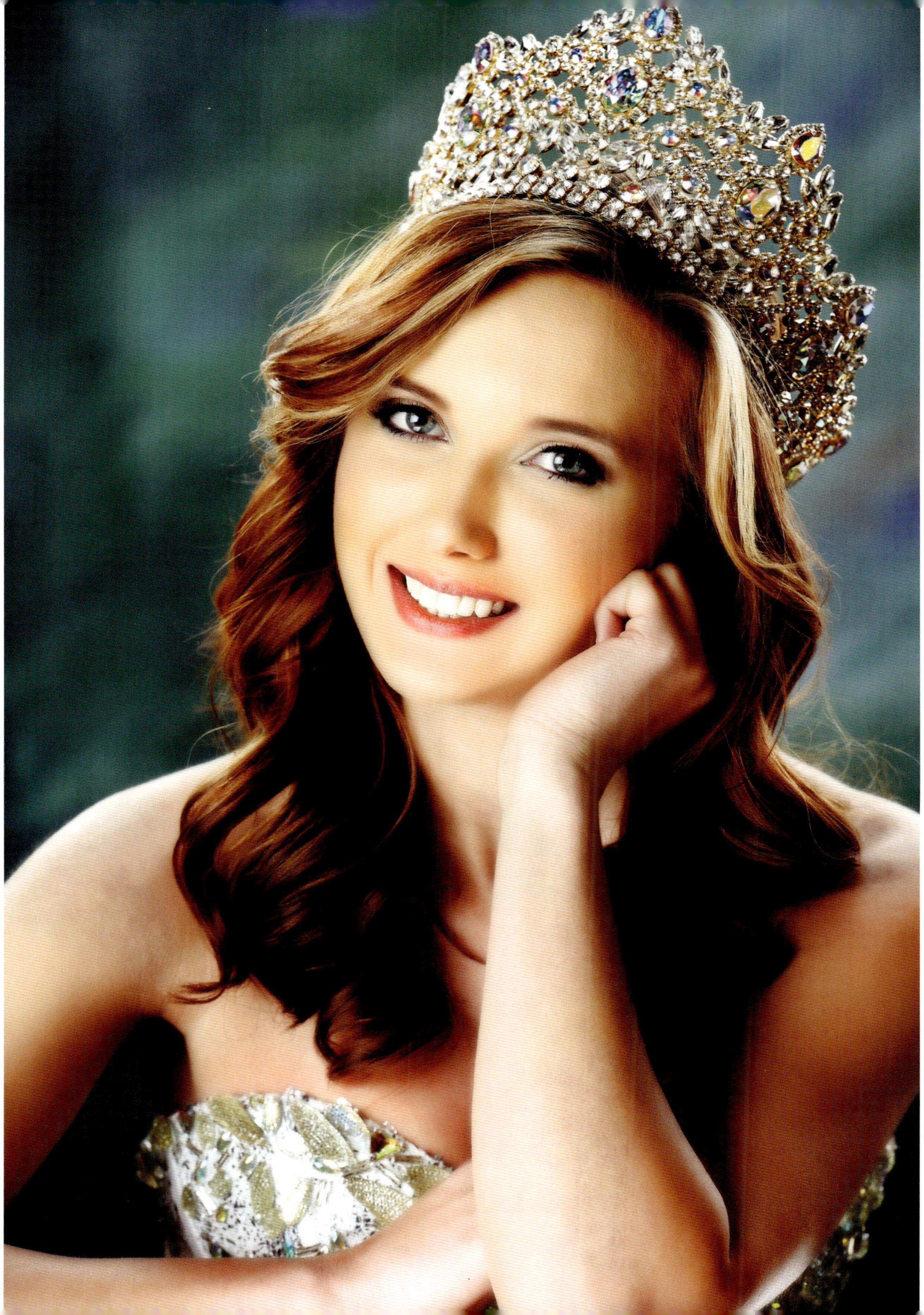

14. **Posing**, Part 2

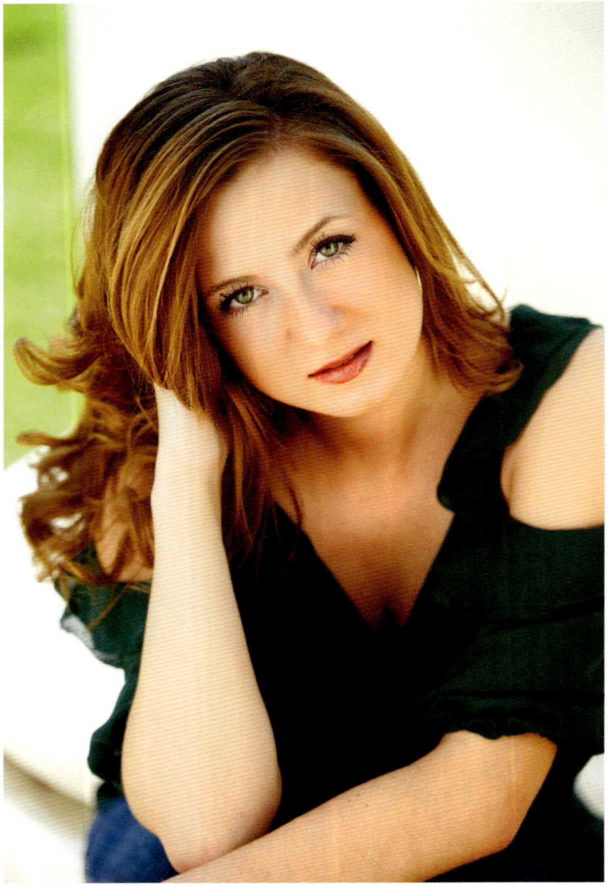

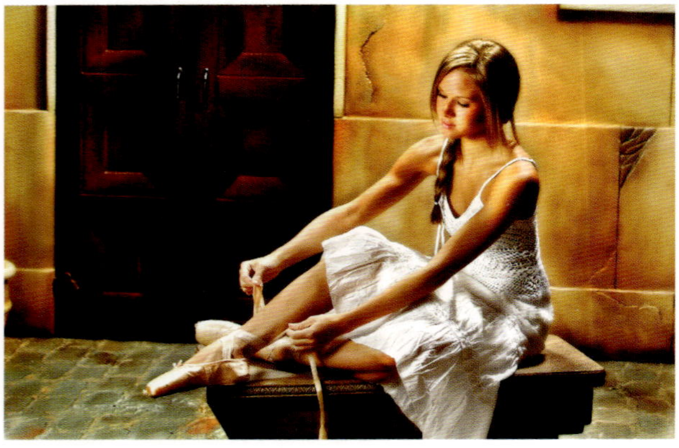

What Do They Want?

The pose has to be tailored to the subject. Sometimes, I have a specific pose in mind for a given subject and scene; other times, it develops more organically as the session progresses. I'll ask them what they want in each scene. Do they want close-ups? A full-body shot? Many subjects also check out my web site and come to the consultation or session with ideas about images they'd like to create. What they want and what works is as different as the individual subjects.

A Personalized Approach

About 85 percent of our clients are young females, and as thin as most of them are, many are still self-conscious about their figures and don't want a full-length image.

I've always had girls all around me (I have two grown daughters and grew up with only sisters—as I noted in a previous section), and that has helped me to be empathetic to their concerns and observant of their tastes.

I can usually get a sense of the differences in their personalities by the clothes they wear and bring for the session. If their outfits are traditional, they'll want traditional images. If they come with clothes that are edgy, I know they want something with a little more of a fashion style. They want to push the envelope a little—always keeping it PG or better, of course.

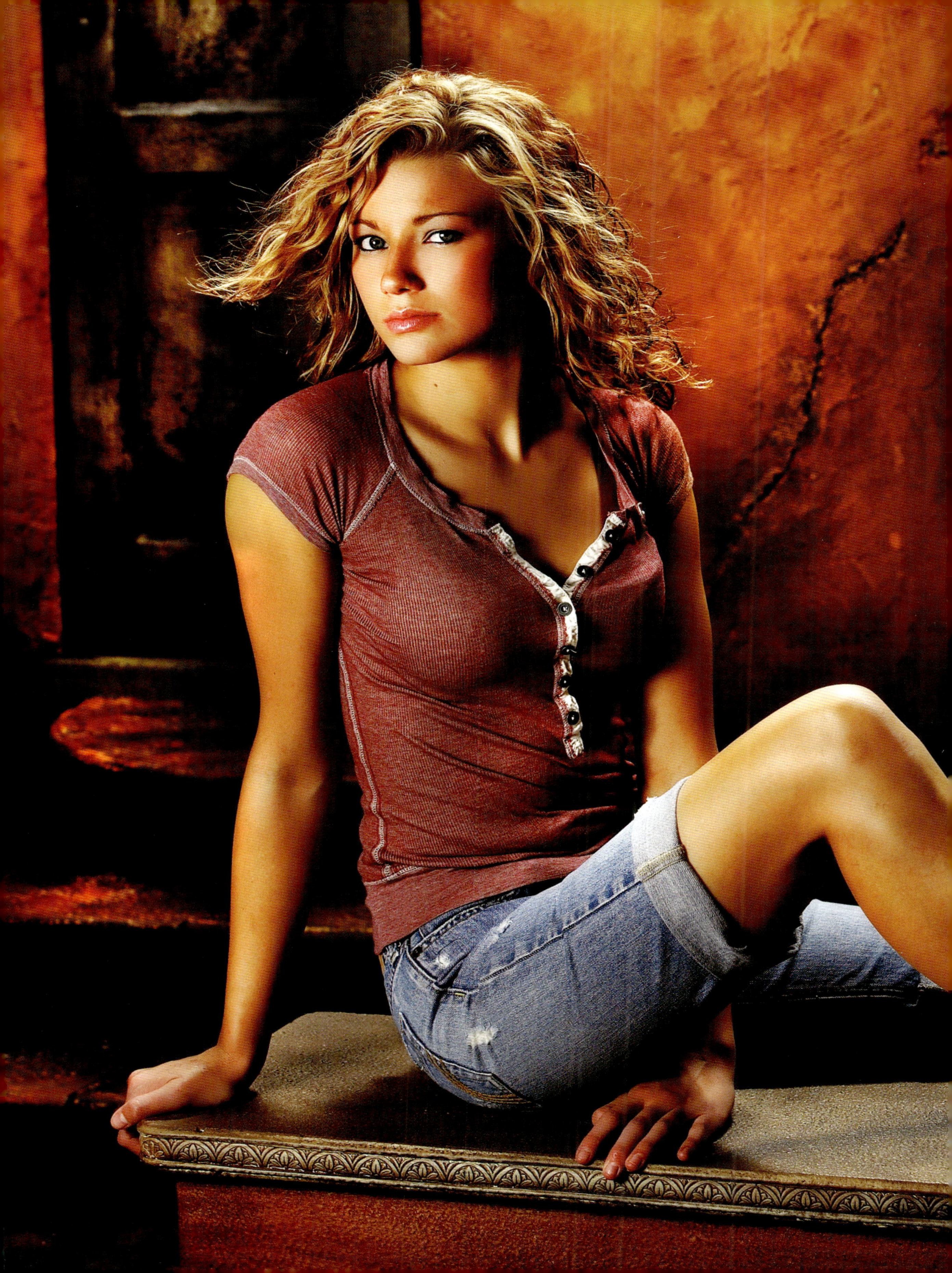

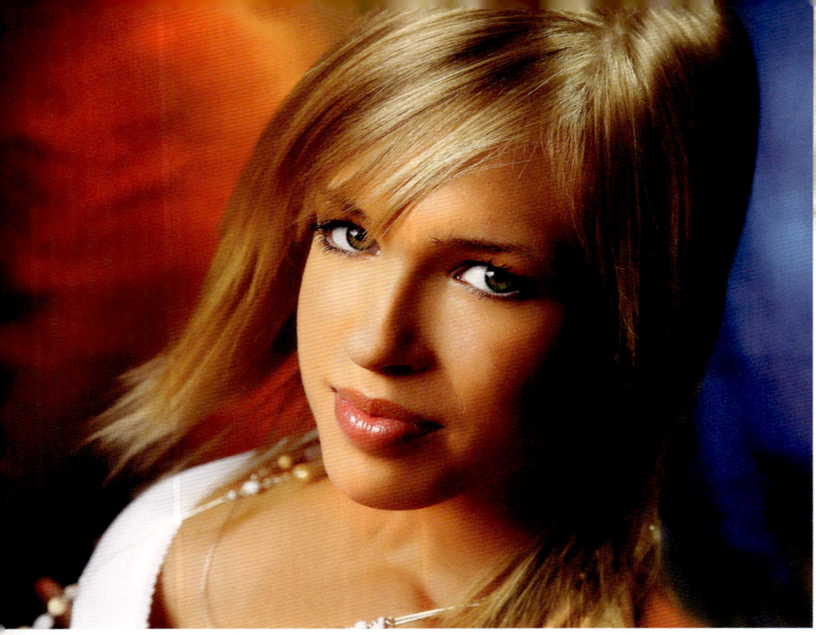

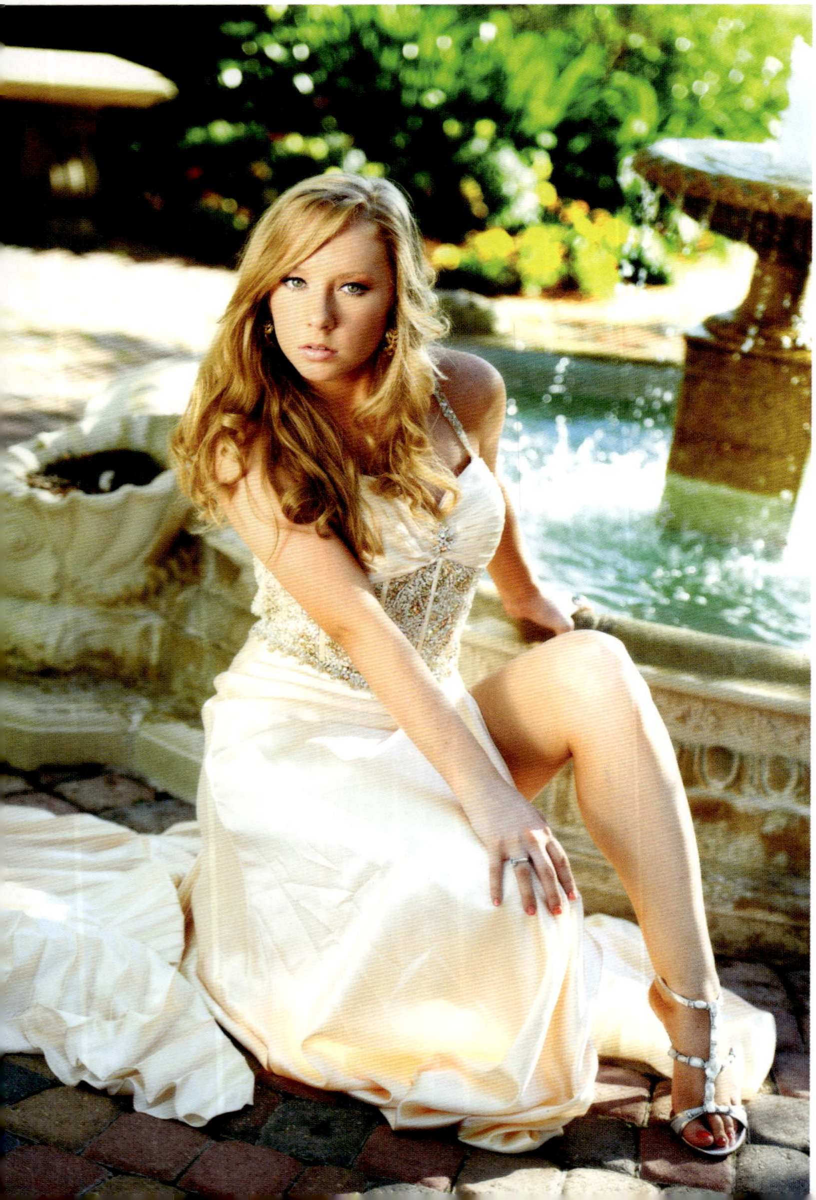

15. **Posing**, Part 3

Objectives: Men vs. Women

While many posing guidelines (not aligning the chin and breastbone, for example) work for both genders, there are some other qualities that tend to make a pose seem more masculine or more feminine.

For women, my poses tend to be soft and bendy. I'm looking for a nice S curve that flows from the shoulders, to the waist and hips, to the legs and feet. Most often, a female subject's head will be tilted toward her higher shoulder.

For men, I tend to go for a pose that more angular. Sharp bends and poses that tend to lean forward tend to read as masculine. Most often, a male subject's head will be tilted toward his lower shoulder.

Rules are made to be broken, of course. The final decision about what makes a pose right must be made on a subject-by-subject basis.

Giving Direction

Most of my subjects aren't experienced in front of the camera and need help to look their very best, so I'll demonstrate the pose for them. Especially when demonstrating poses to the girls, that always gets a laugh. It relaxes them, and they stop seeing me as intimidating and realize that they're going to have a good time.

If the subject still has trouble giving me quite what I want, I'll ask permission, then move their hand or guide their foot into position by touching their knee. We have to honor those basic rules to flatter their form, but still do something a little bit different.

If the subject complains that a pose feels weird (some poses that look great *do* feel weird), showing them the image on the back of the camera usually puts them at ease. I explain that, yes, it feels awkward because you don't normally stand or sit like that—but the reason we're doing it is that we want to create S curves, or it's flattering to the figure. I always explain that to them; it's part of keeping them involved in the session. I don't want anyone to come in and not like their photos because they aren't what they wanted, so I try to get feedback as we go, reading their expressions and listening to what they are saying.

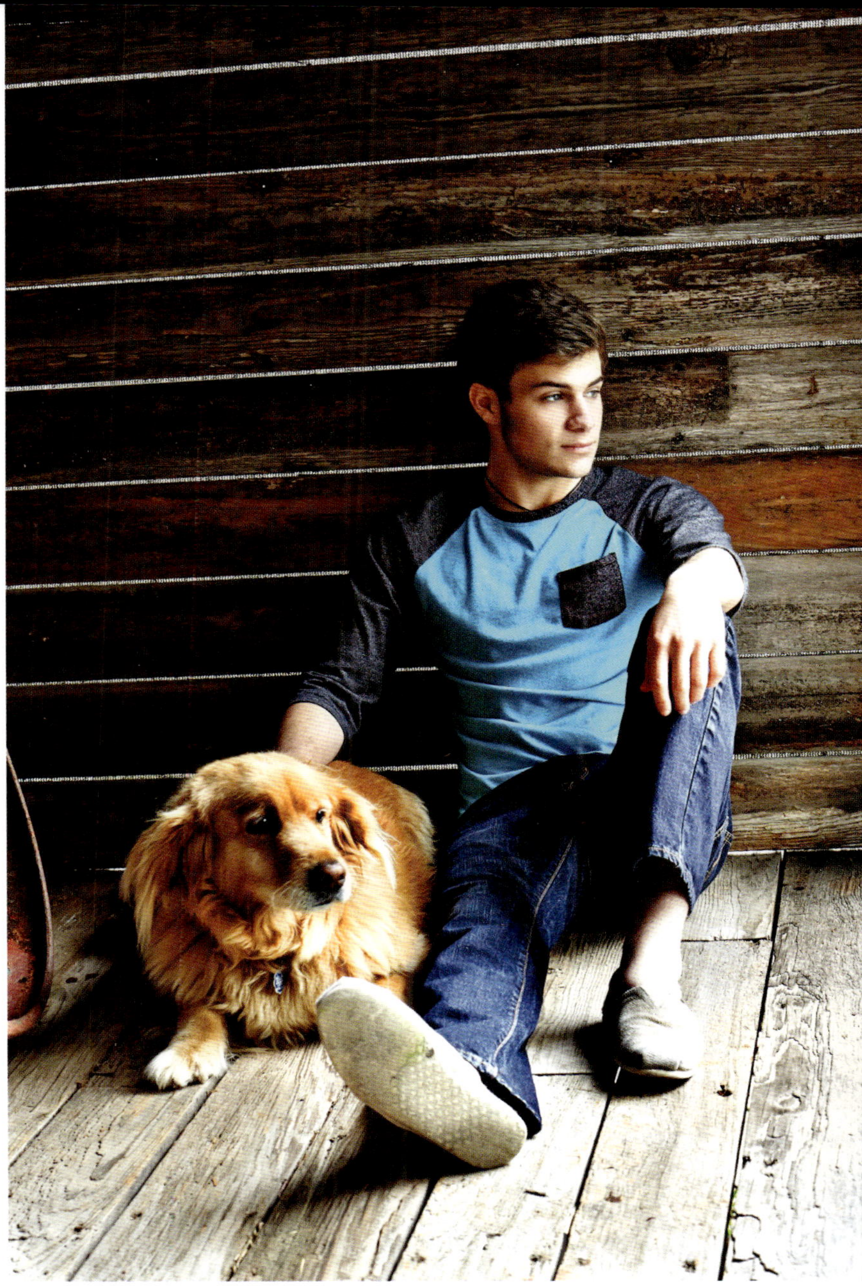

"We have to honor those basic rules to flatter their form, but still do something a little bit different."

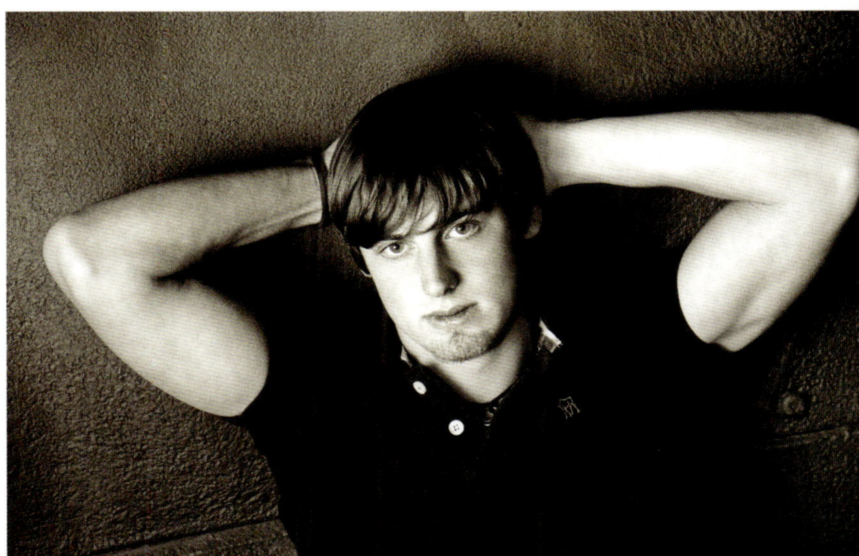

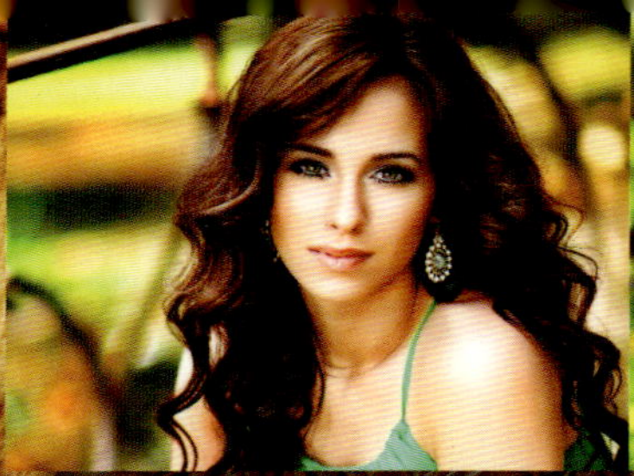

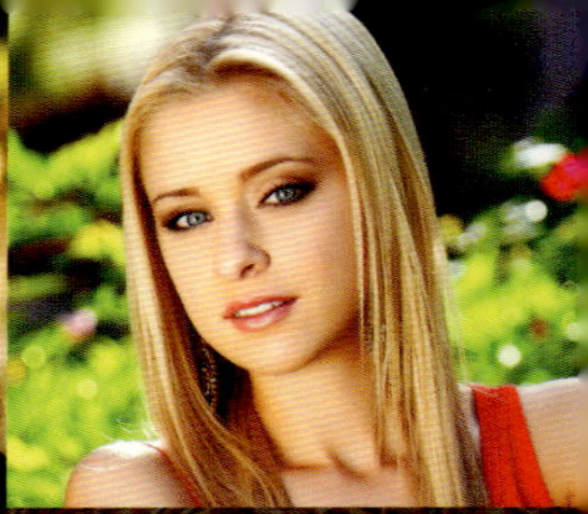

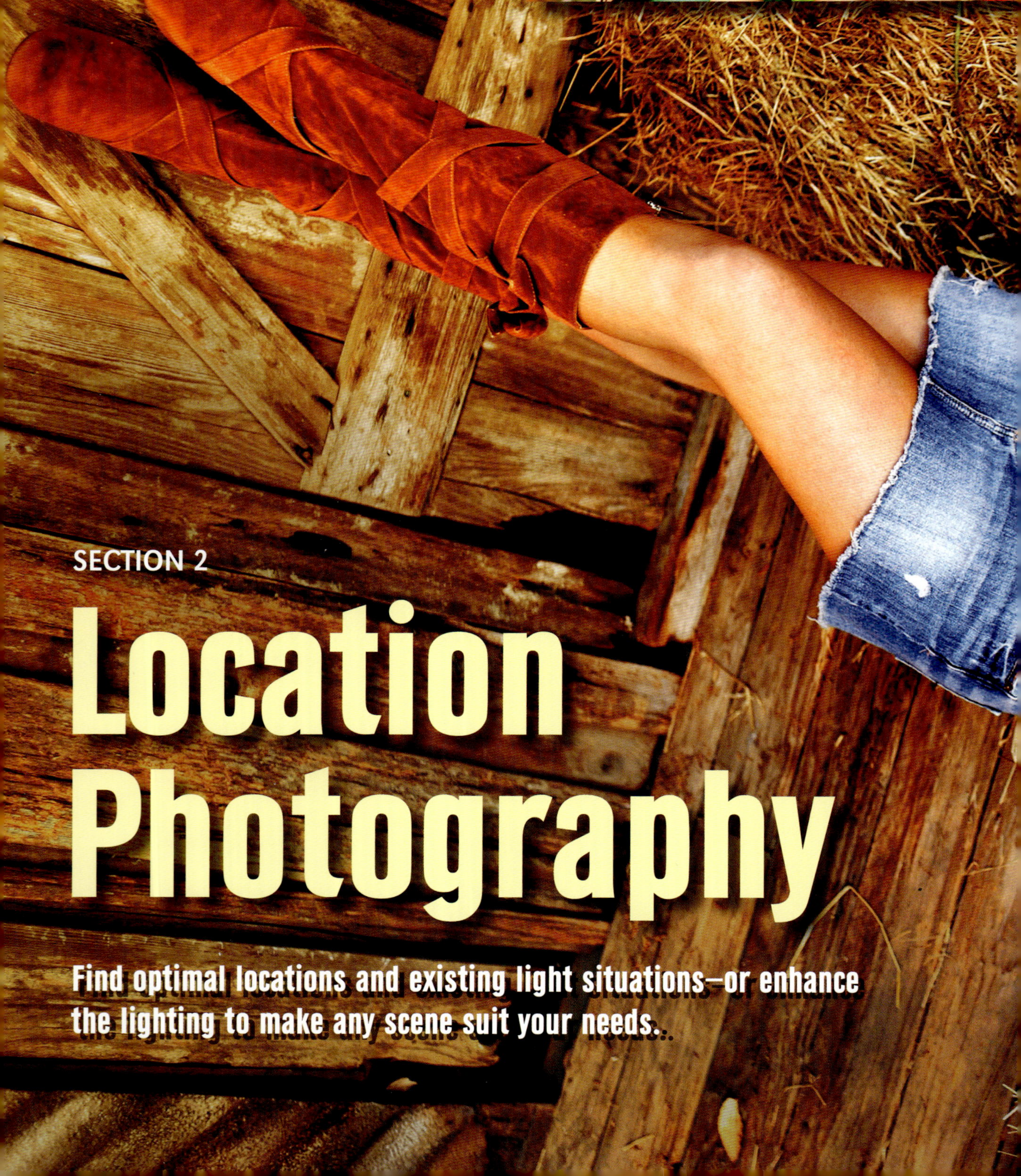

SECTION 2

Location Photography

Find optimal locations and existing light situations—or enhance the lighting to make any scene suit your needs.

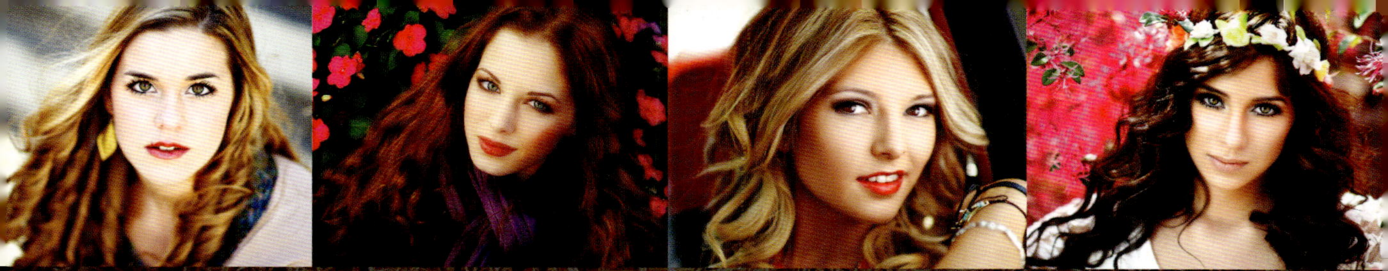
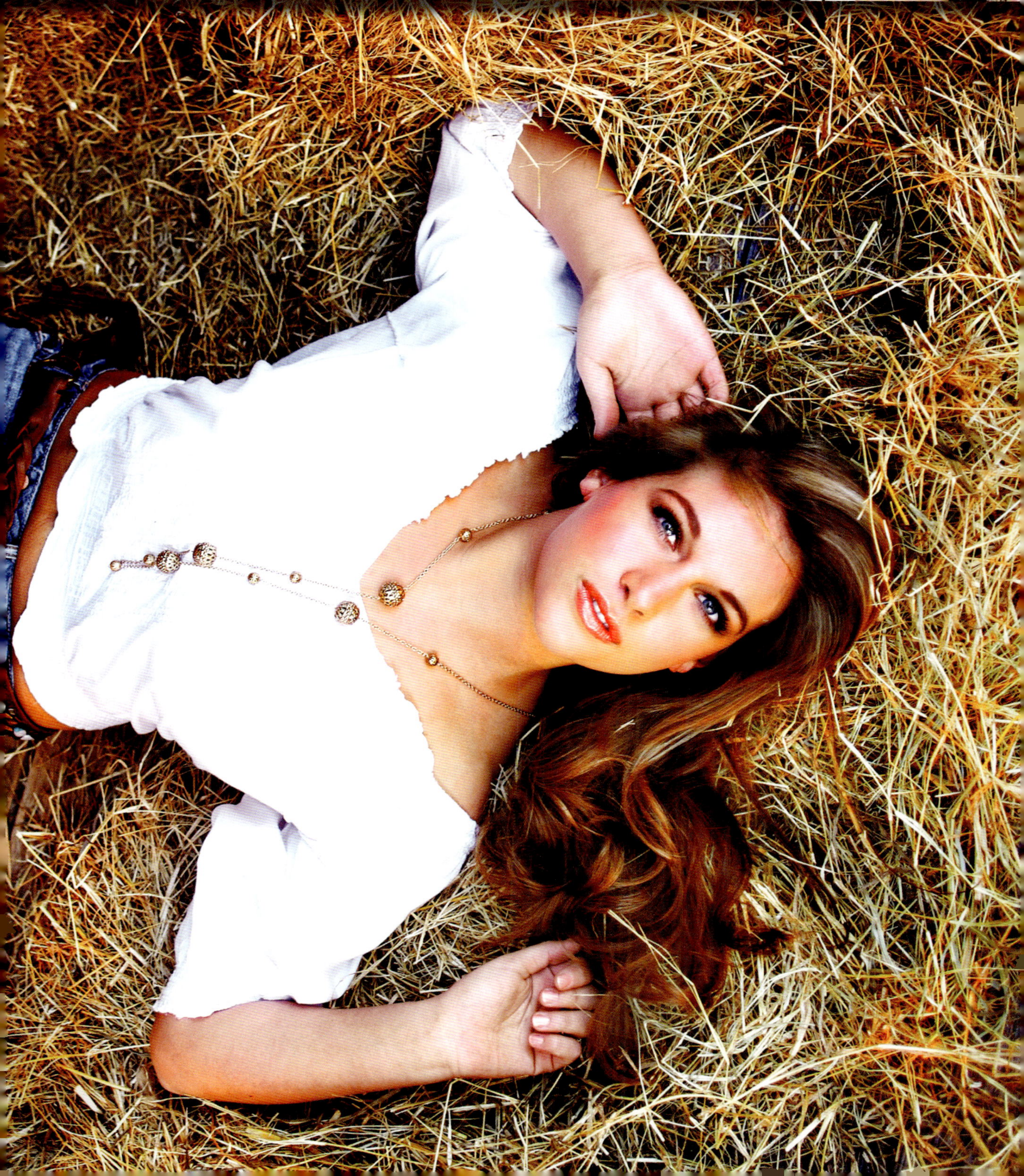

16. Backgrounds: Basic Considerations

A Customized Look

Like the clothing selection, the choice of the background(s) is also something that develops through my dialogue with the subject. I say what I think and try to guide to them toward choices I know will work well—but if there's a certain thing they *must* have, I'm happy to go along with that, too. I just put my spin on it to make it look like a Tim Schooler portrait!

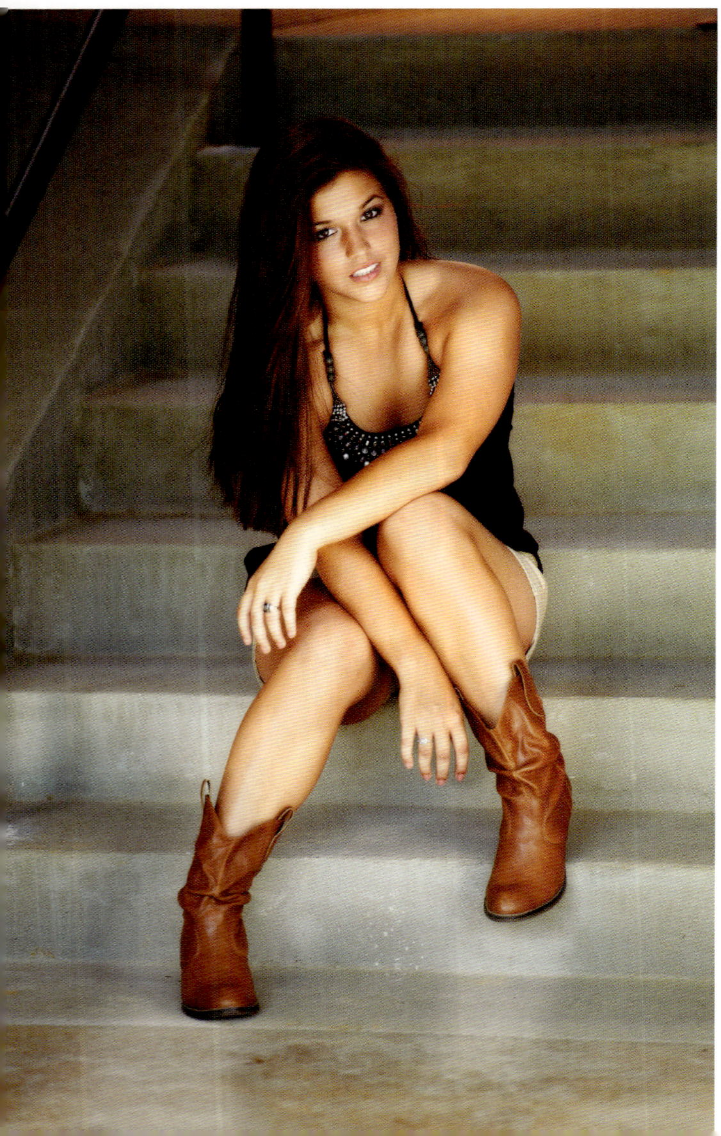

Consider the Clothing

In some cases, a good background choice arises from the clothing selection. If I see a cowboy hat, I might suggest a porch area behind the studio where I have barn-board walls and an old wagon wheel. If the clothing is elegant, the glass walls of a nearby building might be the perfect complement. Did the client show up with her favorite top and a pair of cutoffs? That's a great look for a casual portrait in a field of flowers.

Added Meaning

My clients who are locals often have some ideas of where they'd like to shoot—spots that have some special meaning to them. Once, I traveled with a senior to shoot near a tree on her family's old property; she had special memories of playing there with her grandfather, so it made the portraits especially significant.

On the same note, it's not unusual for clients to want to include a special piece of clothing, like their dad's jersey or a garment handed down from their grandmother, in their portraits. Special items from childhood, like a teddy bear, are also things some seniors bring to make their portraits feel more personalized.

Personal Taste

Portraits should reflect the personality of the subject featured. So I'm always asking clients for their input. Often, they'll go to my web site and bring in images they like—or they may bring in some magazine clippings or photos on their phone that show the looks they are most drawn to.

"Once, I traveled with a senior to shoot near a tree on her family's old property; she had special memories of playing there with her grandfather, so it made the portraits especially significant."

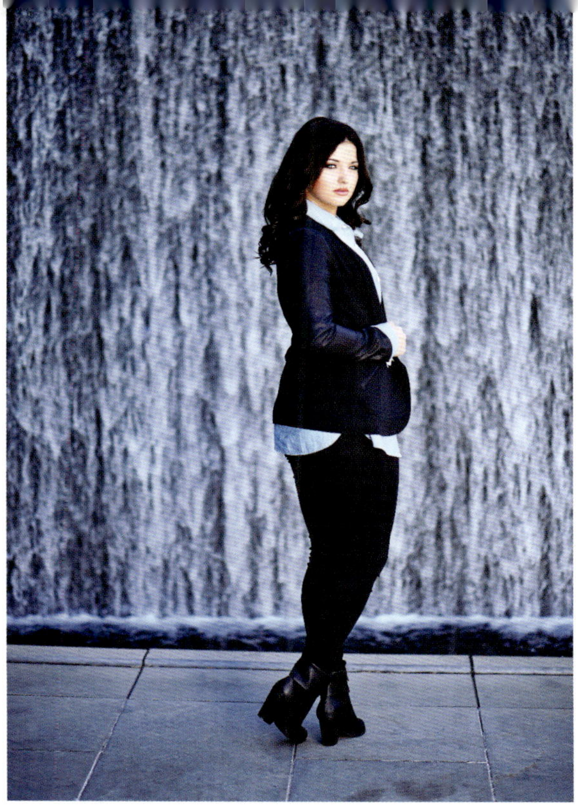

Likewise, I have folders of images on my phone and on my computer that show places we shoot. If the client's "inspiration" image isn't at one of those locations, we can almost always find something with the same basic look and feel. If they like rustic looks, we can shoot at a barn or farm area. If their personal style is more urban, we'll stay in the downtown area around my studio. If they like a natural or traditional feel, a nearby college campus offers nice foliage and classic architecture. For a setting that speaks to our Louisiana culture, there are two sites nearby with restored/re-created Cajun villages that offer nice backgrounds.

In addition to the looks they've selected, I also like to give them some things they didn't specifically ask for. Adding to the variety of looks enhances the overall sale—and often clients are surprised that the unexpected backgrounds are among their favorites.

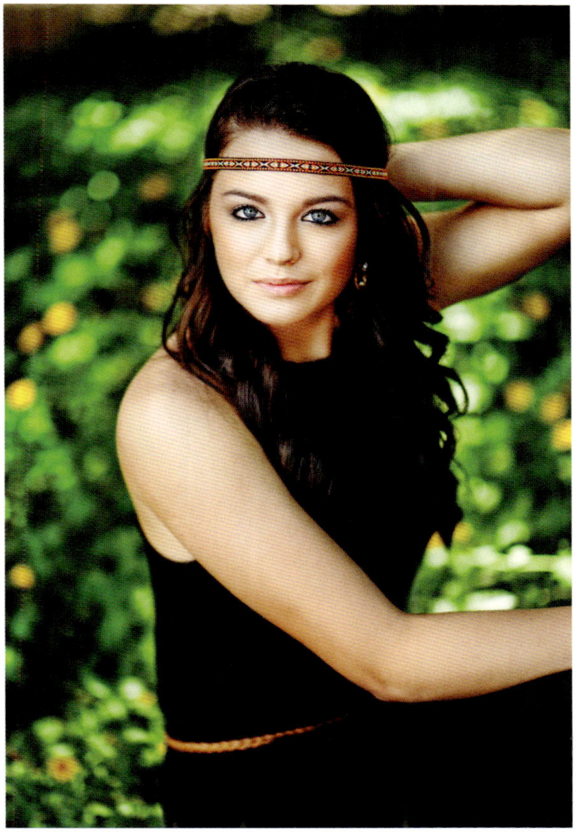

17. Backgrounds: Additional Factors

Seasonal Locations

It's important to keep in mind that many locations change substantially in their look from season to season. Particularly for images with floral backgrounds, we track when/where things are in bloom so we know where to shoot from week to week. This is especially true during the spring, which is our busiest time for senior portrait clients.

Be Considerate!

At many locations that used to be welcoming to photographers, the rules have changed in recent years. New photographers have flooded the portrait market and, unfortunately, some of them have abused these properties. As a result, photography may be prohibited or only permitted with a high fee. Before using a location, investigate their photography policies—and when you get there, be polite and respectful.

Although the temperatures are cool, Thanksgiving time is still a relatively heavy shooting season for us. I love the look of portraits in a scarf, jacket, and jeans—it gives the images a timeless feel. (And some clients even brave the chill to shoot in summer clothes in November!) At this time of year, the grass is usually brown, so we look for areas with evergreens to shoot foliage images. In Louisiana,

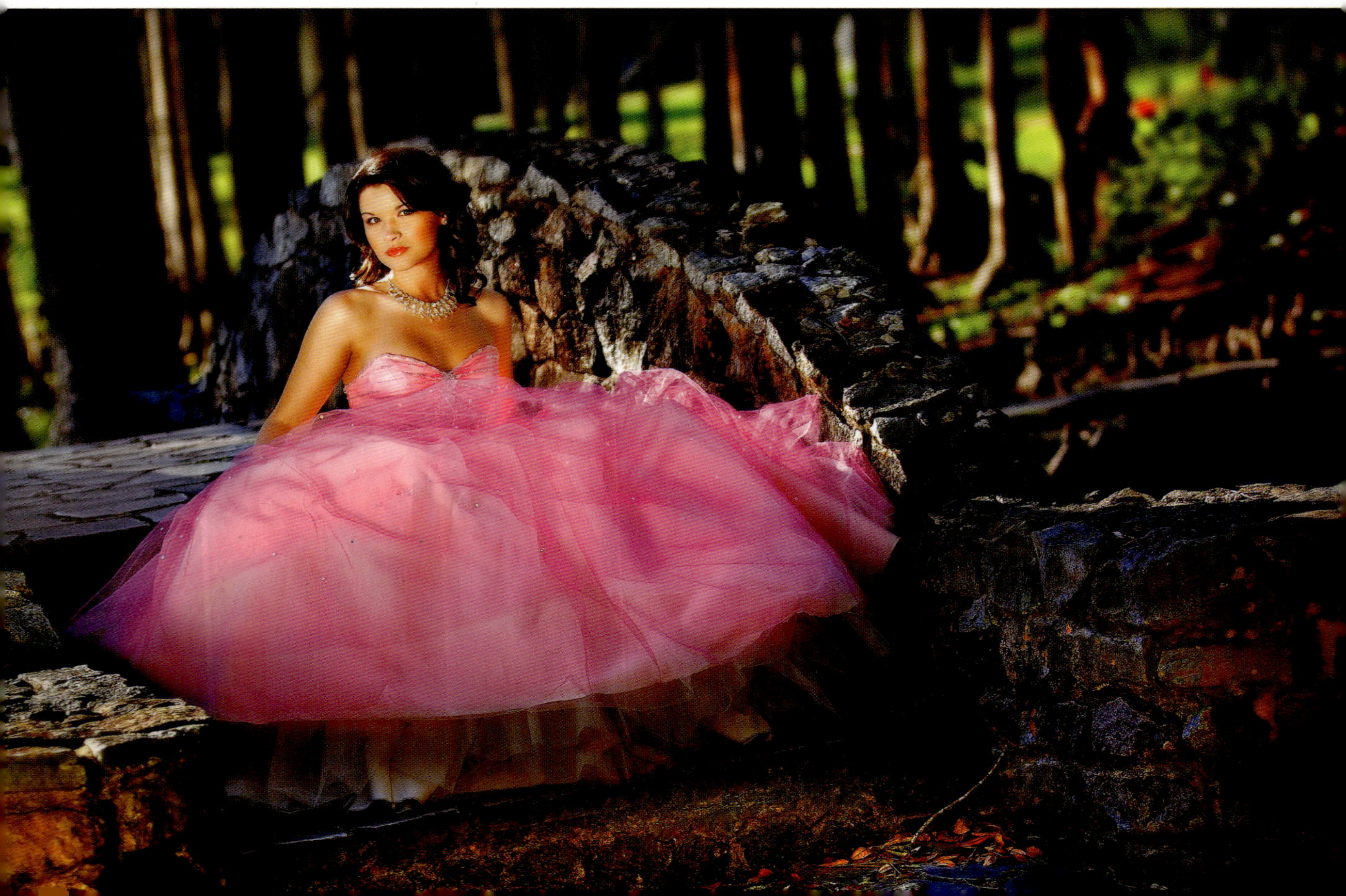

> “It helps to look for things in the scene that will help the subject to pose naturally. Look for something they can rest a hand on, sit on, or lean against.”

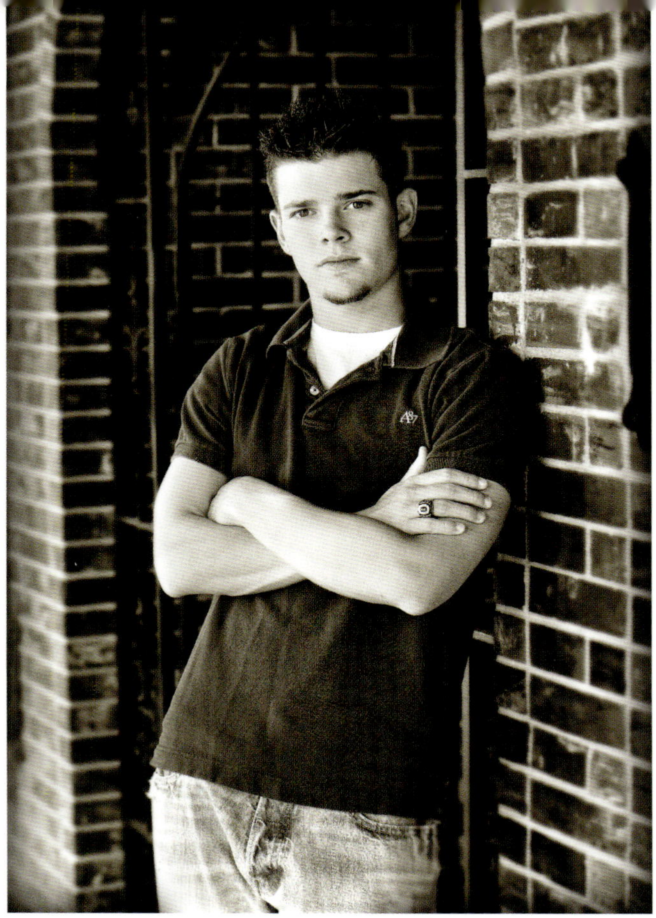

we even have some flowers that bloom during cooler months, so knowing when/where to find those helps expand the range of looks we can create during autumn sessions.

The Weather

The potential is always there for weather problems that can sideline location-shooting plans. As noted in section 8, this is one reason we always meet clients at the studio to start their session. Behind the studio, I have a couple setups with overhead blockers that create directional light and allow us to create outdoor looks without getting wet. One is a barnboard wall for rustic looks. The other is a rock waterfall for more nature-themed portraits. There are also a few nearby buildings that have overhangs; these, too, let us create outdoor looks for our clients without having to reschedule the session.

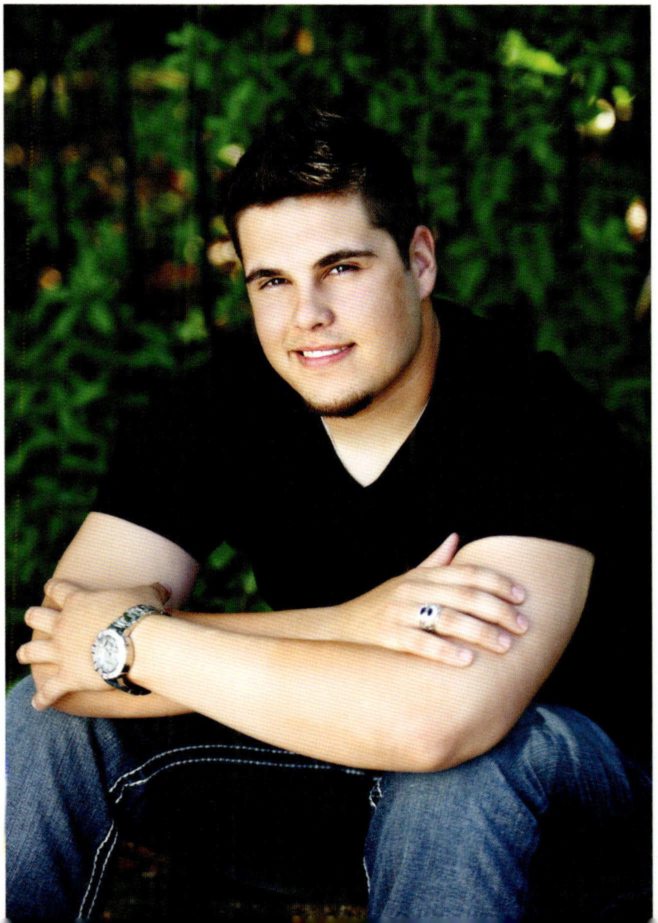

Posing Aids

It helps to look for things in the scene that will help the subject to pose naturally. (It’s hard to pose a portrait subject beautifully when they are just standing isolated in a field!) Find something they can rest a hand on, sit on, or lean against.

18. Backgrounds: Men vs. Women

Masculine

For portraits of male subjects, it's best to opt for scenes that feature rough textures, glass, or hard lines (*below*). Urban scenes, industrial settings, warehouses, brick walls, parking garages with old pipes—these all make good settings for masculine images.

Feminine

Women can cross over into most of the same settings, but also look good photographed with softer backgrounds (*facing page*). Ivy and flowers, for example, are nice settings for more feminine images. Green foliage also provides a classic background for almost any subject.

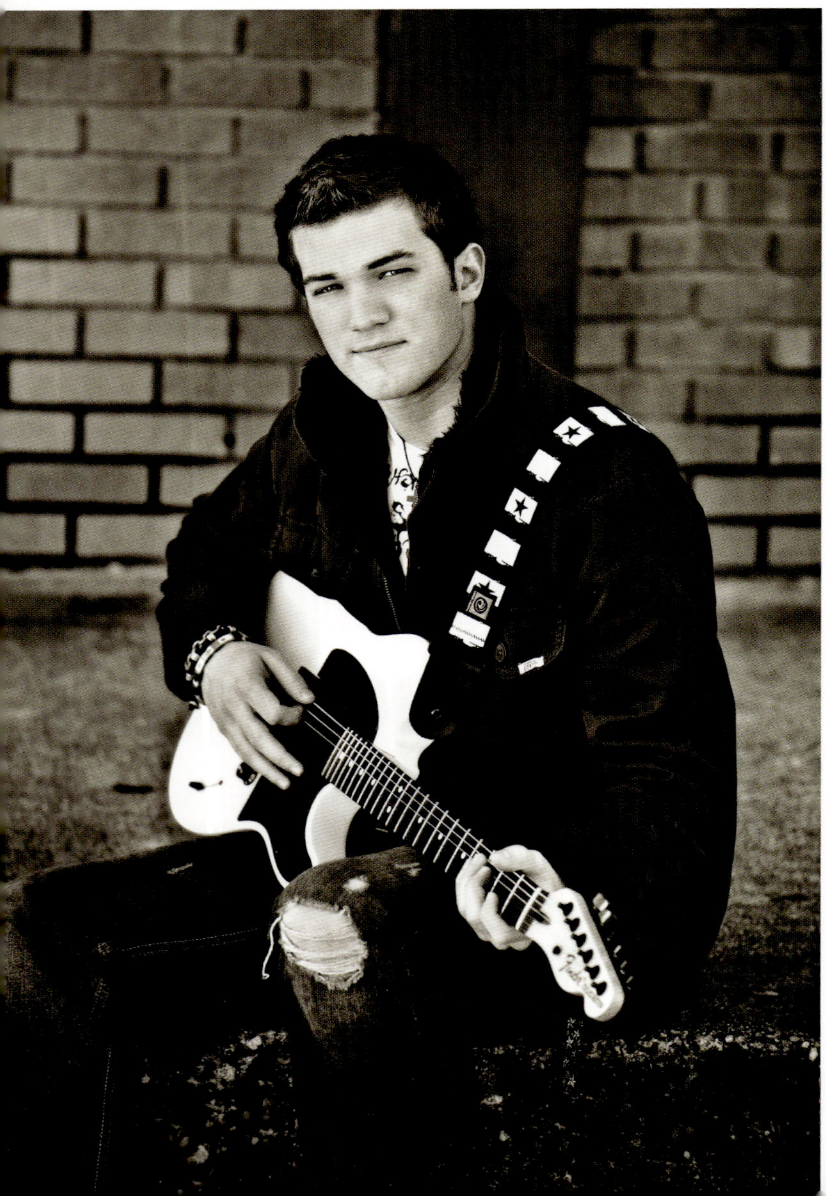

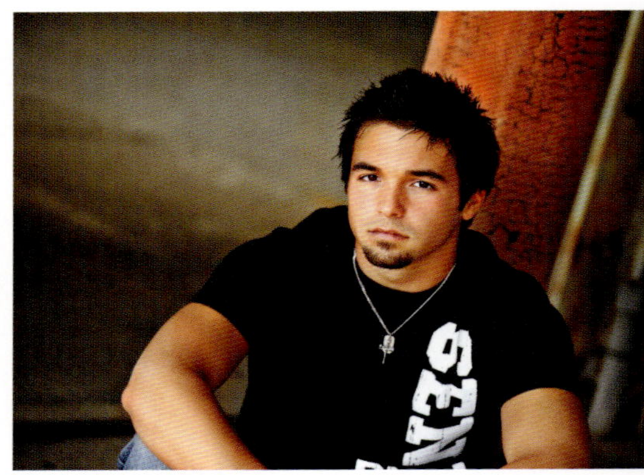

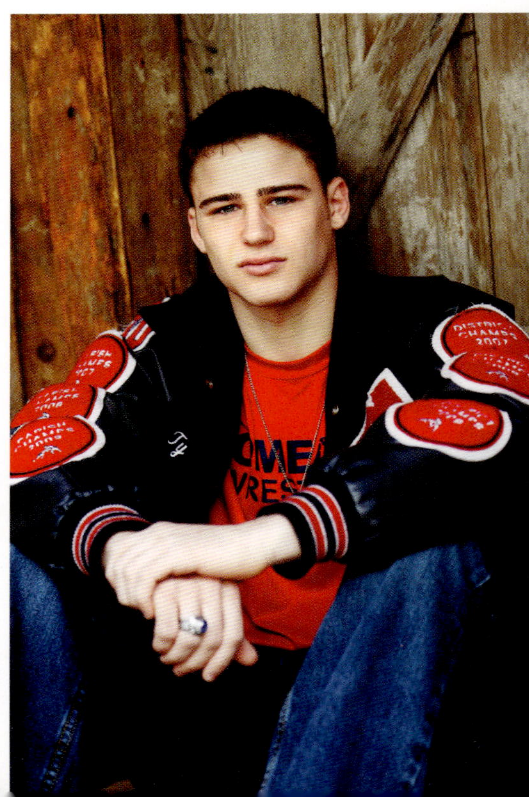

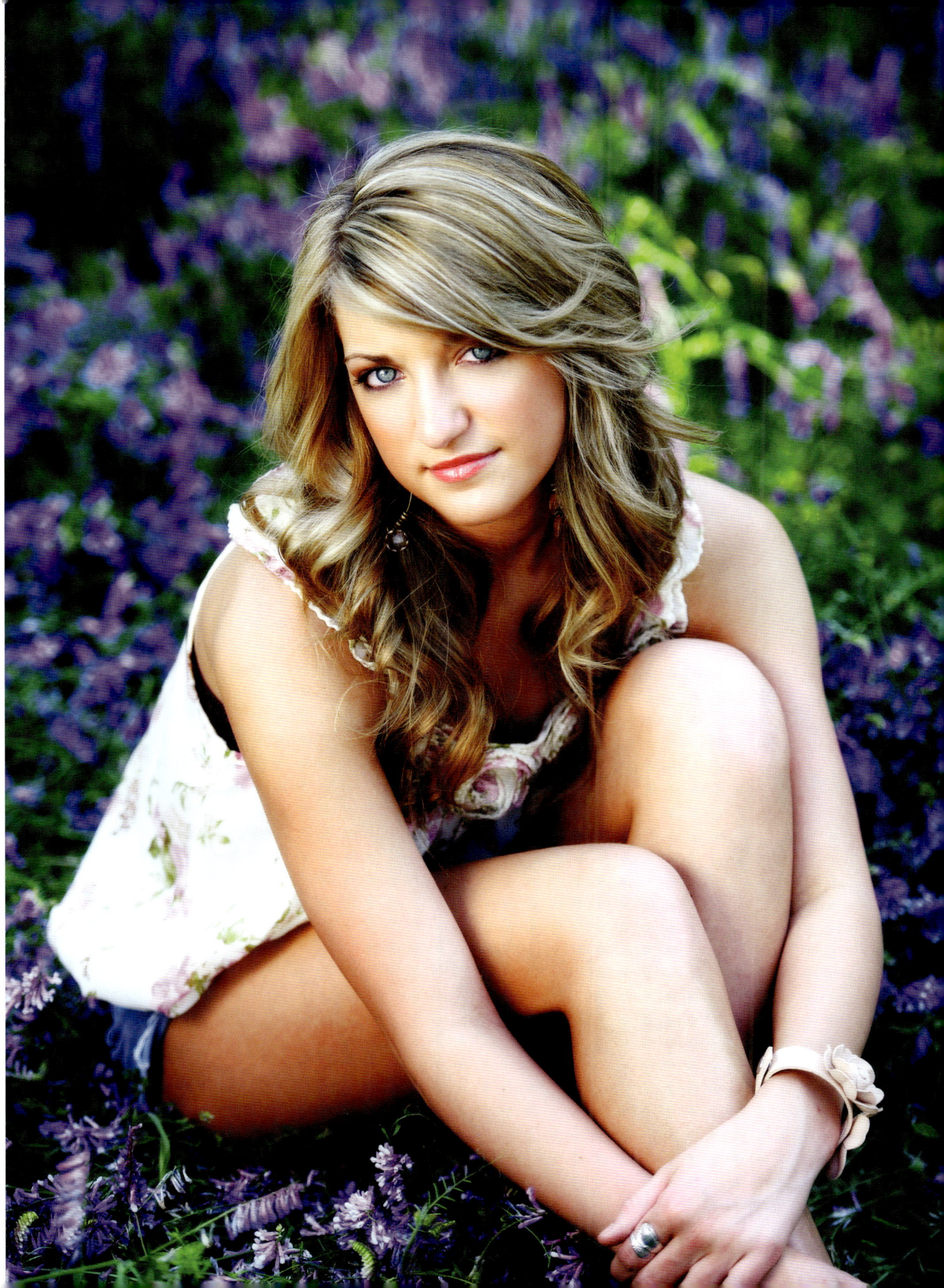

19. Find the Light

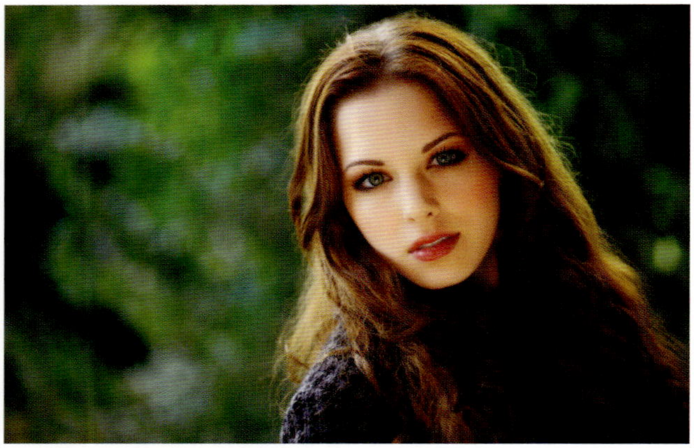

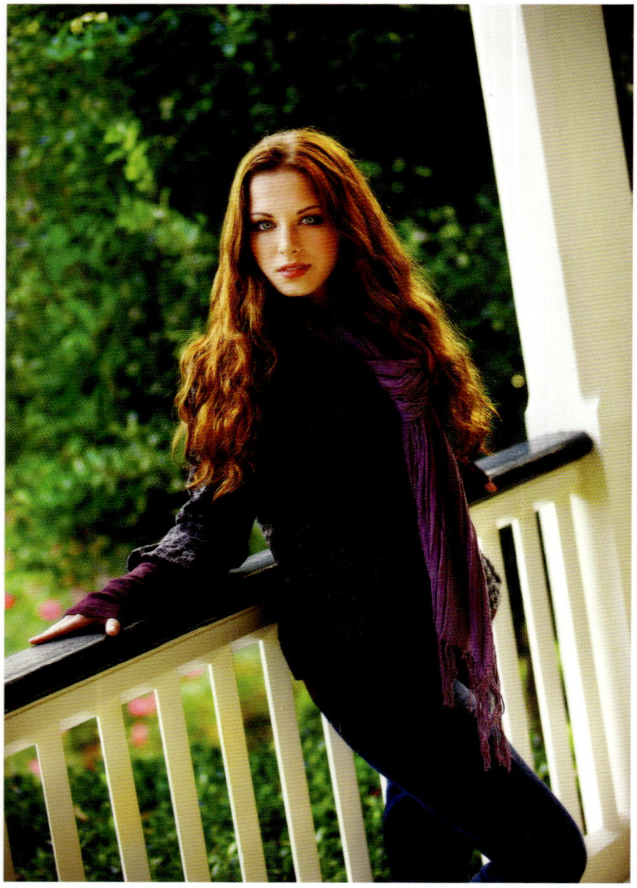

The Top Concern

While selecting the right background for your subject is very important for the overall look and feel of the portrait, the most critical consideration when setting up a location shot needs to be the lighting. A nice background won't save your image from unflattering lighting on the subject.

Directional Light Is Key

The sense of depth we like to see in a professional photograph comes from the interplay of light and shade. Light and shade are what reveal contours and make a two-dimensional image seem more three-dimensional. In studio lighting, we create this by adjusting our main light's height and angle relative to the subject. When using available lighting, we have to 1) find spaces with directional lighting and 2) position our subjects relative to that lighting for a flattering look.

Portraits on a Porch

For these images, shot on a porch, the light came from camera left. A wall to camera right blocked the light from that side, creating a nice pattern of light and shadow on my subject's face. The brighter sun behind her added nice edge lighting on her hair, highlighting its beautiful color. With a few simple posing variations, I was able to create several nice images here—using just the available light.

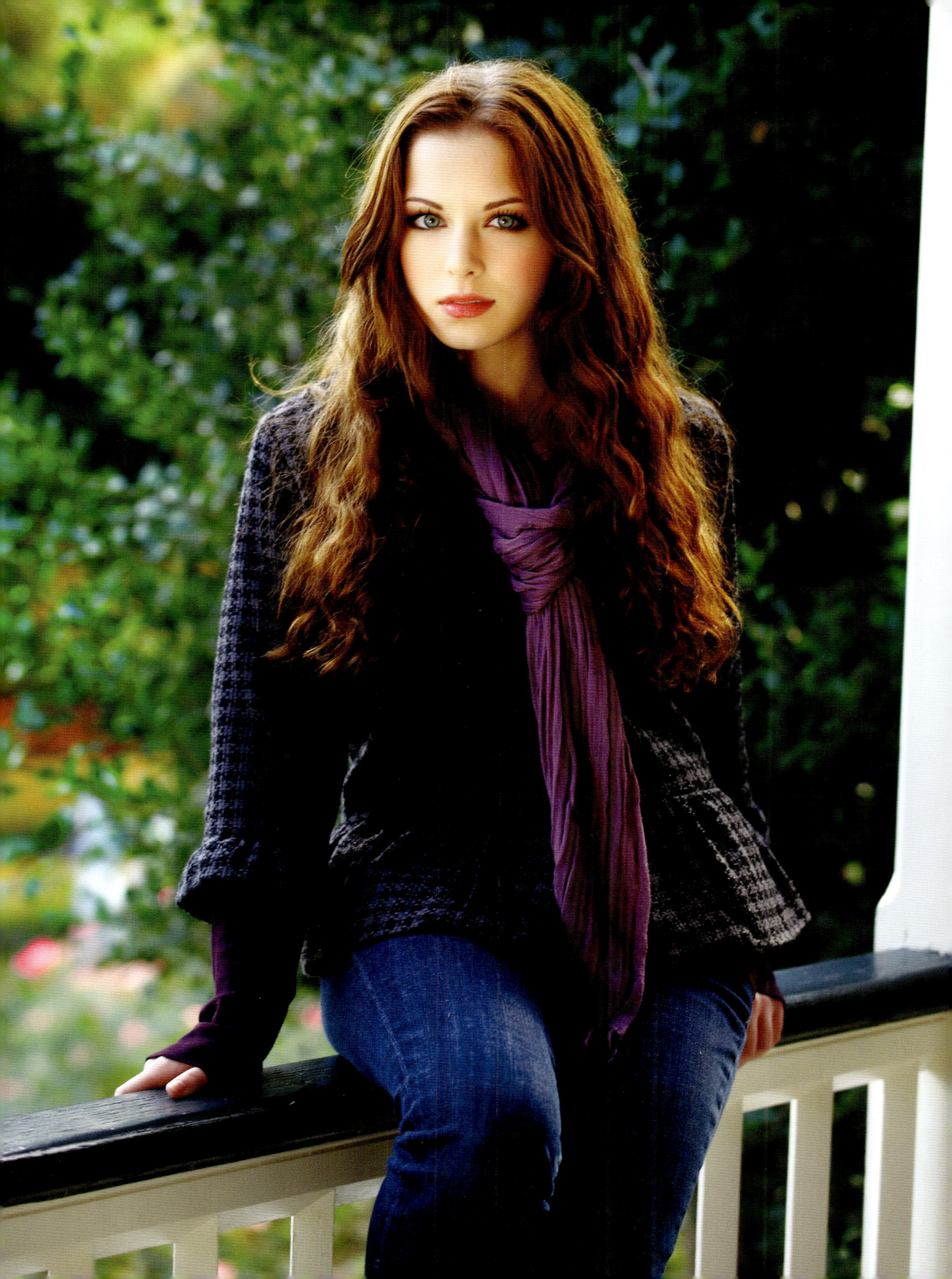

20. **Block the Overhead Light**

Lowering the Angle

Light that comes from too high an angle tends to create too much shadowing on the eyes and an overall unflattering look that lacks direction.

If you're shooting at sunrise or sunset, the available light will naturally come from a low angle that produces directional lighting on your subject. At all the other times of day, the times when most of us actually shoot, you can get a nice directional look by simply blocking the overhead light. This is the kind of lighting you find under an overhang—be it the roof of a porch (as we just saw in section 19), the branches of a tree, or some other feature of the scene. When the overhead light is blocked, the remaining light falls on the subject from a lower angle—more like where you'd place the main light in a studio portrait.

Portico Portrait

For the image on the facing page, I posed my model in a long portico and had her look back at me in the opening at the end (with the sun behind me). The lighting pattern is more subtle, but the low angle of the light lit her eyes and smile fully and beautifully.

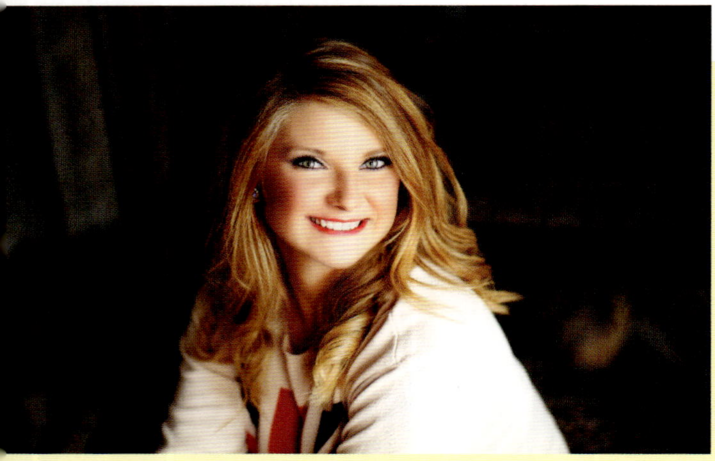

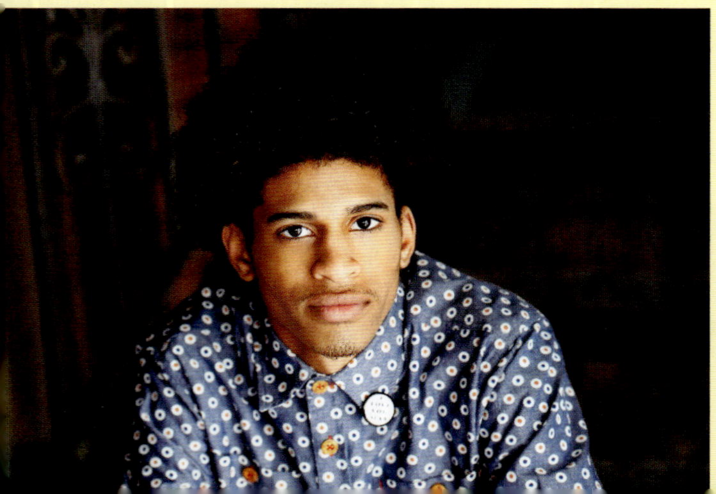

Watch the Catchlights

The two portraits to the left were shot in the same location—outside a bail-bonds shop! The facade of the old brink building features multiple arched openings, as you can see reflected in the subjects' eyes (*below*). A covered location like this is perfect for portraits on days when the weather isn't perfect—and the fact that the light is very directional makes the resulting portraits very flattering. On the overcast days when I shot these images, the direct light from the sky was flat and unattractive. Also, check out the background. The girl's portrait was shot at f/1.4; the guy's portrait was at f/2.8. That one-stop adjustment changed the look quite a bit.

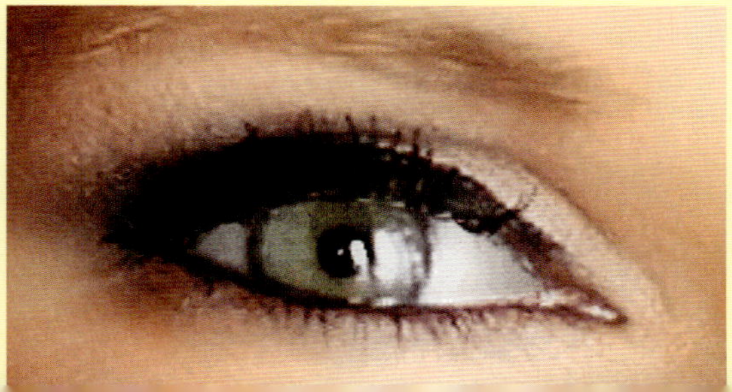

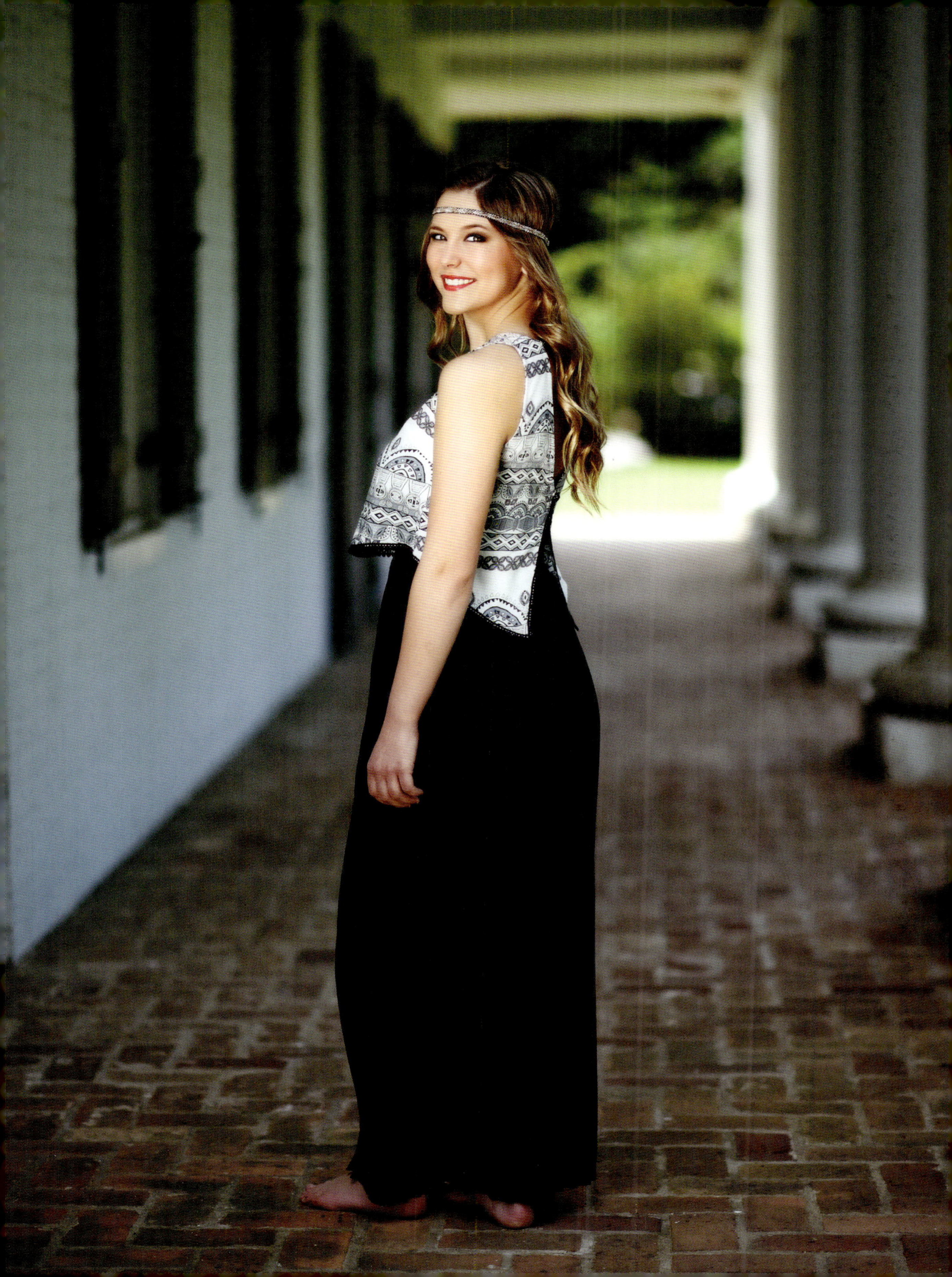

21. **Add a Reflector**

Positioning the Reflector

While I was always taught to use a reflector for fill light, I actually prefer to use the reflected light as the main light source in my outdoor portraits—creating the primary pattern of light and shadow on my subject's face. Instead of allowing the sun to fall on the subject's face, I place it *behind* them to function as a hair light (for shine and texture on the hair) and as a kicker (for highlights on the body).

Which Reflector to Use

As noted in section 9, I keep several reflectors in my location lighting kit. I most often shoot with the white side of the big Photoflex reflector. This will light the subject's whole body. And I can have Mom hold it, because she can rest it on the ground and easily keep it in just the right position.

In my area, seniors are allowed to wear white prom dresses (underclassmen must wear colored gowns). For these portraits, the 74-inch white reflector is too big—it will blow out all the detail in the dress. So I switch to a 42-inch round reflector that I can aim just at the face. The same technique works for brides or people with darker complexions who are wearing light-colored clothes.

The Tri-Grip reflector is even smaller—but its size and handle make it something that I can handle myself, for shoots when no assistant or parent is available.

The gold and white reflector is something I use on overcast days where I need a little more punch than the white reflector can provide.

Soft and Beautiful

The image on the facing page is one of my favorites. I created it at a nearby college campus while the sun was quite high in the sky. I posed my subject under a tree with sun behind her. A large white reflector, held by her mom, was positioned in a spot where the light was breaking through the trees—in this case, just a bit out of frame to the left. That's it! I had soft and beautiful lighting on her face.

If I'd had to move the reflector back farther to catch the light, I could have flipped it to the silver side to kick enough back onto the subject. Switching to the silver side does make the effect a bit specular. To my eye, it's not *quite* as pretty—but it's still directional and appealing.

Portrait Lighting Terms

Main light—The light source that creates the primary pattern of light and shadow on the subject's face.

Fill light—A secondary light sources added to brighten the shadows created by the main light.

Hair light—Light from above and behind (or to the side of) the subject that adds accents on the hair, giving it texture and shine.

Kicker light—Light from above and behind (or to the side of) the subject that adds accents on the body for a greater sense of depth and background separation.

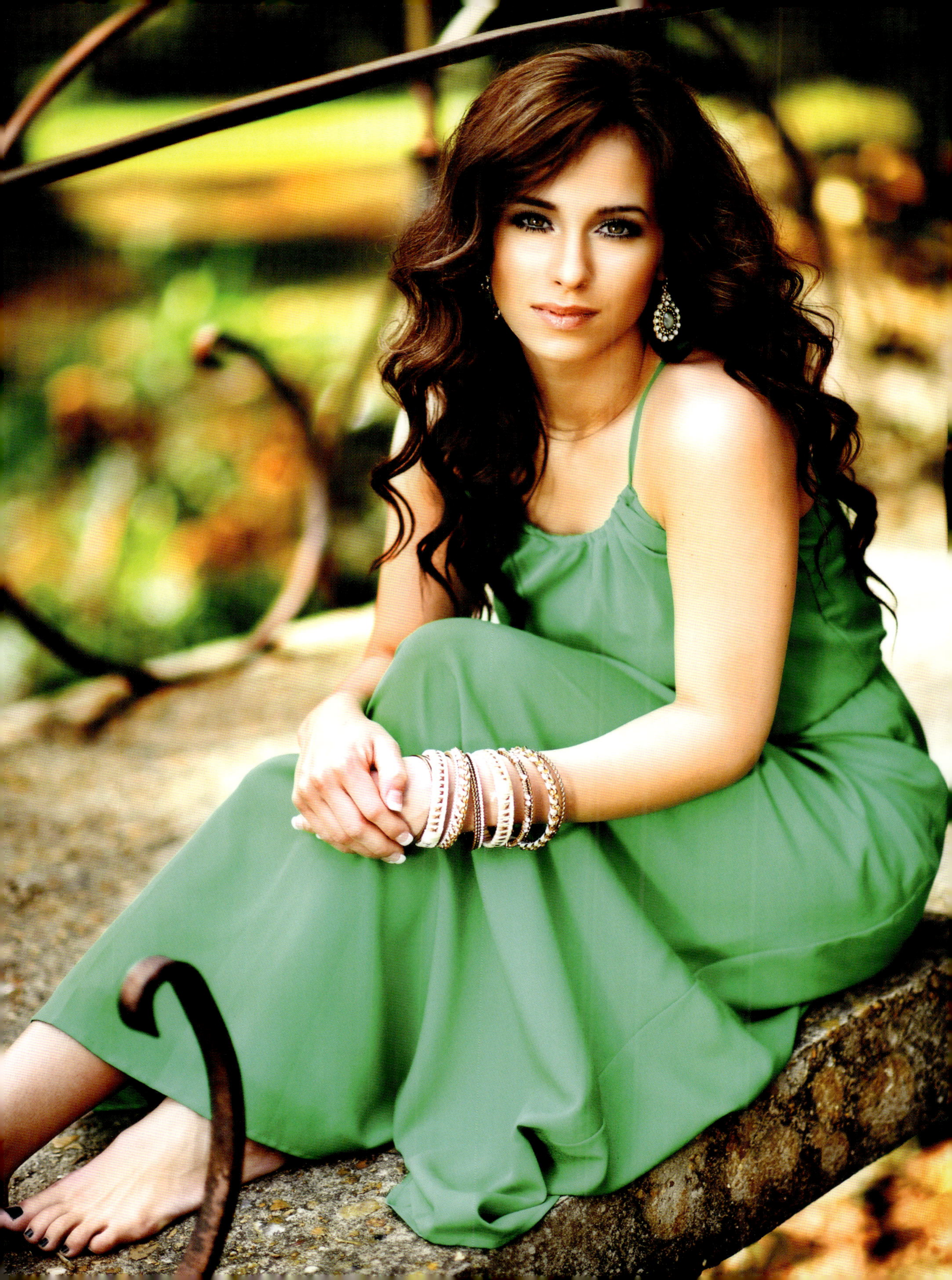

22. Subject Position

Edge of the Sunlight

These photos were taken on some steps across the street from my studio. For the facing-page image, I positioned my subject at the edge of the direct sunlight and added a reflector to bounce very soft, even light onto her face. The bright sun behind her blew out the detail on her hair and the edge of her right leg. It's kind of a fashion look—and it's one that girls like, so I don't worry about the loss of detail.

Into the Shade

To keep the detail in the hair and keep my subject in the same position, I could have added a scrim overhead to cut down on the top light. On this day, though, I didn't have an extra person on hand to hold a scrim in place. To get a similar look, I moved her over just a little into the shade, as seen in the image below.

Get Mom Involved

Moms and friends like to get involved. A small reflector is hard for them to keep in place, but a large one that rests on the ground is easy. It also separates them from the subject a bit and distracts them from coaching or preening the person whose photo is being taken.

Watch the Eyes

Note, however, that the catchlights in the image below are not quite as prominent as those in the image on the facing page. That's because my model was in the shade. The bigger catchlights in the more sunlit portrait are desirable; they make the eyes more attractive. So it's a trade-off: shifting the subject position improved the highlight details, but to the slight detriment of the lighting on the eyes.

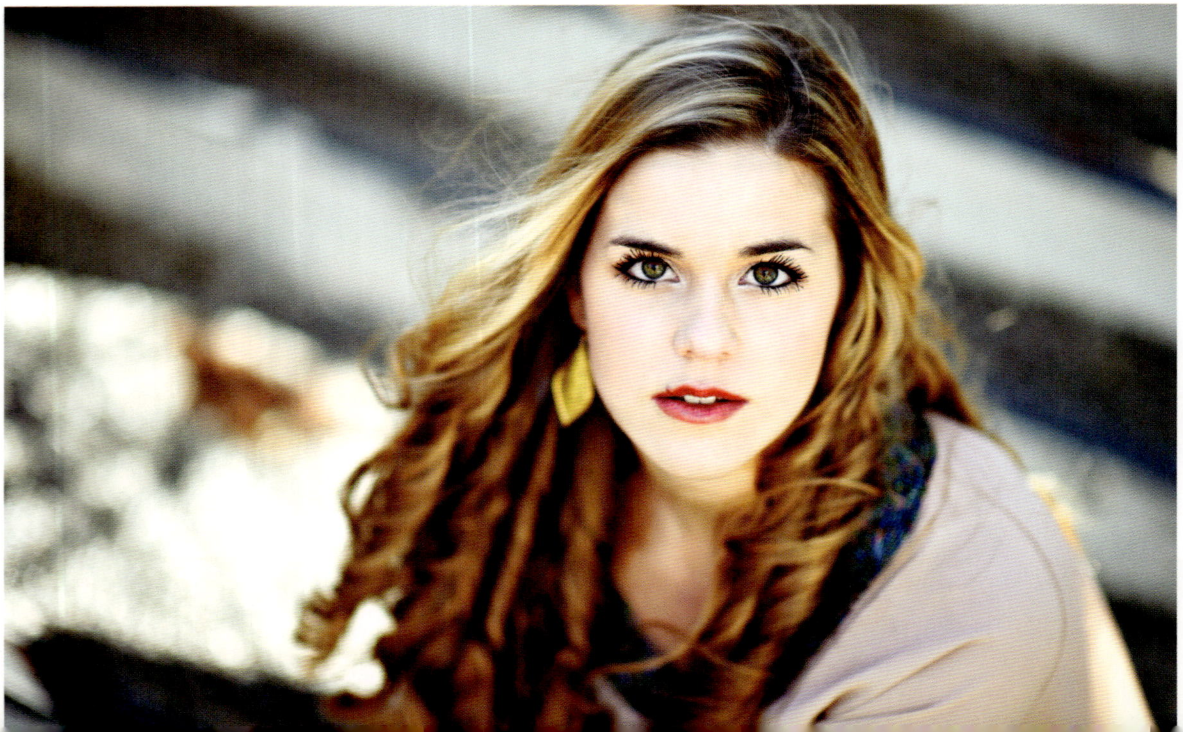

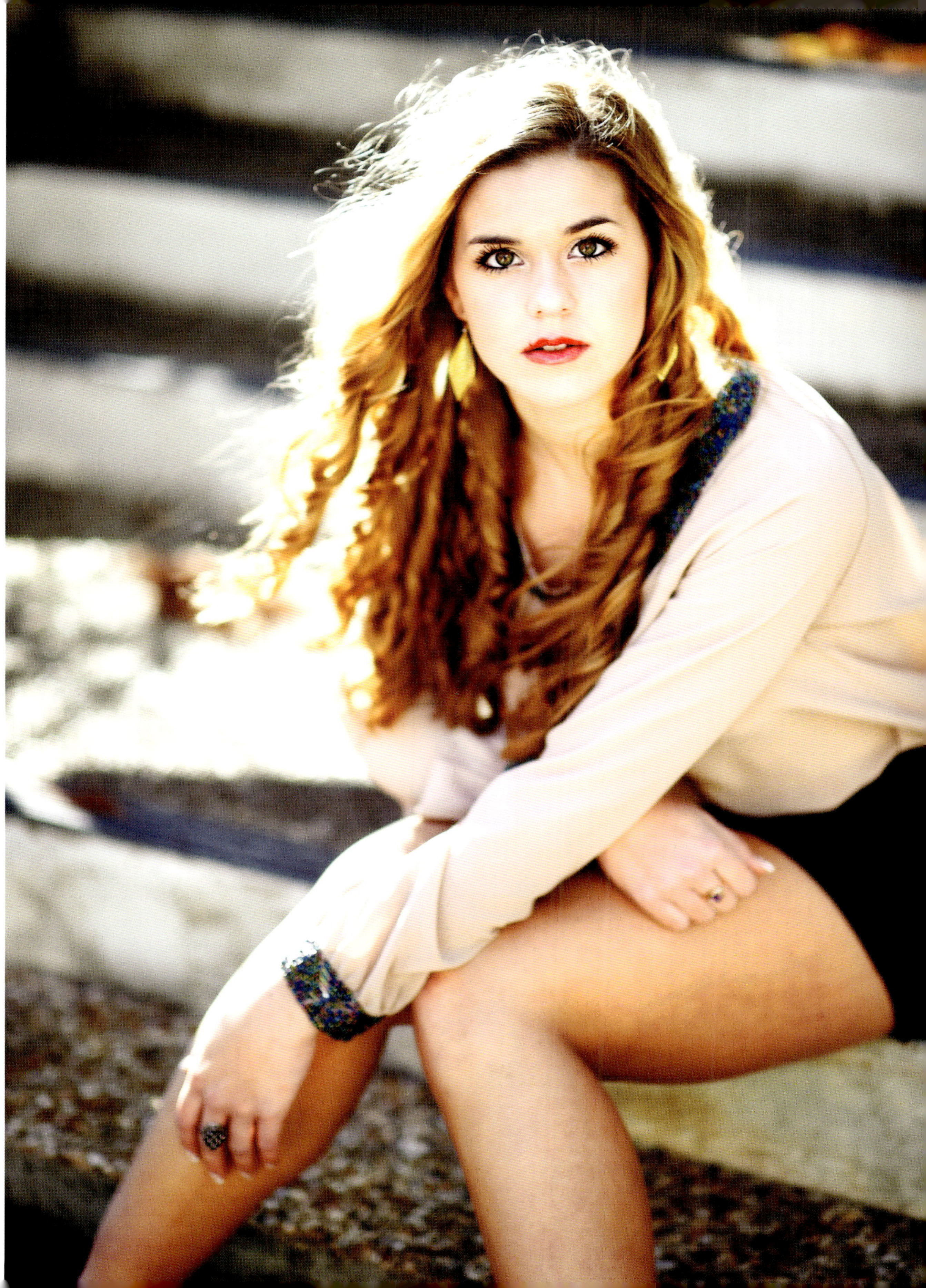

23. Which Direction?

Short Lighting

We've looked at how important it is to have directional light, but *which direction* should it come from?

Close to 90 percent of my images use short lighting. This means that, when the subject's face is turned to at least a slight angle (not facing dead-on into the camera), the light falls on the side of the face that is less visible to the camera—the "short" side. Lighting the narrower side of the face naturally slims the subject's appearance, which almost everyone finds more flattering.

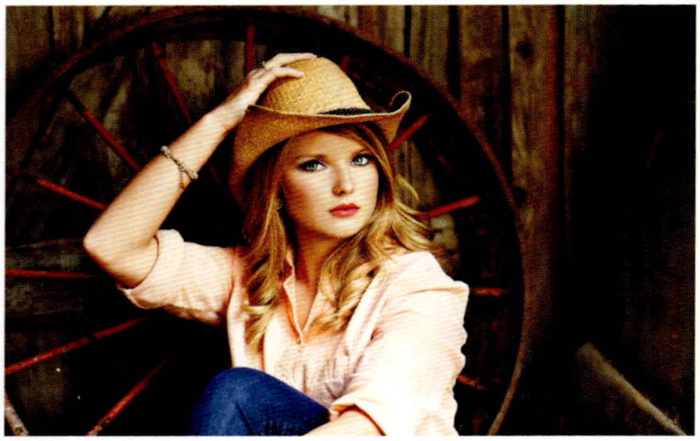

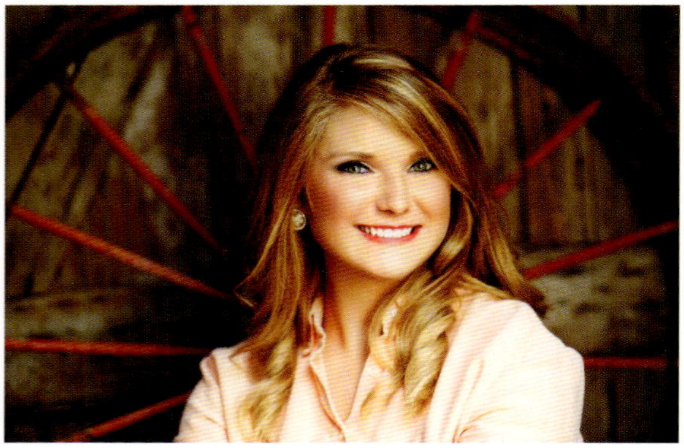

Broad lighting, putting the main light on the more visible ("broad") side of the face, is a look that I use more selectively—usually for very slim people with especially narrow faces.

Studio Porch

The short-light portraits on this page were shot on the porch behind my studio where a tin roof obstructed the overhead sun from behind the camera. This is a perfect opportunity to control the light by catching it in the adjacent alley and bouncing it onto the subject from the side with a reflector. With my subject seated on the floor, I created two variations using simple changes to the props and posing. (The background is cypress wood reclaimed from a 150-year-old rice mill; it has a great texture that works perfectly as a background.)

Your Web Site: Fresh But Consistent

People today are exposed to a lot of great photography and are more style-conscious than ever—and that's especially true for senior portrait clients. So keep evolving and keep freshening up your web site. At the same time it's important to maintain your brand. On our site, we've updated the images and basic look over the years, but we've always kept the same overall feel and a consistent logo.

Don't hesitate to ask clients for feedback. For example, I once mentioned to a senior that I thought it was about time to change the music on the site—but she said to keep it. It was so recognizable that when kids at school heard it in the computer lab, they immediately knew that someone was on my web site!

Townhouse Porch

Near my studio are some beautiful townhouses, occupied mostly by retired people—and they don't mind letting us shoot there. The image to the right was created on a porch with a nice overhang and columns I used to block the light. I turned the model's face toward the light from the overcast sky; that was the main light. Her hair was going too dark on the shadow side, so I added a reflector to camera left for fill.

Plantation Home

On the porch of this plantation home (below) there was a lot of light bouncing around. I positioned my subject in the shade of the column then placed a reflector to camera left to serve as the main light and add some direction to the lighting. I used just the edge of the reflected beam to keep the lighting soft—with just enough shadow to show the shape of her face.

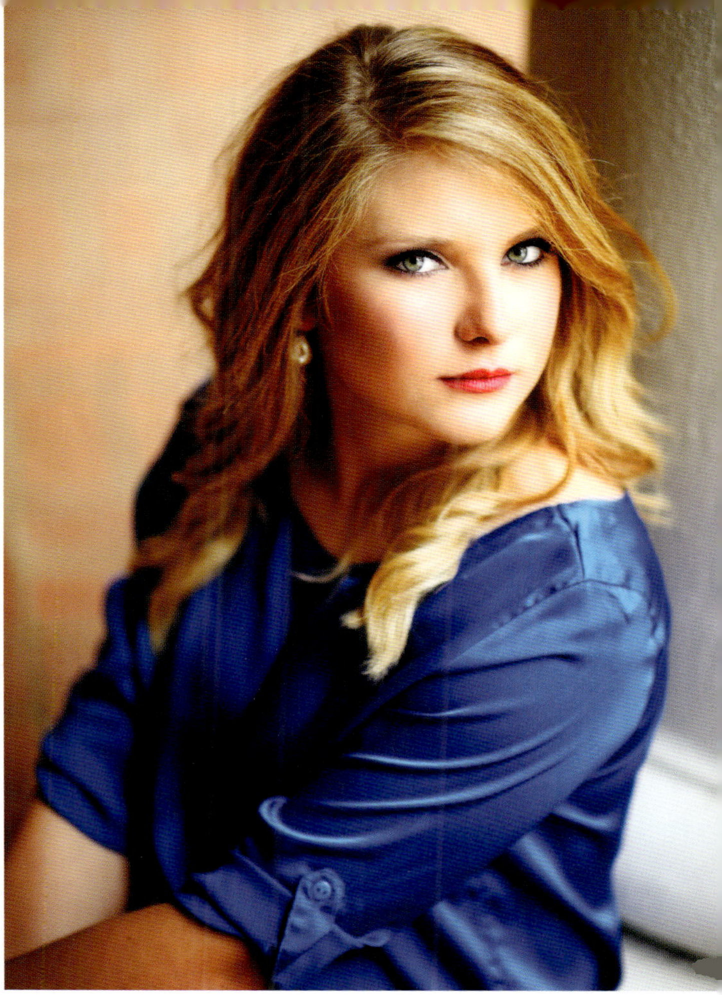

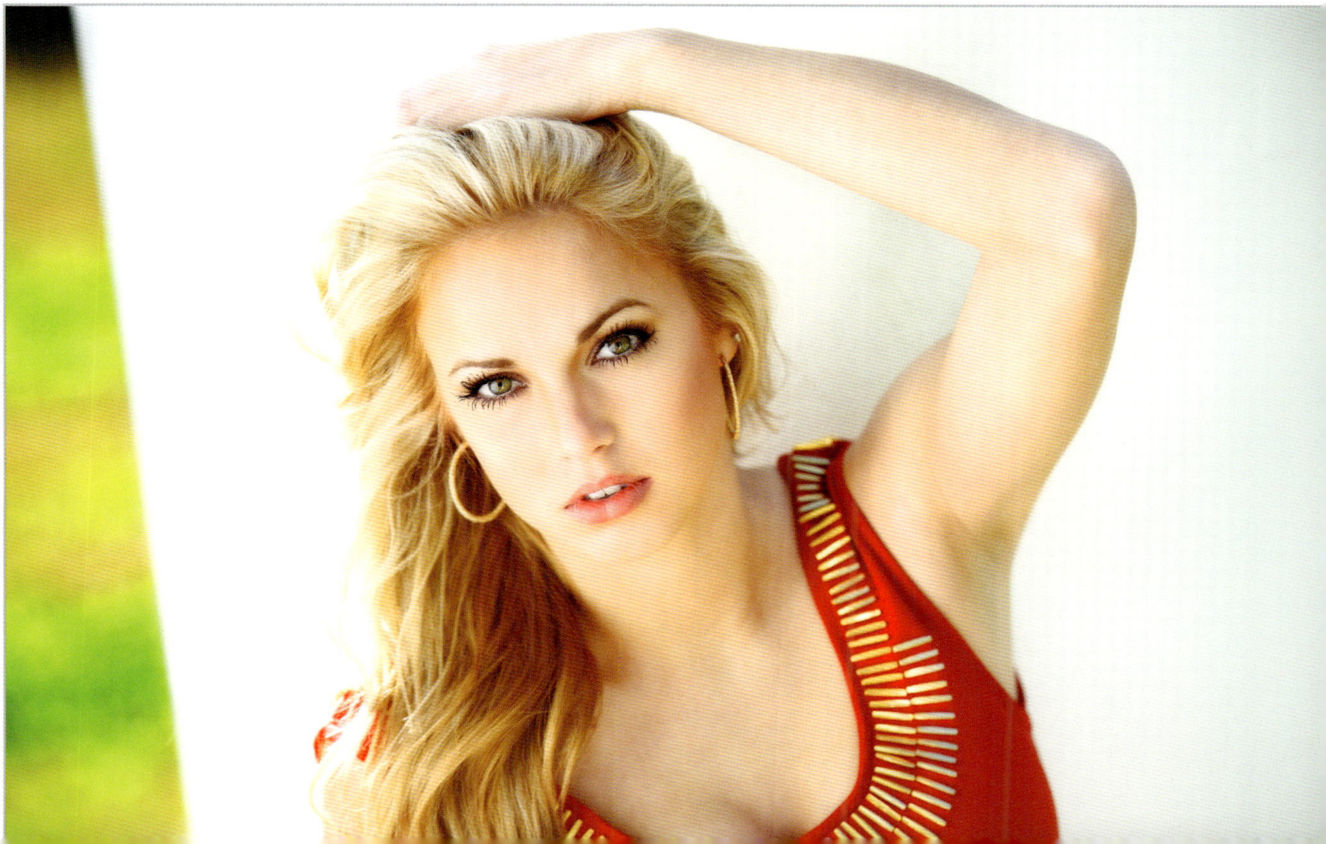

24. **A White Dress**

Location

Seniors love trees, flowers, and fields, so we often head to a nicely landscaped college campus for their portraits. Here, I loved how the tree trunks framed my subject, surrounding her in a perfect dark vignette that make your eyes go right to her.

Lighting

I posed her with her face in the shade and just the back of her head in the sunlight. In this spot, the natural light created studio-quality lighting on her beautiful hair. To create equally beautiful lighting on her face, I brought in a white reflector.

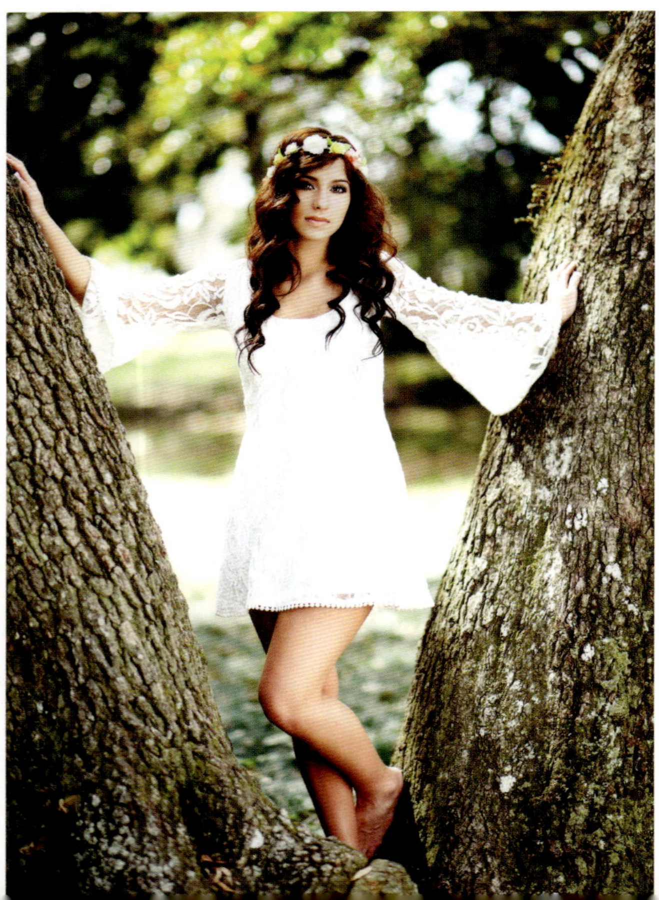

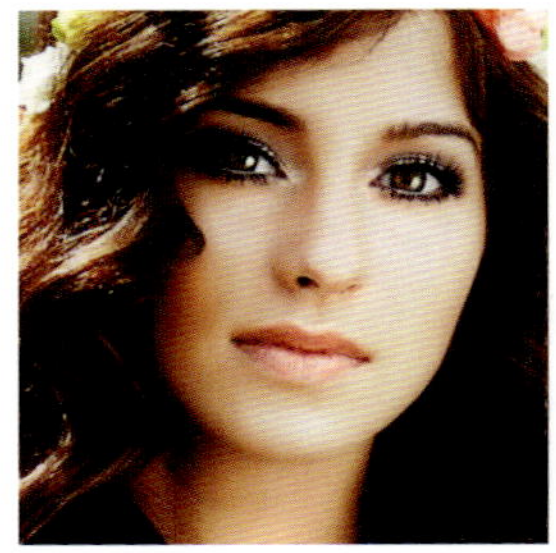

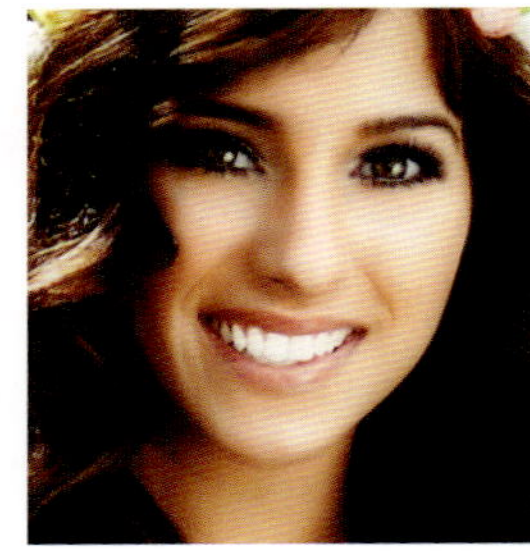

Posing and Expression

For the image on the facing page, I had my model drop her chin just a little bit. This forces the subject to look in a slightly upward direction. It creates better eye contact and opens the eyes up for more impact and a more compelling expression. Check out the inset images above for a closer look.

An Exposure Challenge

Do you notice a potential issue, though? The light on her face is perfect—but it's a bit too much on her dress. There's enough detail in the whites for this to be a pleasing client image. However, if I had it to do over again, I'd choose an outfit of a different color. If that wasn't an option—say, in the case of a bridal portrait or a commercial image—I'd probably make a second lower exposure to use as an overlay for the dress area in postproduction.

Be on the Lookout for Great Light

Sometimes when we're driving, I scare my wife by shouting, "Look! Look at that!" Her first thought is that we're about to crash–but I'm usually shouting about some great lighting I've spotted. As you drive around or watch movies and television, observe the light and think about how you could use it or re-create it.

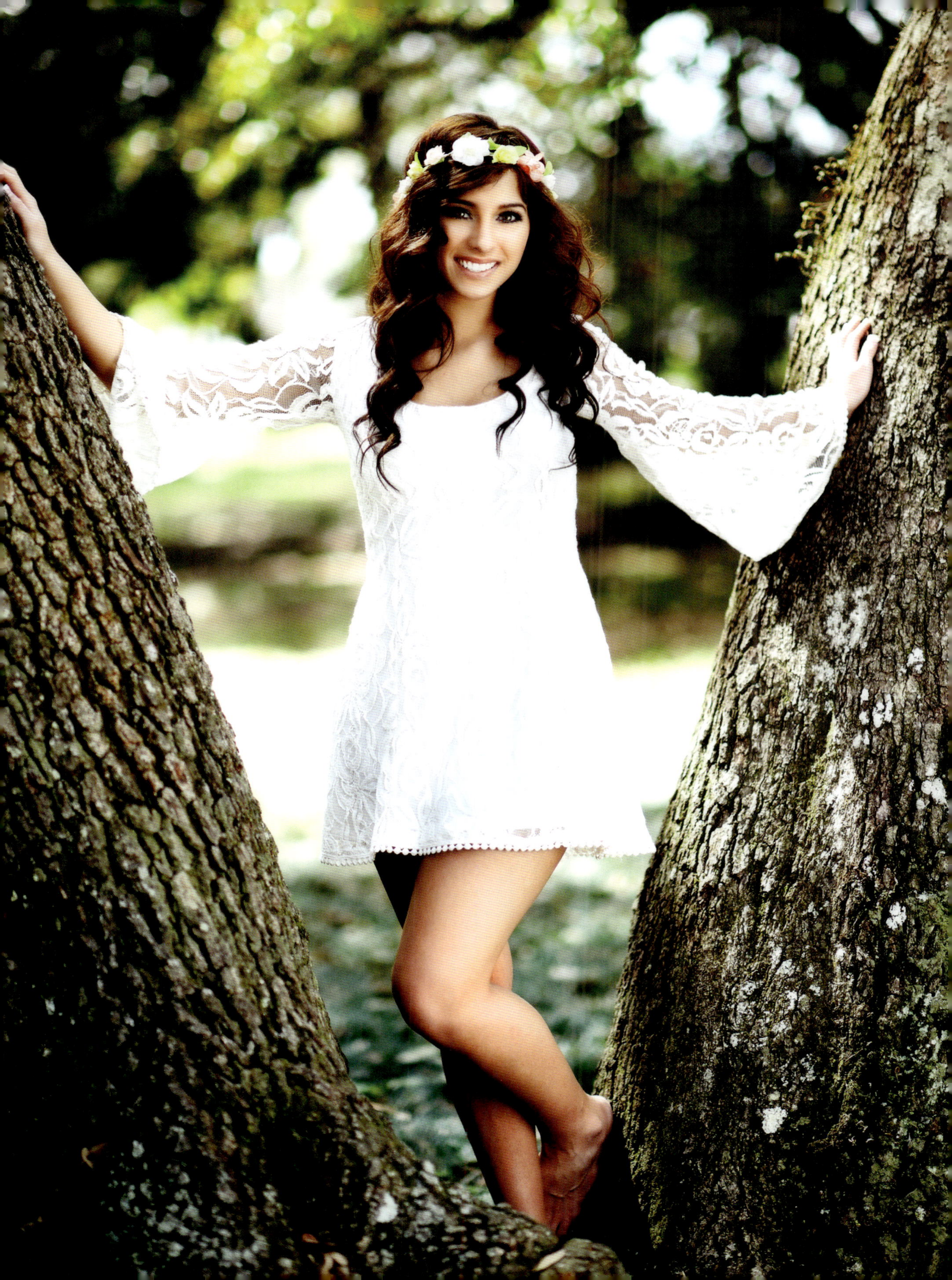

25. **Reflections**

A Clean Background

For more dressed-up looks, I often head to a building with a large glass face. If you look at this straight on, you can see right in—but when you shoot from an angle, it creates a wonderful reflection that my female clients especially like. Just make sure that you, your gear, and any other distractions stay *out* of the reflected area when you're shooting!

Lens Selection

Shooting with an 85mm f/1.4 lens isolated my subjects against a wash of color. Clients love these images where they seem to pop off the page—and they know that their mom's camera doesn't take pictures that look like this!

Lighting

A narrow overhang on this building blocks the overhead light if I go at the right time of day (and keep in mind that this "right time" will change over the course of the year).

The sun's angle relative to the overhead blocker makes a big difference. In the bottom-left and facing page images, the subject was in a very narrow band of shade—the sun was about to peak over and hit the model. As a result, the background is very light.

In the bottom-right portrait, on the other hand, the band of shade was quite deep, so the color and tone in the background is deeper. It contrasts nicely with this subject's red dress.

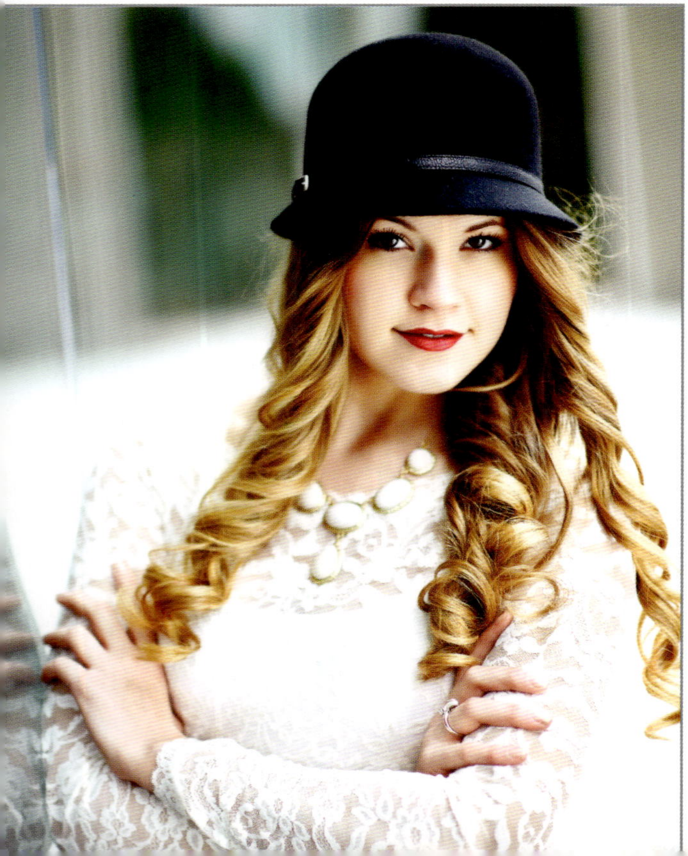

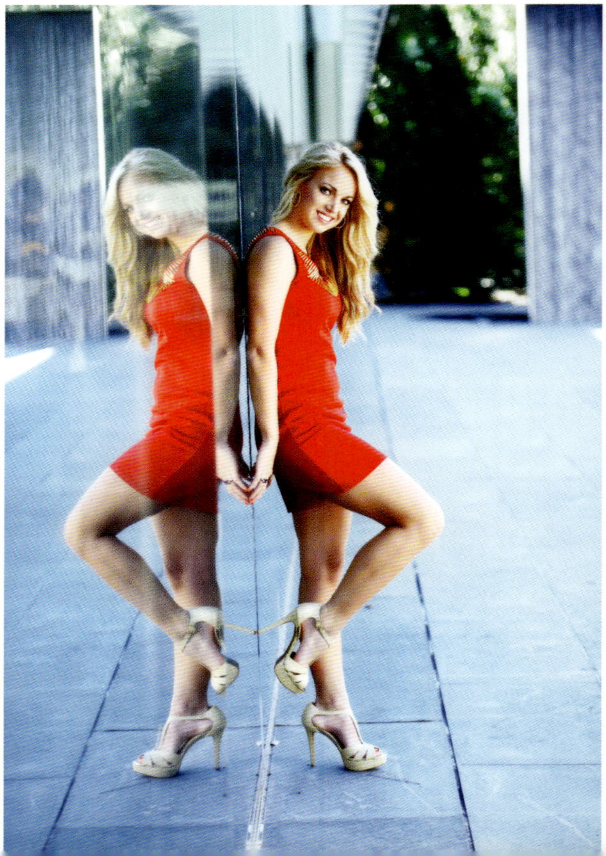

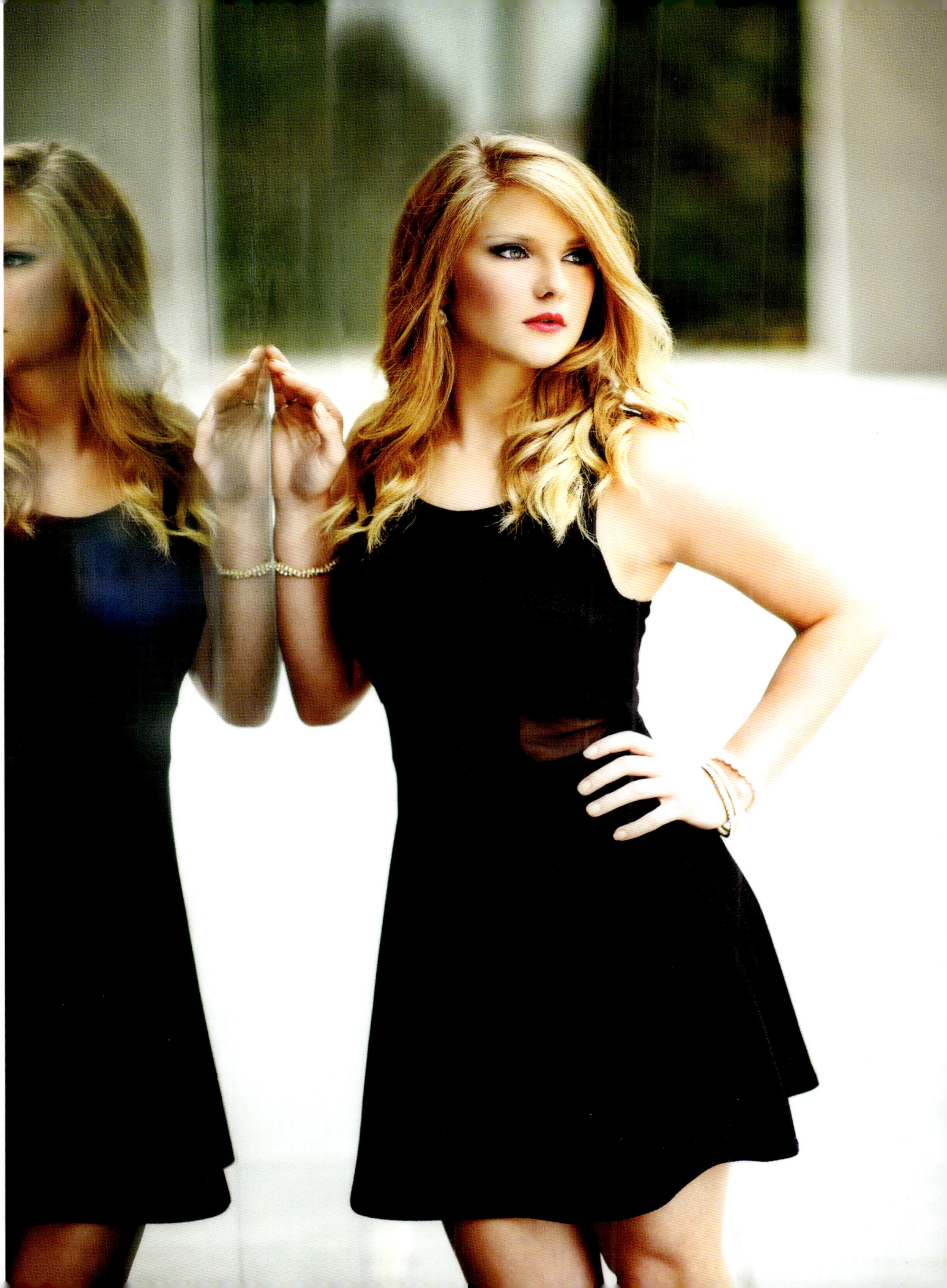

26. Vibrant Colors

Not Just Green

While we tend to associate outdoor portraits with green foliage, there are lots of opportunities to integrate color into your images. Keep your eyes open for them and use them when you find them!

Winter Flowers

Shooting in November, we came across a vibrant patch of flowers (*below*). As soon as I saw them, I knew they'd make a perfect background for my auburn-haired subject who was wearing a purple scarf and sweater (an autumn look that's one of my favorites).

Since the flowers were low to the ground, I did something I almost never do: I posed her lying down (propped up slightly on her elbows) and photographer her from above with a wide-angle lens. To get this perspective, I had to stand so I was nearly straddling her!

The image was lit with natural light breaking through the overhead trees from behind her to the left. A reflector to camera right bounced some of this light back onto her face.

Spring Flowers

During a spring session (*facing page, top*), my senior portrait client and I came across a

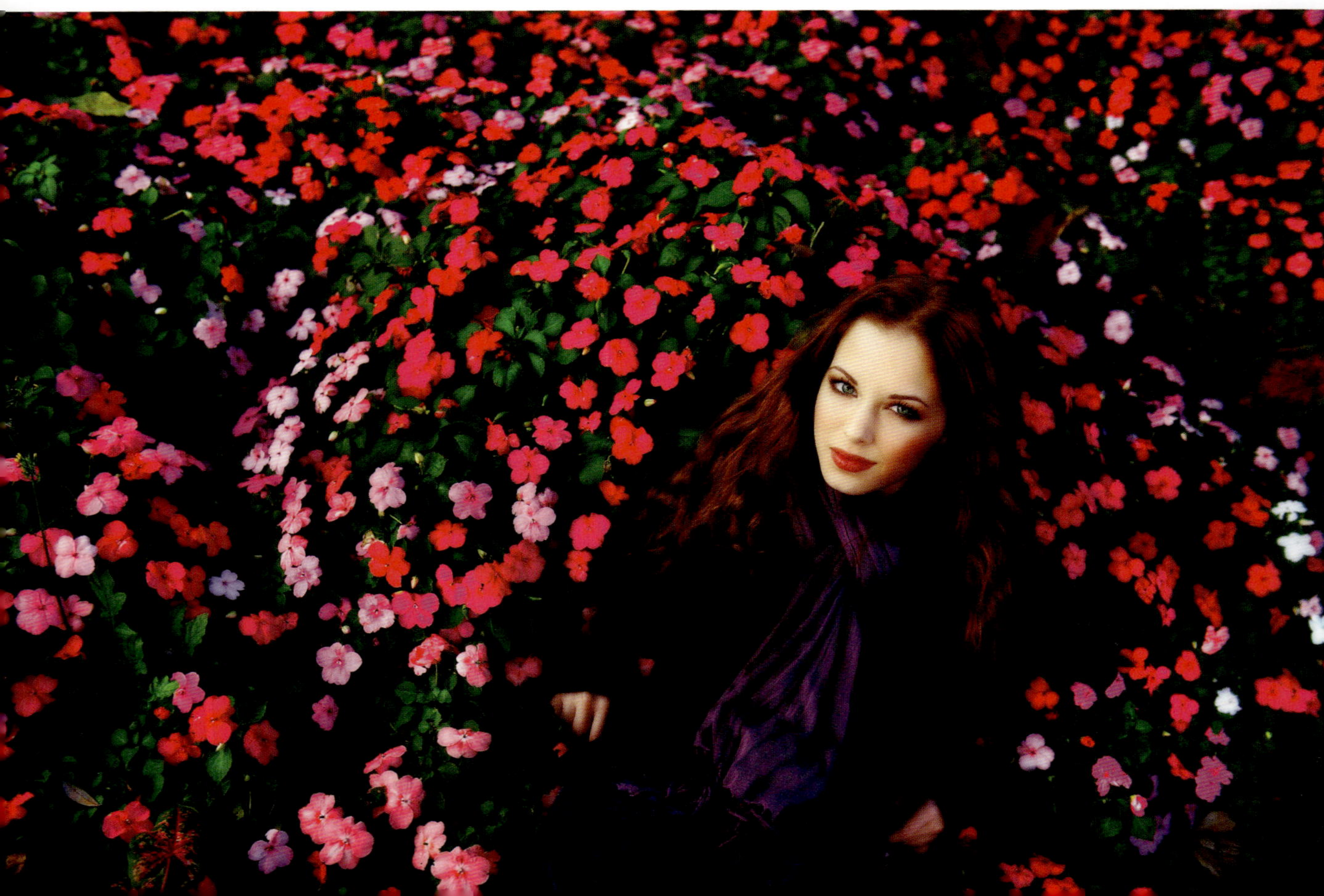

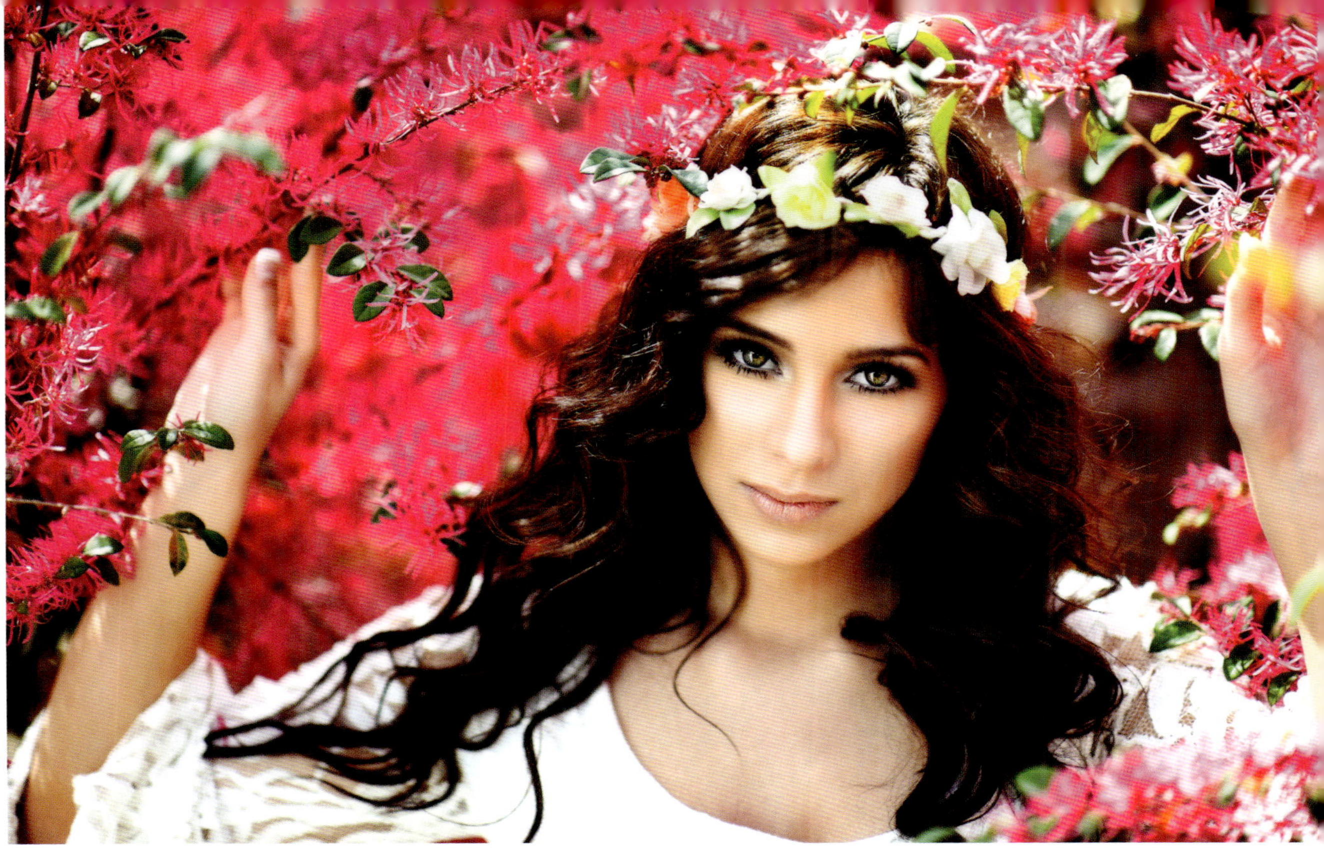

colorful tree—it was absolutely covered in hot-pink flowers and looked like something from a Dr. Seuss book! I tucked her into the very minimal shade and kept making minor position adjustments until I had nice light on her face. An inch in any direction, the light was totally different (you can see a little of it catching on her hair to camera left). A big reflector in close gave me soft light and huge catchlights.

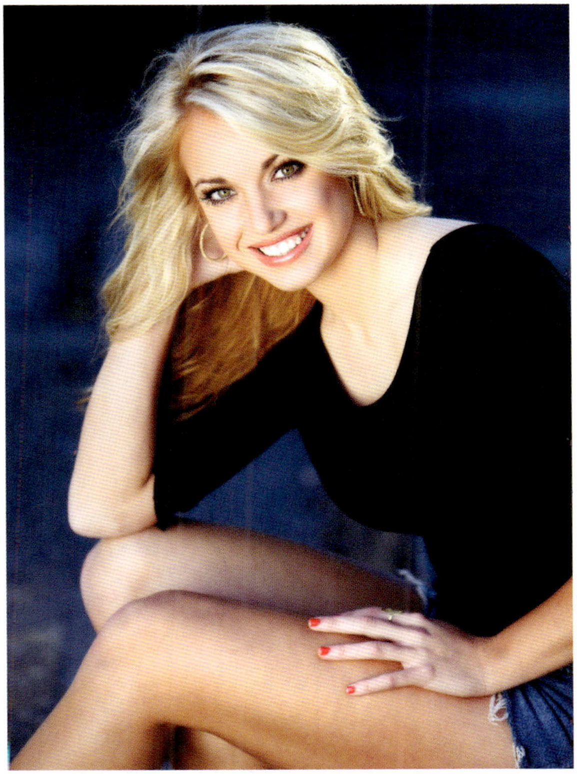

Cool Blue

For the image to the right, my subject was posed on the cusp of the open shade with deep shade. This let me bounce very bright light onto her using a super-close reflector. In comparison, it almost looks like night behind her. The sidewalk and street in the background went very blue because the area was in such deep shade. It's another way to use color!

27. Simple Changes, Big Variety

A Classic

This senior-portrait client's dad was able to borrow a classic Chevy pickup truck from a coworker. They thought it would be cool for photos—and I agreed!

Natural Light (with a Reflector)

We parked the truck under a tree in front of an art museum. I had the young lady's father stand at the edge of the shade where he could catch bright light with a reflector and bounce it back onto her as she posed in the cabin of the truck.

We never moved the truck and made only slight changes in the position of the reflector to make sure we kept the catchlights in her eyes. Otherwise, all of these looks were created by adjusting my camera position relative to the subject or adjusting her position relative to the windows (letting light in) and the frame of the truck (blocking light).

Although some purists might argue, I contend that shooting with a reflector *is* shooting with natural light; you're just redirecting it as needed. I tend to call myself an "available light" photographer.

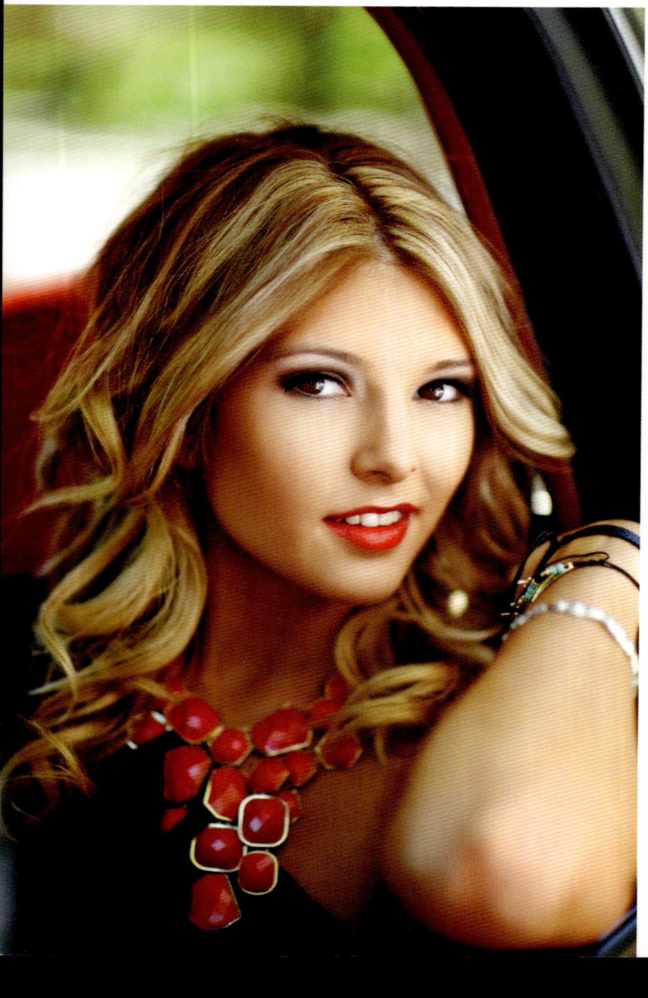

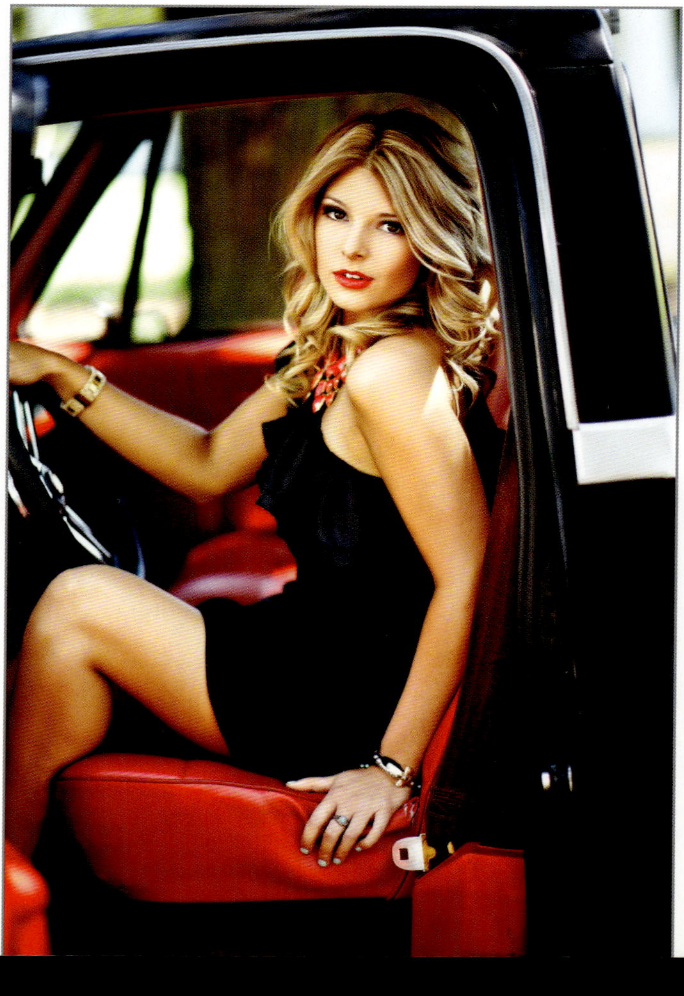

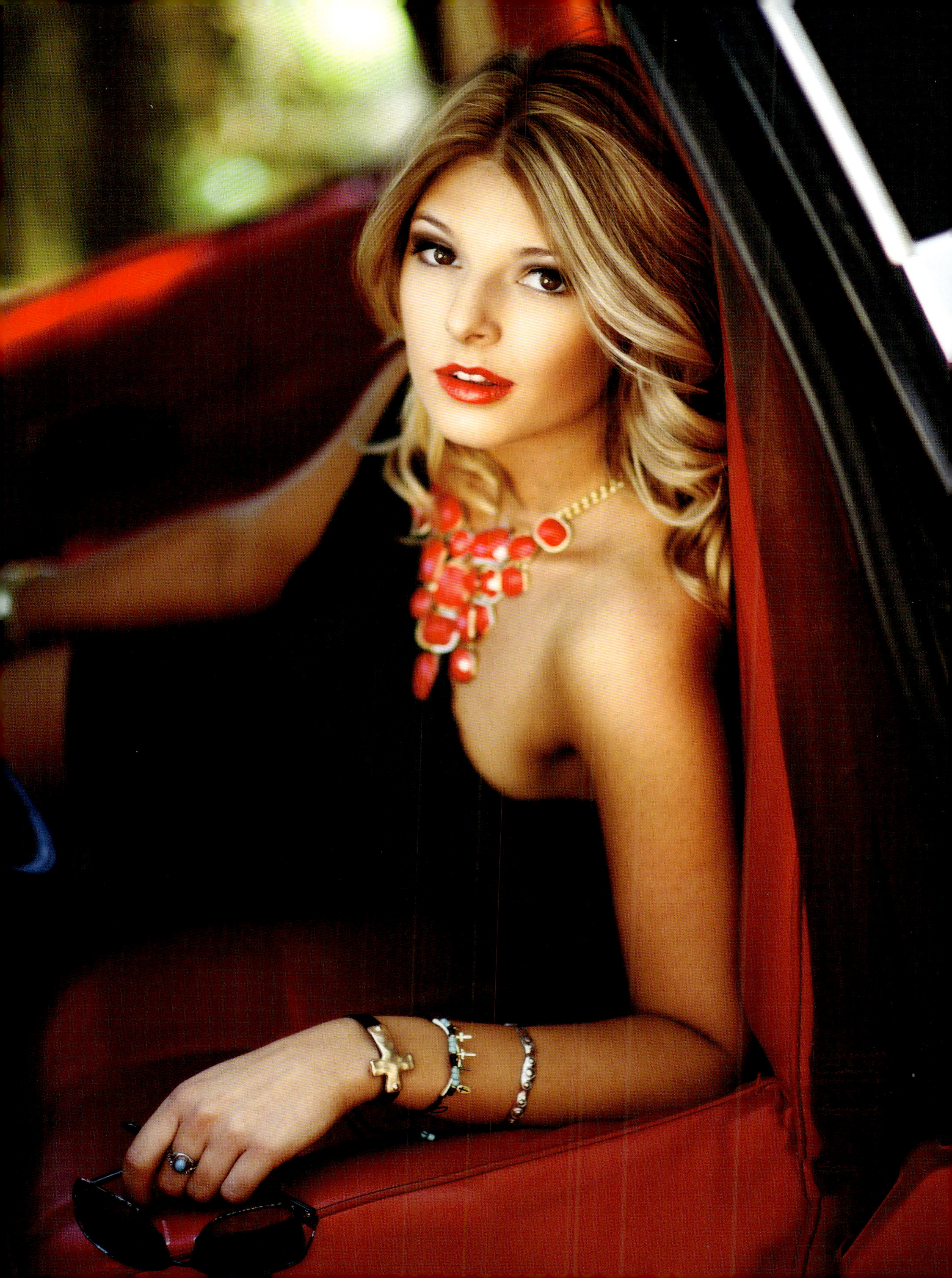

28. The Face and Eyes

The Point of the Portrait

When shooting portraits, you'll pick nice outfits and coordinating backgrounds, but those are just gravy. The real meat of any portrait, the area where viewers should focus their attention, is the face—and especially the eyes. In these portraits, that objective was achieved through careful lighting, posing, composition, color control, and selective focusing. The subject's face is the first thing you look at in each image.

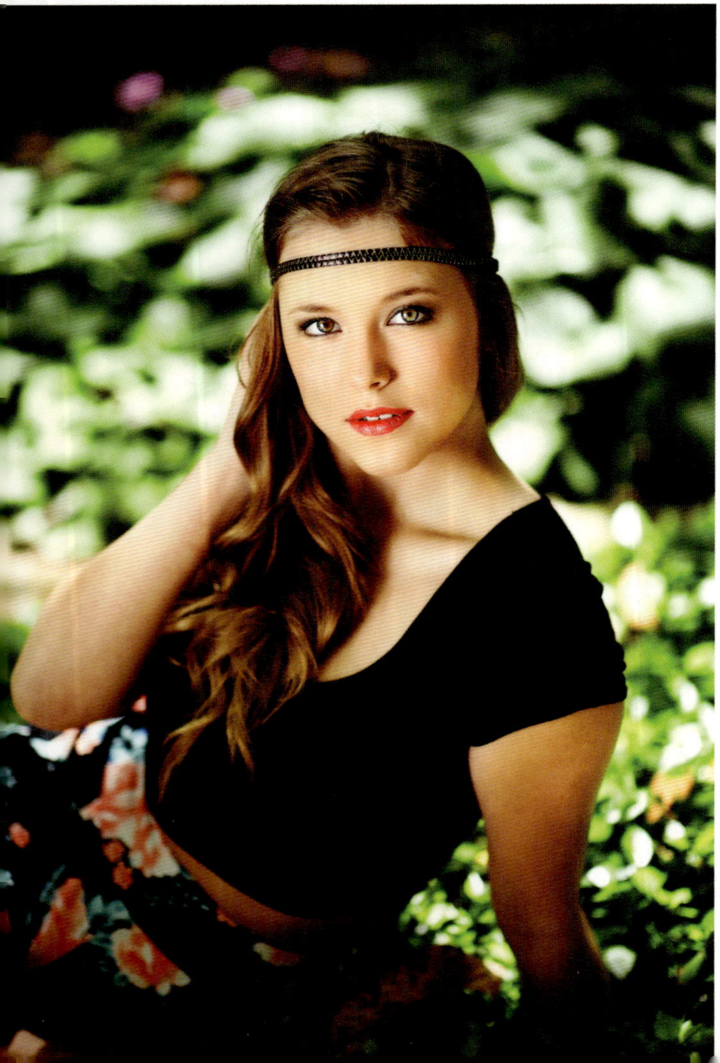

A Bright Background

In the image to the left, my subject was seated on the grass, surrounded by really strong lighting. I positioned her in a tiny spot of shade and bounced light onto her face. This balanced her against the scene. Shooting with my 85mm lens at f/1.4 transformed the high-contrast foliage into a variegated wash of color and helped further emphasize that her face is the center of interest.

Similar factors are at work in the top image on the facing page. Shot at f/3.5, the background has a bit more detail, but her warm-toned face stands out nicely from the cool-toned background. The more directional look to the lighting came from shooting later in the day.

A Natural Vignette

For the facing-page bottom image, I had my subject posed on a porch. She was leaning up against an urn that coordinated with her hair color and contrasted with her green eyes. Against these darker tones, her skin and eye color stand out nicely. Her arms and hands further frame her face.

For this shot, the sun was to camera left. The light already had a nice directional quality because the porch roof blocked it from overhead. I placed a reflector to camera left, quite close to my subject, to amp up the effect and provide a very dramatic look.

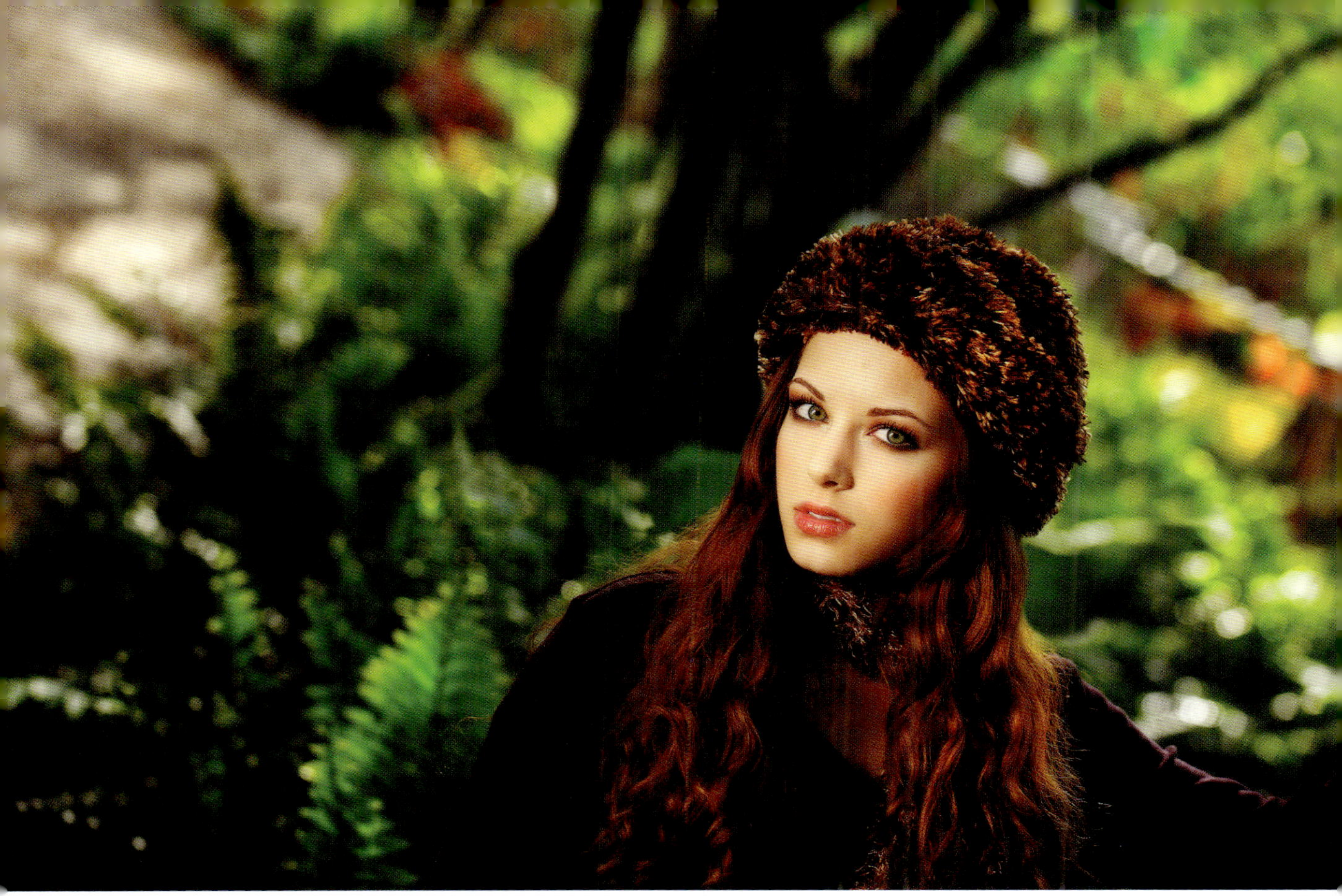

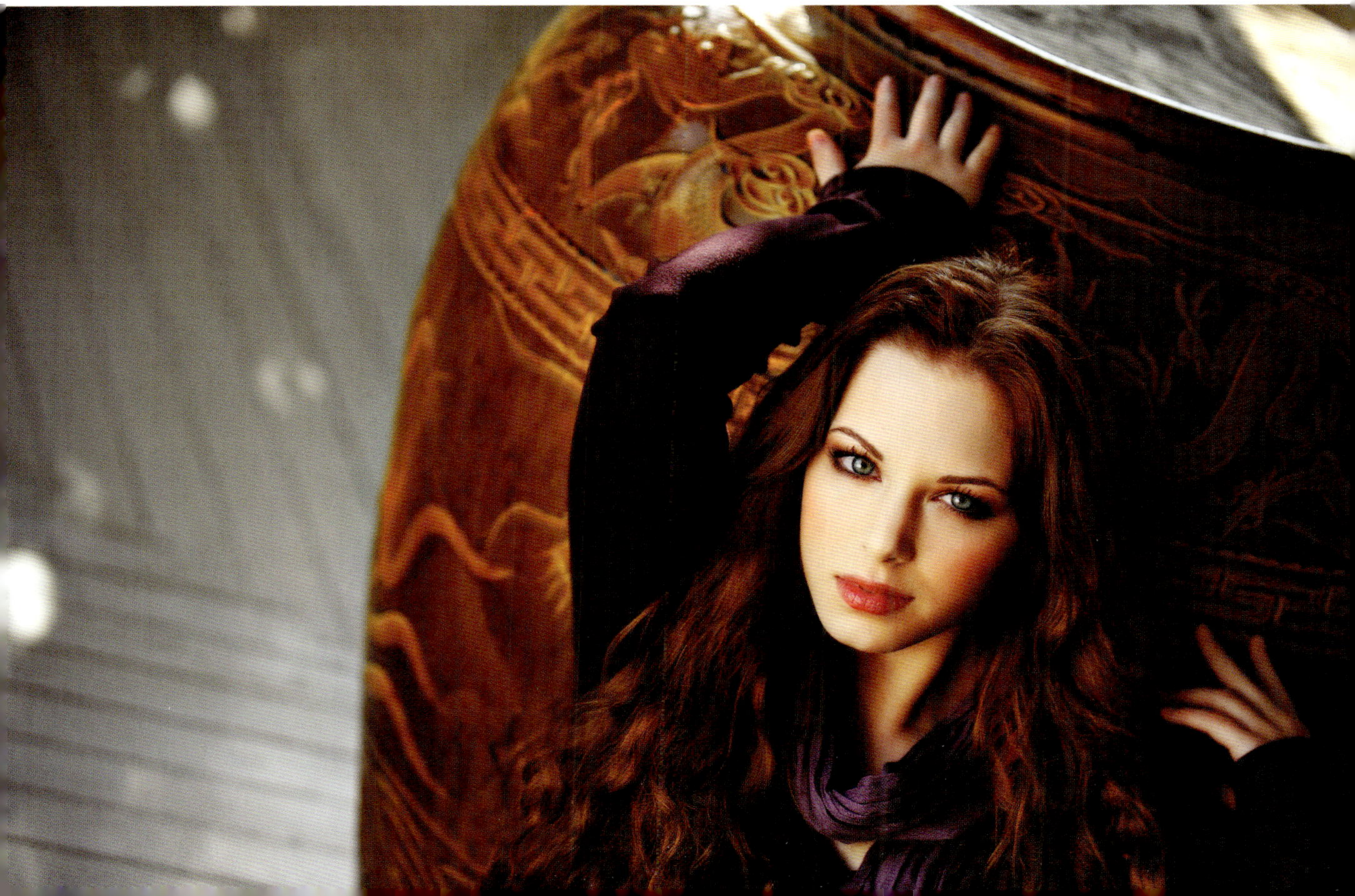

29. Enhancing Variety

Take Advantage of Your Surroundings

Part of what's great about shooting outdoors is the endless assortment of backgrounds at your fingertips. You probably won't have to go too far afield to find backgrounds to create a nice variety of looks during a single session.

Garden Look

As we drove around during this young lady's session, we came across an area with flowers a few blocks from my studio (*below*). I had her sit on the ground with her back to the sun for nice edge lighting. A reflector kicked light back onto her face. It's a nice, casual look.

Gritty, Fashion Flair

At another area, also just a few blocks from my studio, I posed her on a staircase for a more fashion-oriented look (*facing page*). Again, the sun was behind her, blocked from overhead by a building, and a reflector to camera left bounced in the main light. A texture overlay added in postproduction added to the gritty feel of the final image.

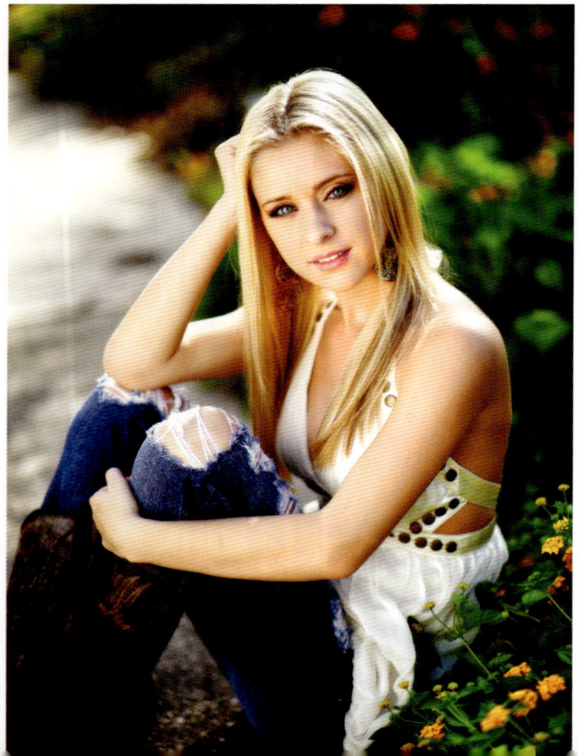

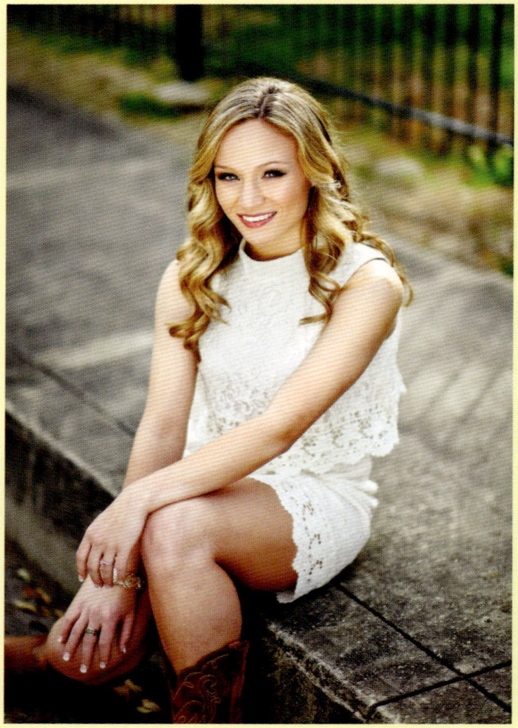

Light and Angle Transform the Scene

Flip back to section 26 and look at the young lady against the deep blue background. Believe it or not, the portrait above was created in the same spot. My angle was a little different and the sun was higher in the sky, so there's a lot more light getting to the area of the sidewalk behind her (making the background much lighter). Again, I posed my subject at the edge of the shade and bounced light back onto her with a reflector.

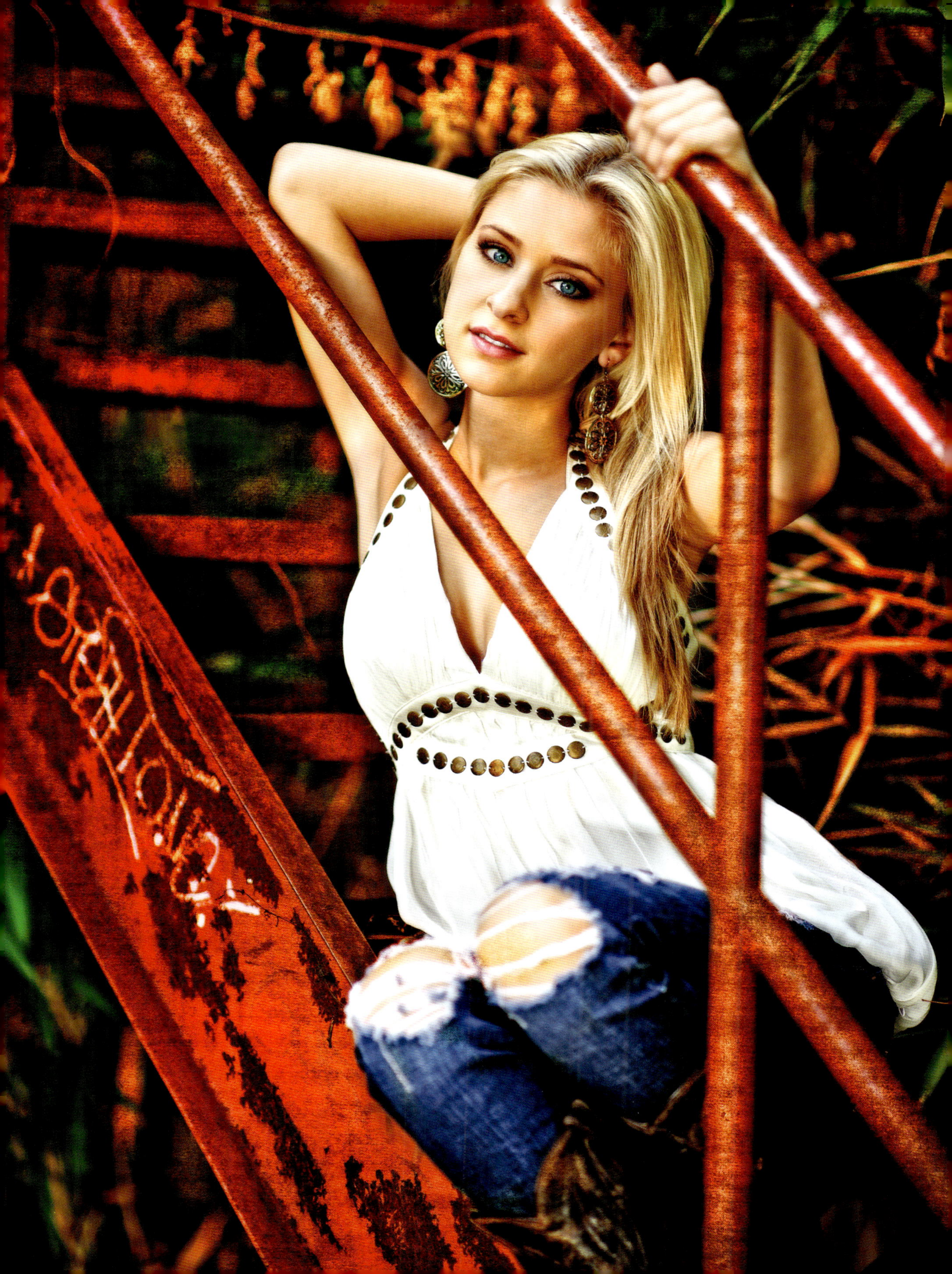

30. Adding Strobe in Outdoor Scenes

Pros and Cons

I prefer to use available light or reflectors, but when I have to add artificial light I will. Most often this is when I can't find or add an overhead blocker with the chosen background. Adding light is also an option when wind makes it difficult to use a reflector. If I absolutely must, I'll even add on-camera flash for a pop of light in the eyes (we do what we have to!). To me, this looks a little flat, but it's not something that clients will perceive; they'll still be happy with their images.

The drawbacks of adding strobe? For one thing, it requires more gear and setup time than shooting with natural light plus a reflector. Additionally, the strobe puts out so much light that it can be hard to work at the wide apertures I like in order to blur out the background and make the subject stand out. (This is also more of a photographer thing; clients usually won't notice if the background is a little sharper than *I* might prefer it to be.)

A Bright Scene

In the image below, the fountain on which my subject is posed was out in the middle of a shopping area—there was no way to block the direct afternoon sun from overhead. To get

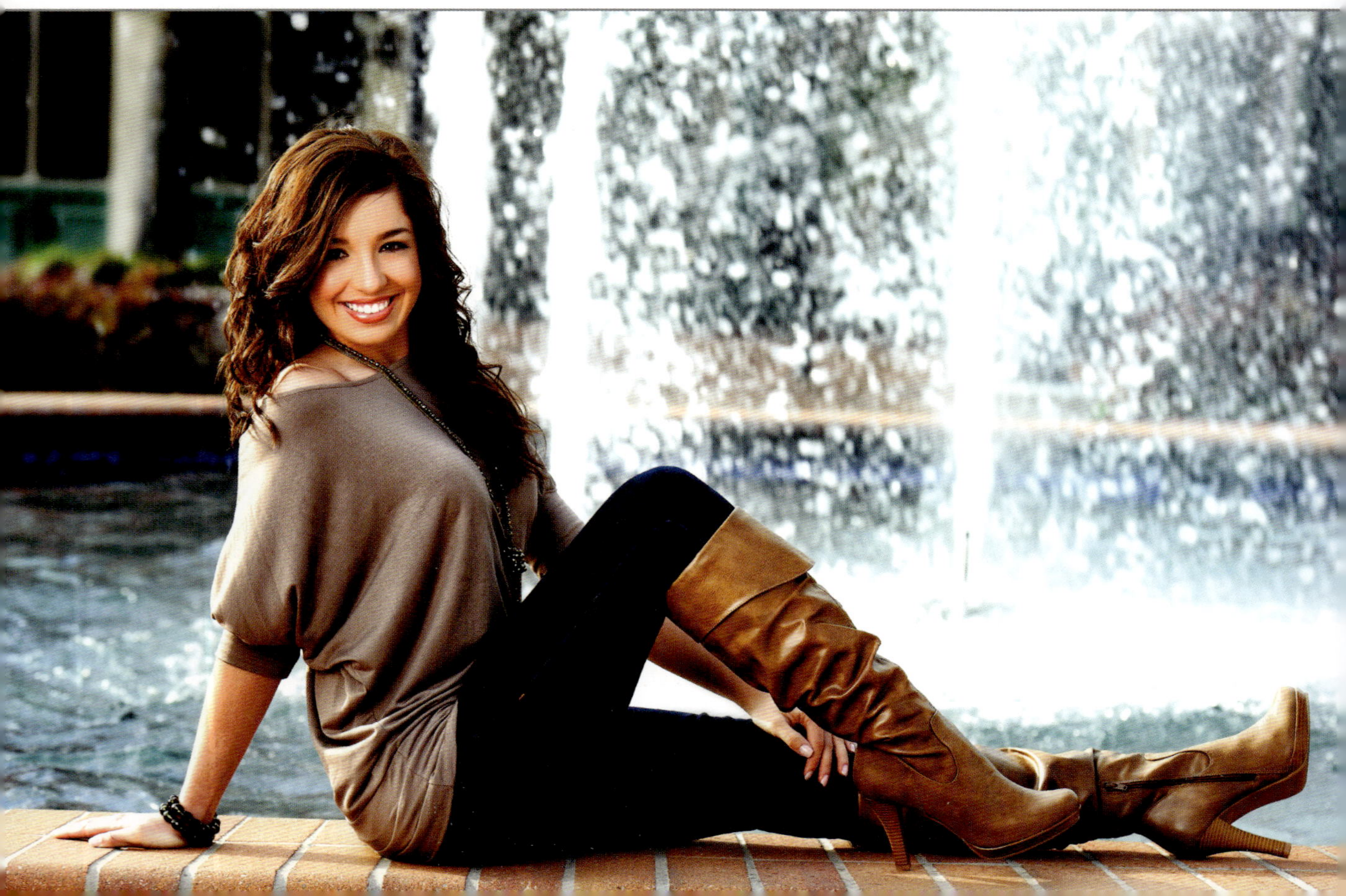

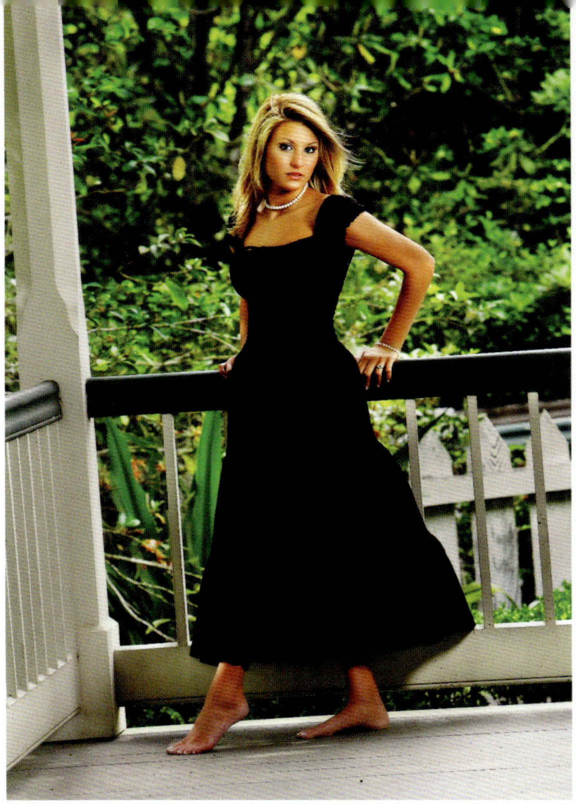

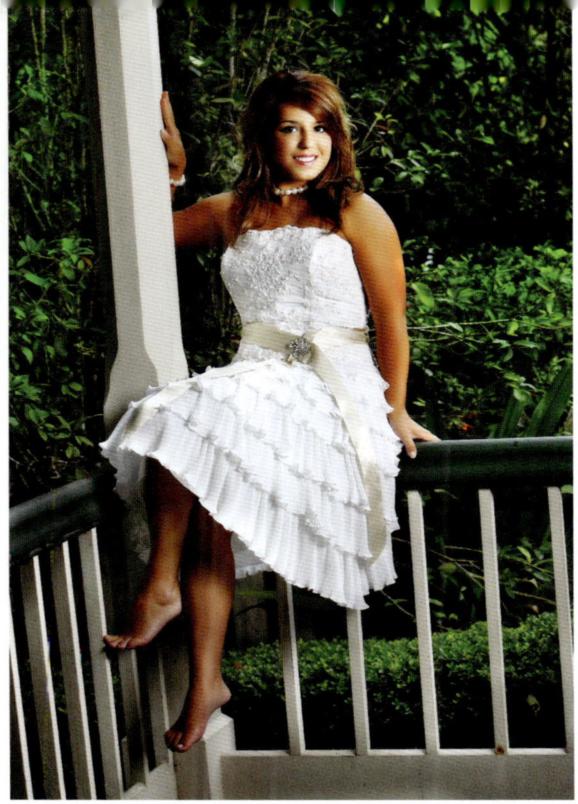

the photo I wanted, I had to overpower the sun with strobe. I still used the natural light, though; I positioned my model so it fell on her from behind and to the left, adding nice shine on her hair and a highlight on her shoulder and arm.

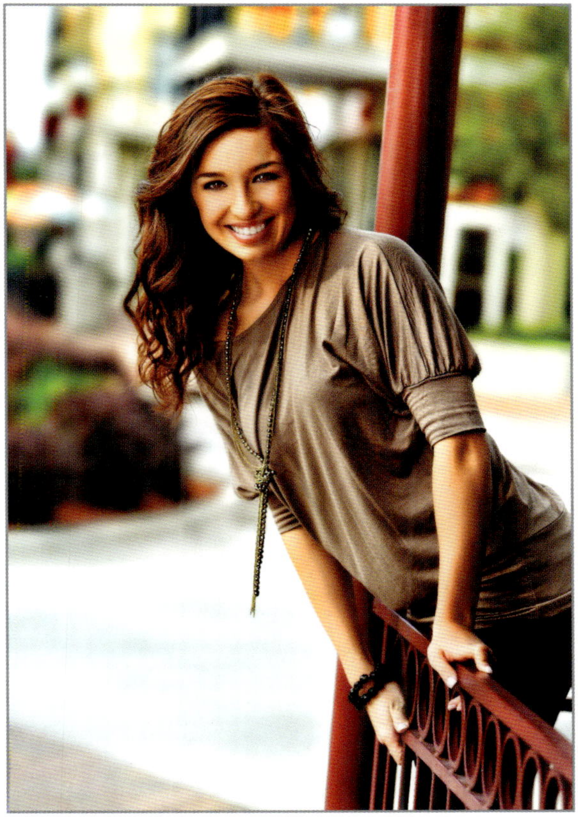

Very Overcast

Adding light can also be a necessity when the day is so overcast that there's too little direction to the light for it to serve as the main light. If there's *any* direction to the light (often there's not), I put it behind my subject as a hair light. Then I pull in a large light source, like my 47-inch octabox, close to their face for soft light with enough shadows to sculpt the face. That's the approach I used for the photos shown on this page. While they were taken in different locations, the quality of the light is consistent and flattering.

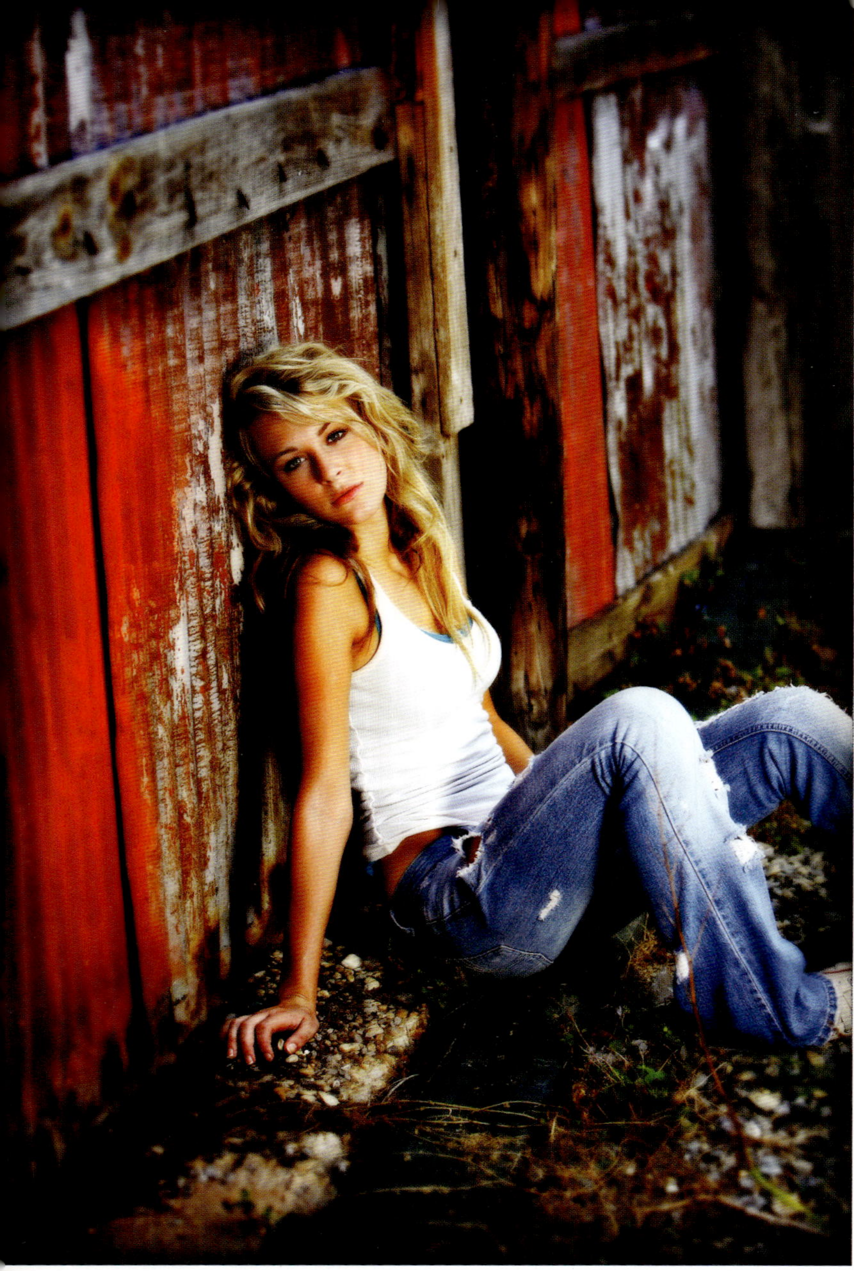

31. A Little Grunge

Lines and Texture

Many people are drawn to scenes of rustic and urban decay. As you can see in these images, the rigid lines and rough textures also make a nice background for portraits.

Posing and Clothing

A pose with plenty of diagonals helps develop a nice contrast between the hard scene and the softer subject. Casual clothes, relaxed poses, and subdued expressions seem to suit these scenes well.

Lighting

Lighting for a softer look on the skin provides a nice complement to a textured scene. It can be directional for a little more drama or more flat for an editorial edge.

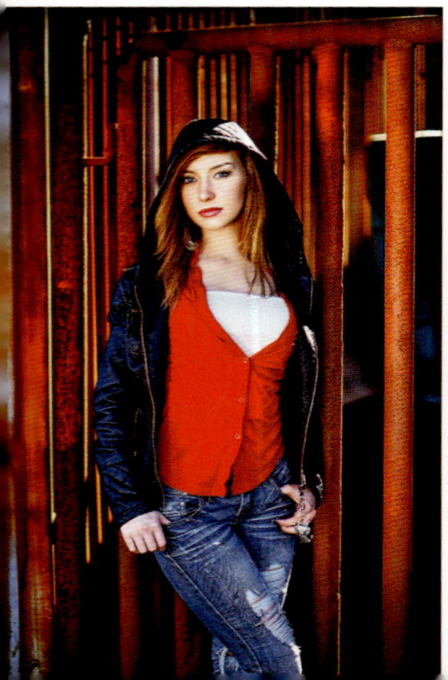

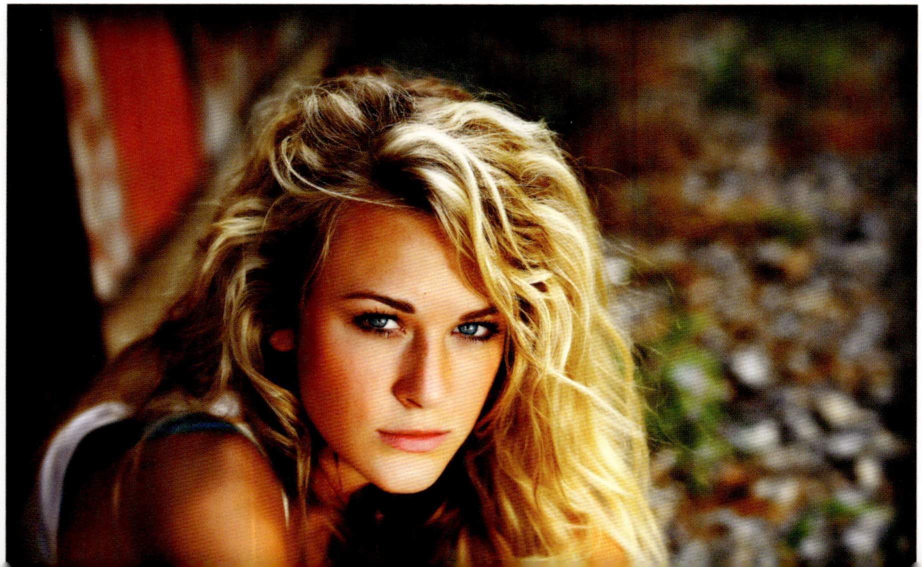

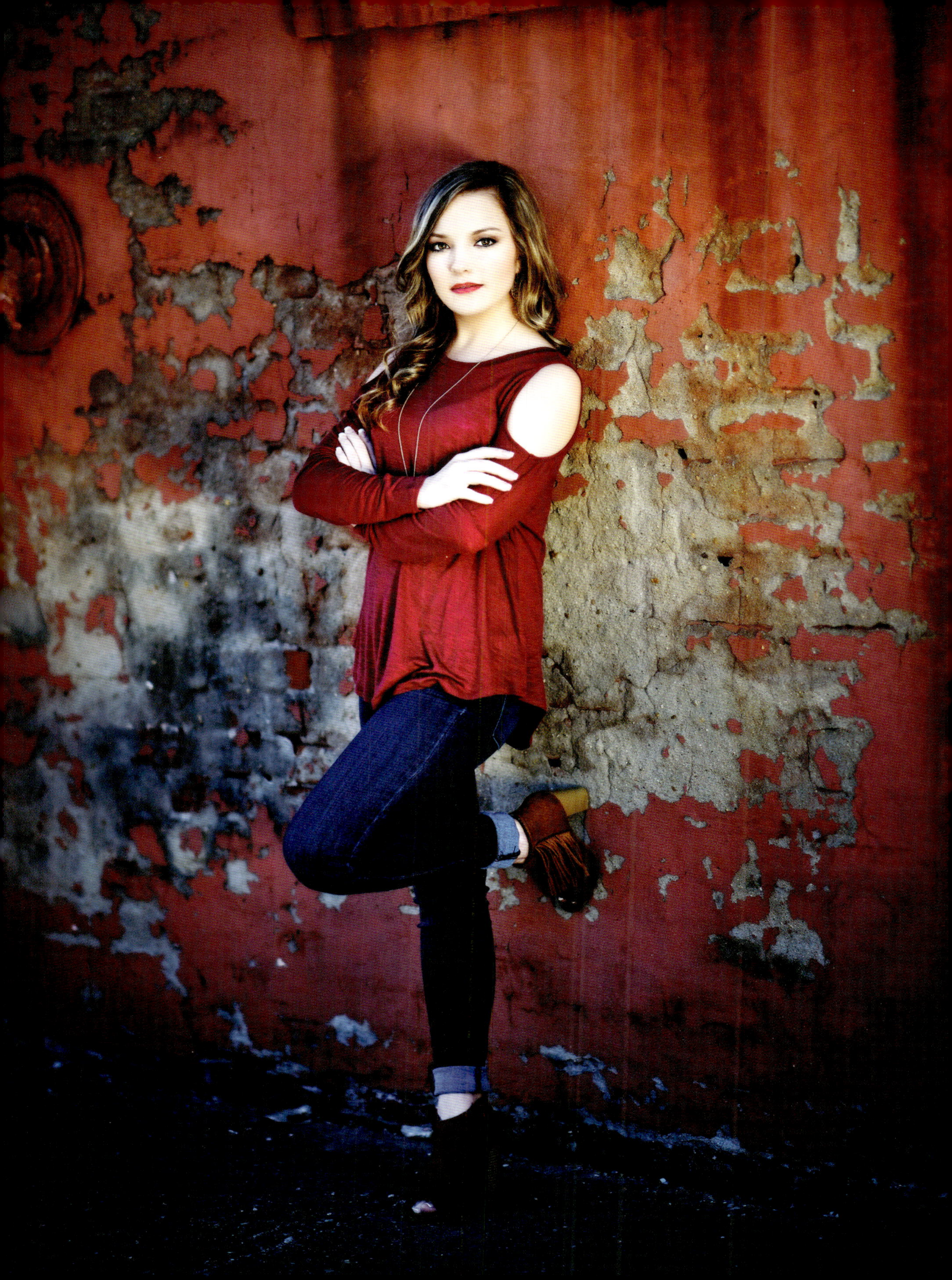

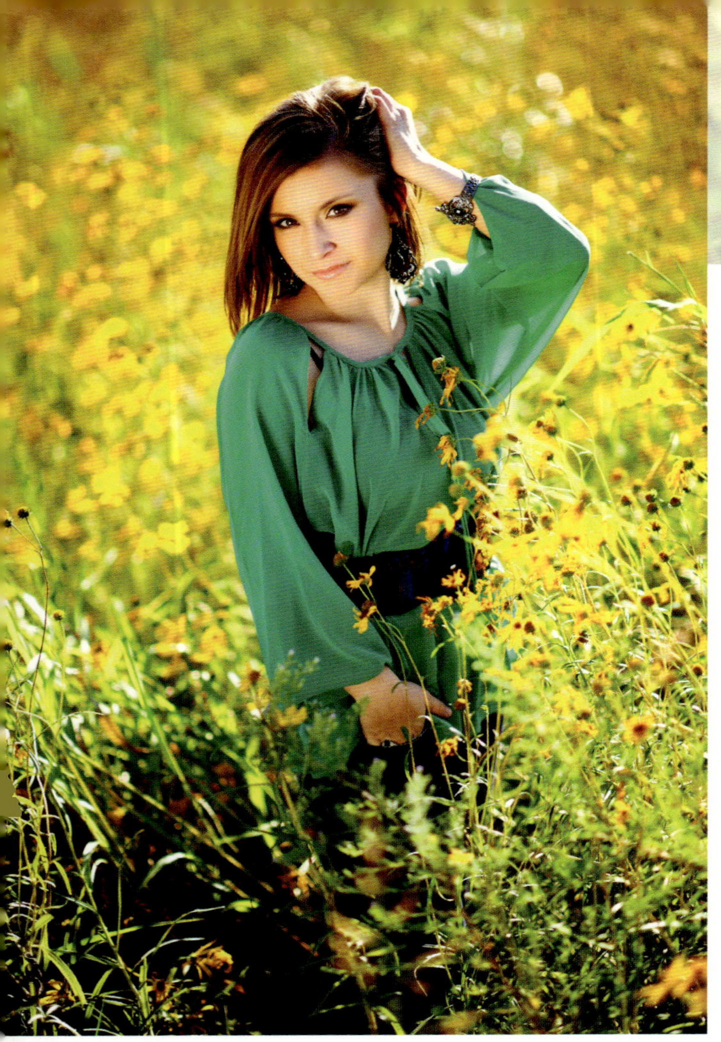

32. Camera Height

Background Control

Changing the camera height is a powerful way to control the background. Here, I got up high and shot down toward the ground to fill the background with these yellow flowers and keep the emphasis on my subject.

Lighting

For this image, the sun provided the back lighting, giving me nice highlights on her hair and arm. I used a reflector to camera left to kick plenty of nice light back onto her face.

Variations

Simply going from a smile to a more subdued expression created one variation. Having her slip into her red coat produced another look.

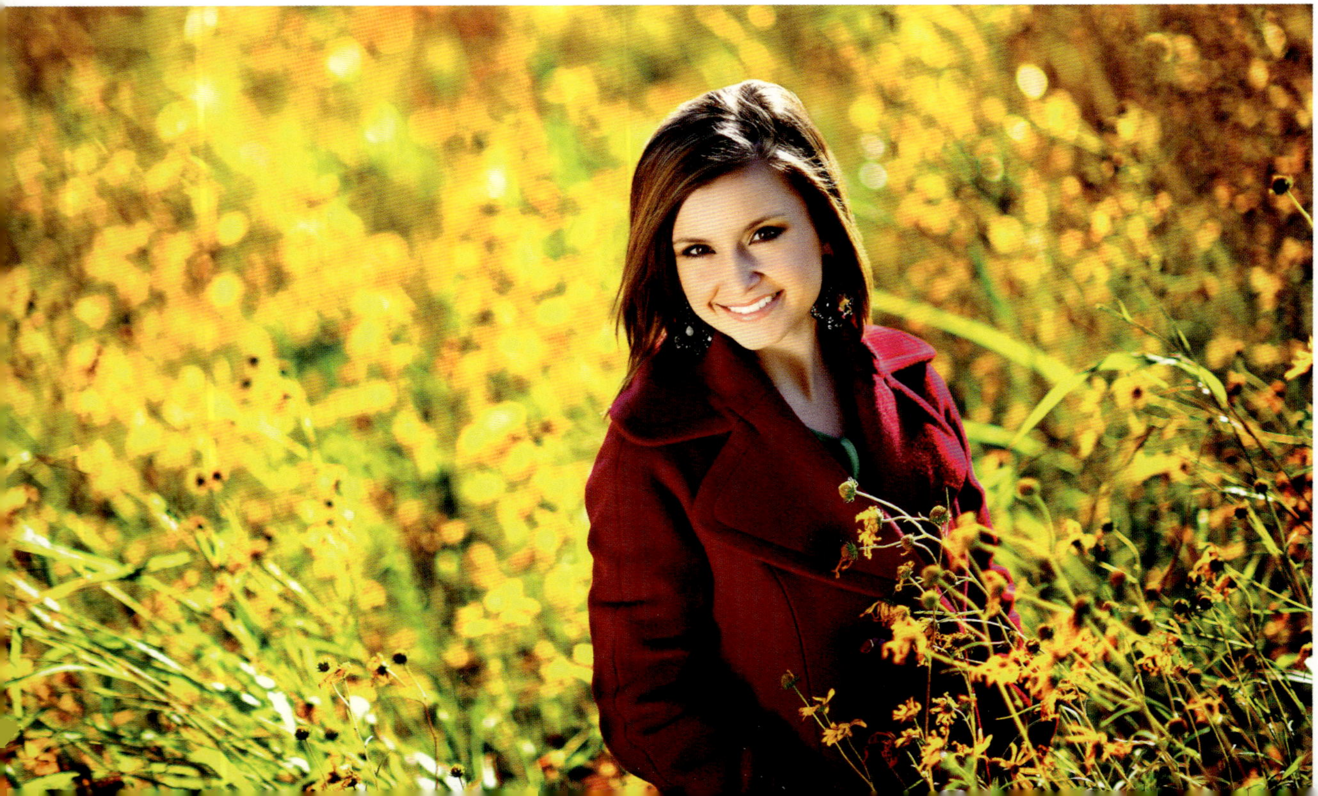

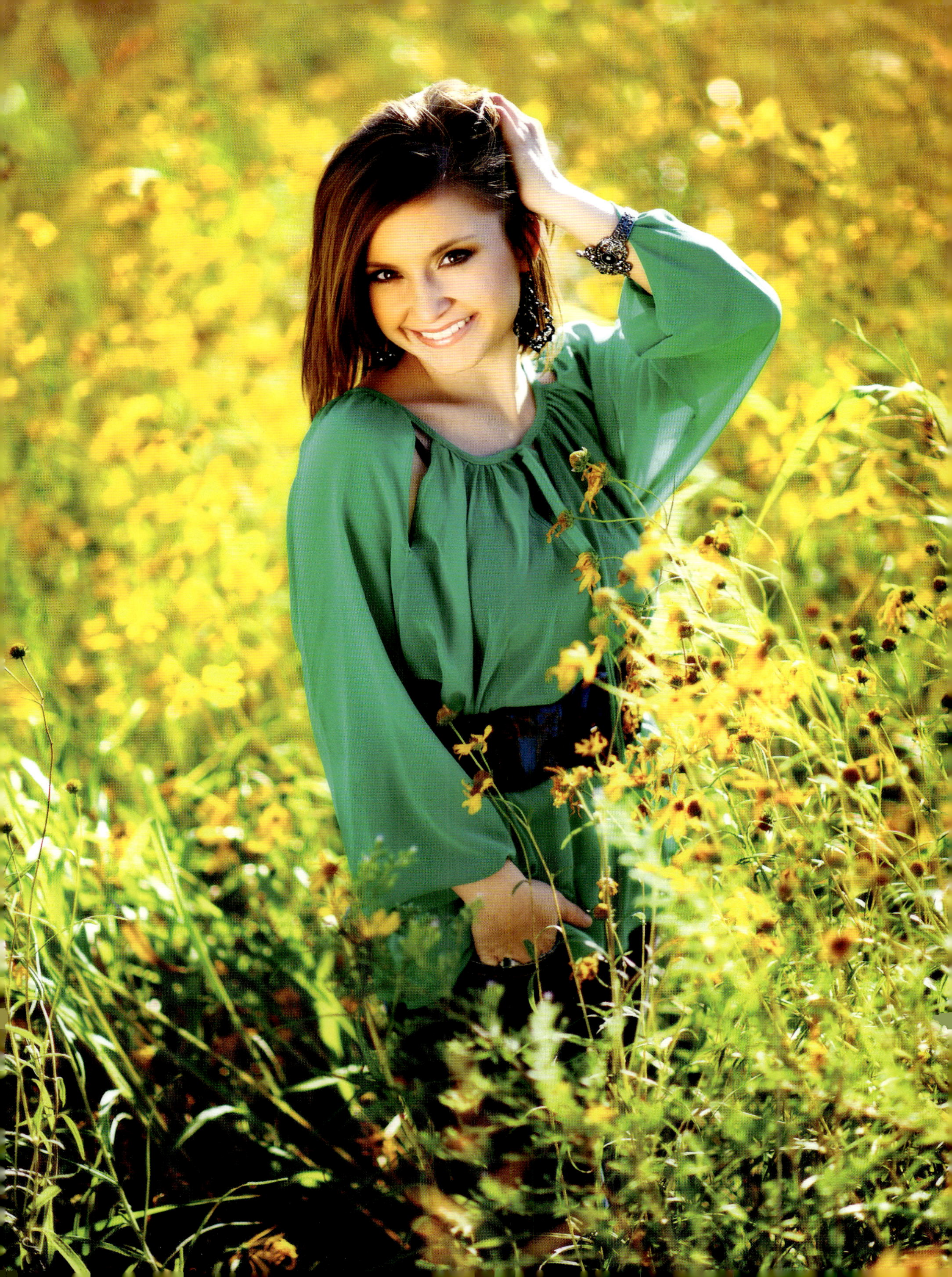

33. Don't Forget the Props

Not Just for the Studio

Props might spring to mind more commonly in a studio portrait, but there's no reason to ignore them in your outdoor portraits. Pets, instruments, sports equipment, and more all work well outside. Or, try adding something unexpected—like a record player (*facing page*).

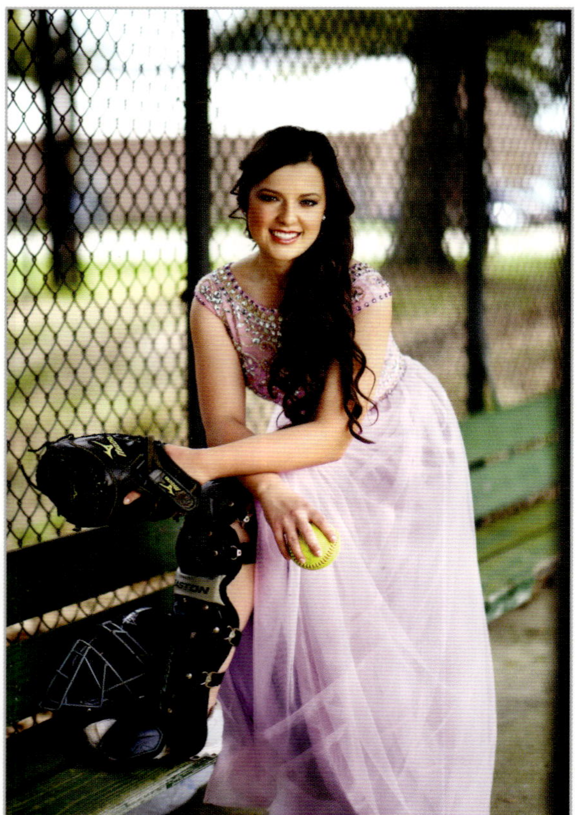

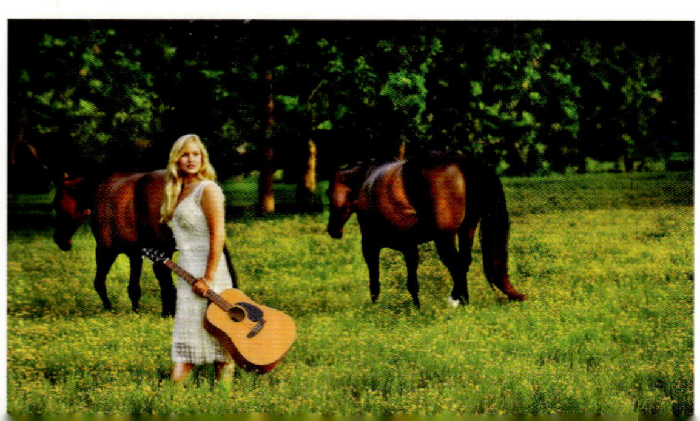

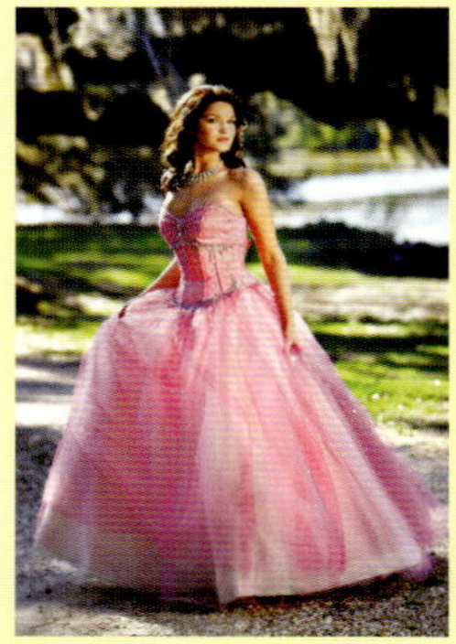

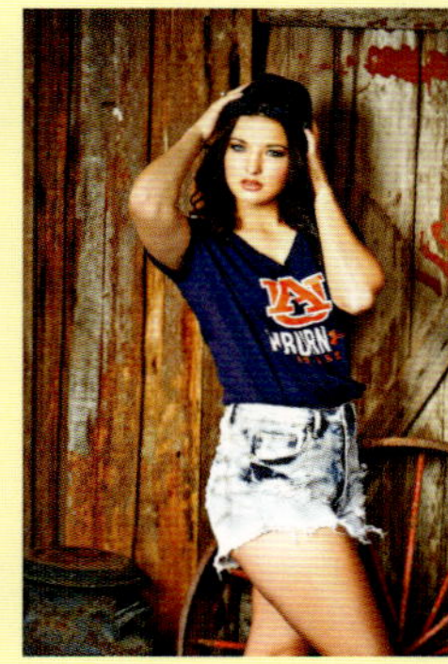

Clothing Can Add Personality

Seniors often have special clothing that reflects this stage of their life. Formal gowns. tuxedos, sports uniforms, t-shirts from their chosen university, and other outfits can all add personality to your outdoor senior portraits.

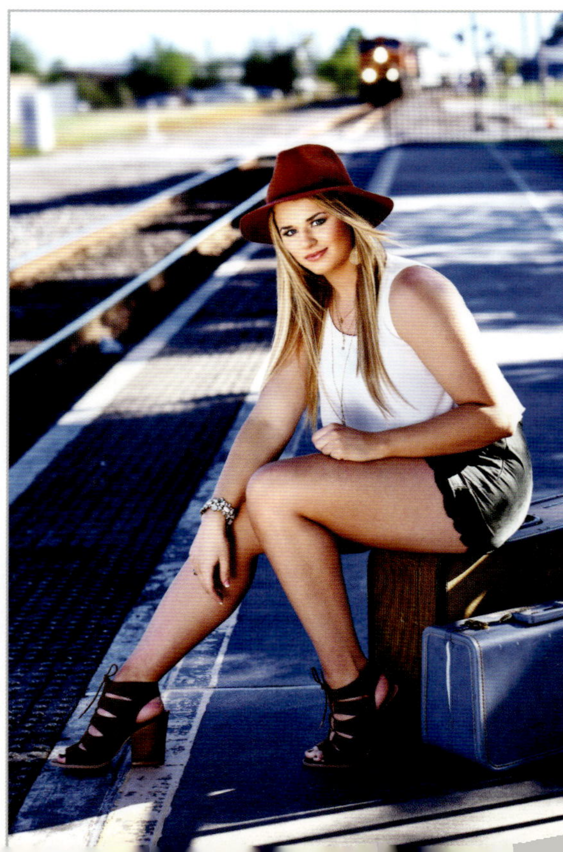

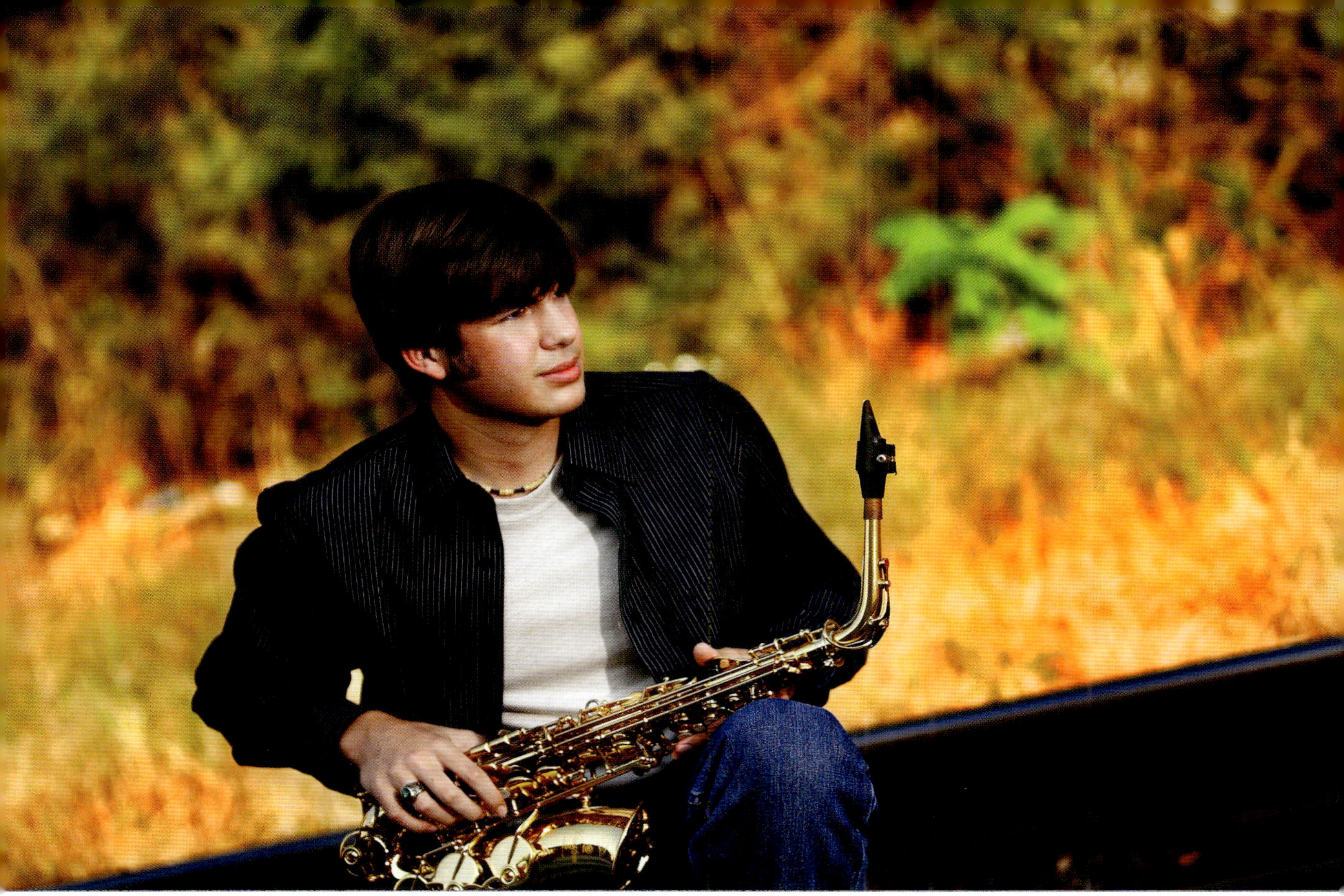

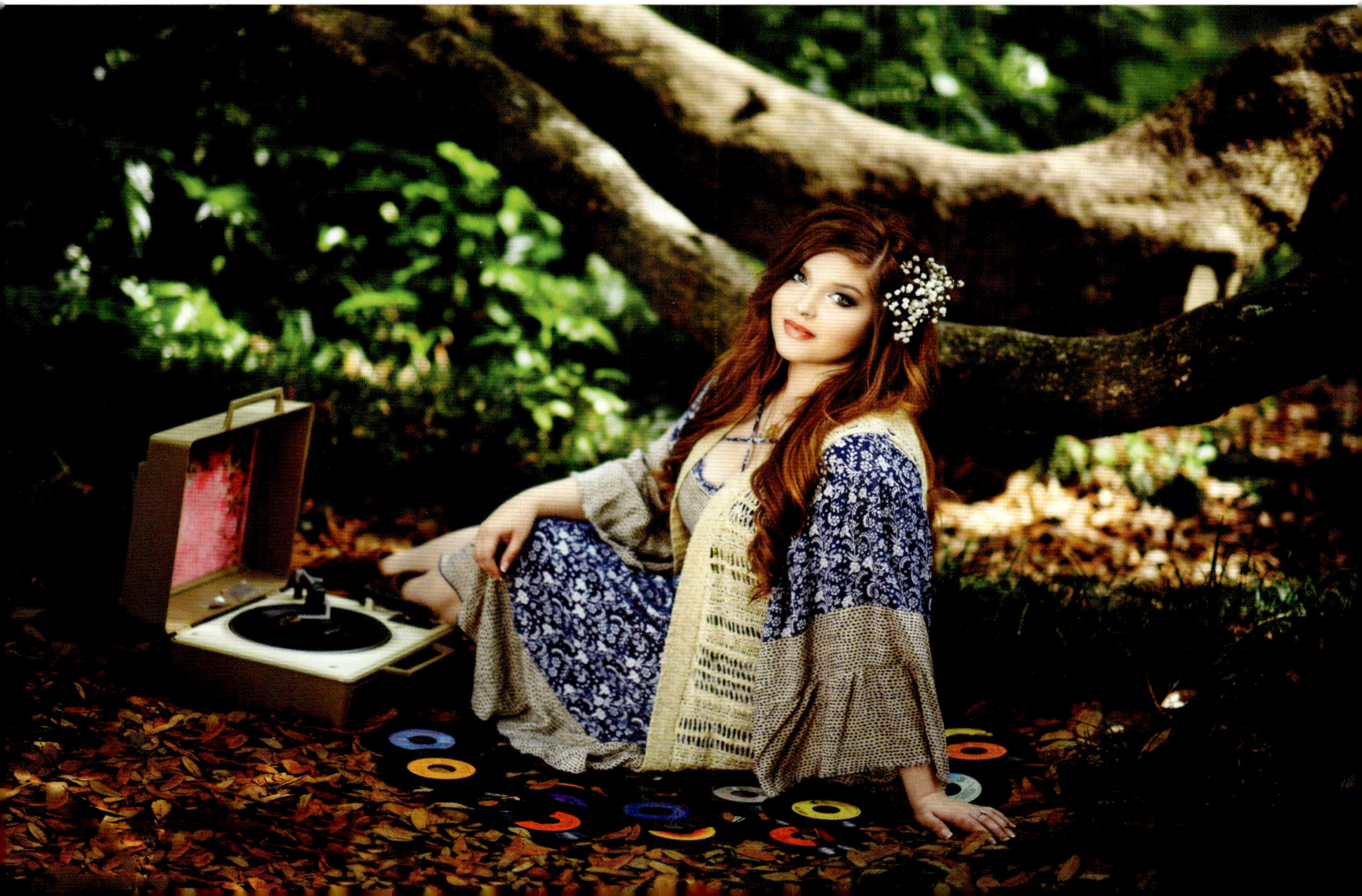

34. Use the Scene

The Lines

Look for ways to use the scene to your advantage. In the photo below, notice how the diagonal lines in the background were presented at an angle. I then posed my subject to create an opposite diagonal. These diagonals meet at her head and shoulders—the focus of the image. In a closer shot (*facing page*), the same criss-cross effect is happening with the line on the background and the line of her eyes.

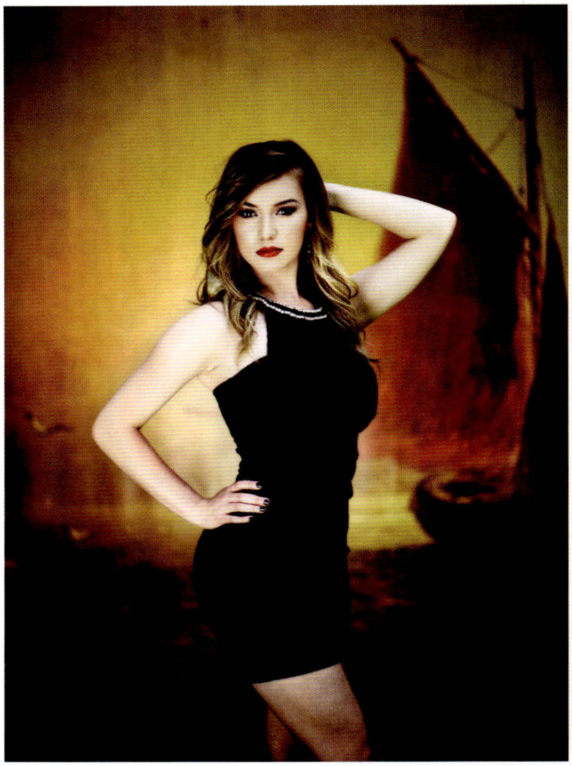

The Tones

In the image to the right, notice how the gradation of background tones blends with her dress in the lower part of the image. Our eyes go right to the area of greatest contrast—her face, slim arms and waist, and her pretty hair against the gold area of the painting.

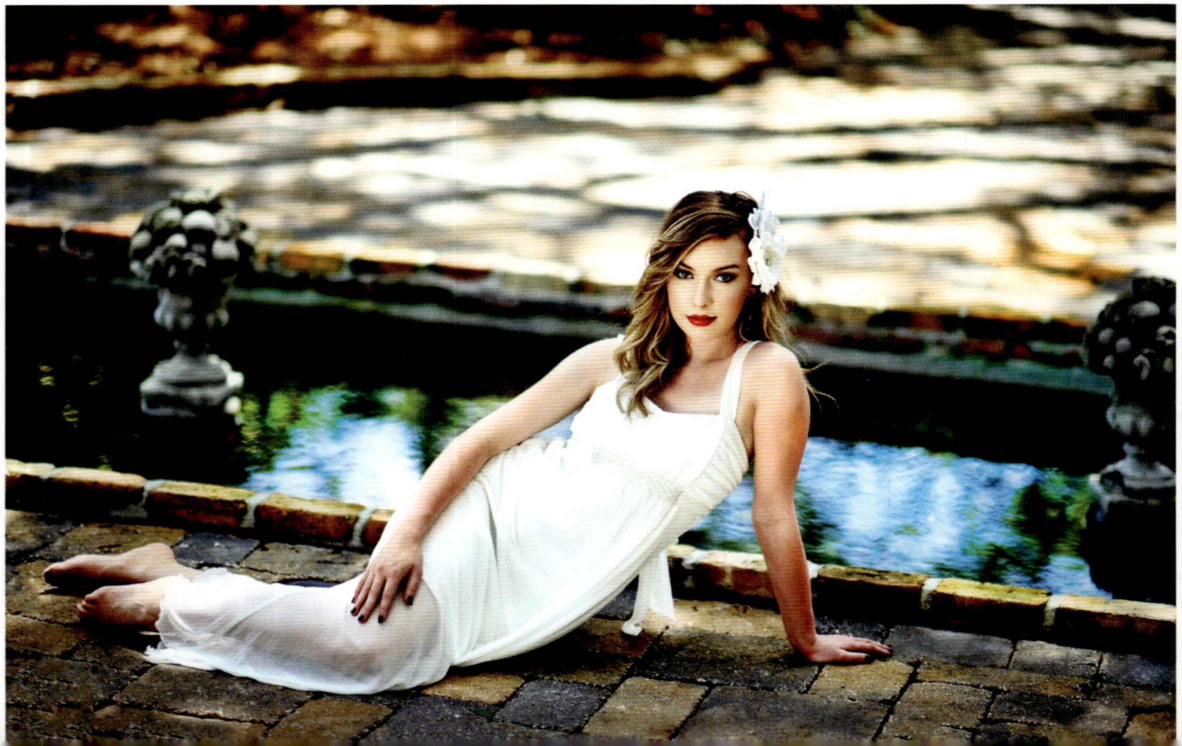

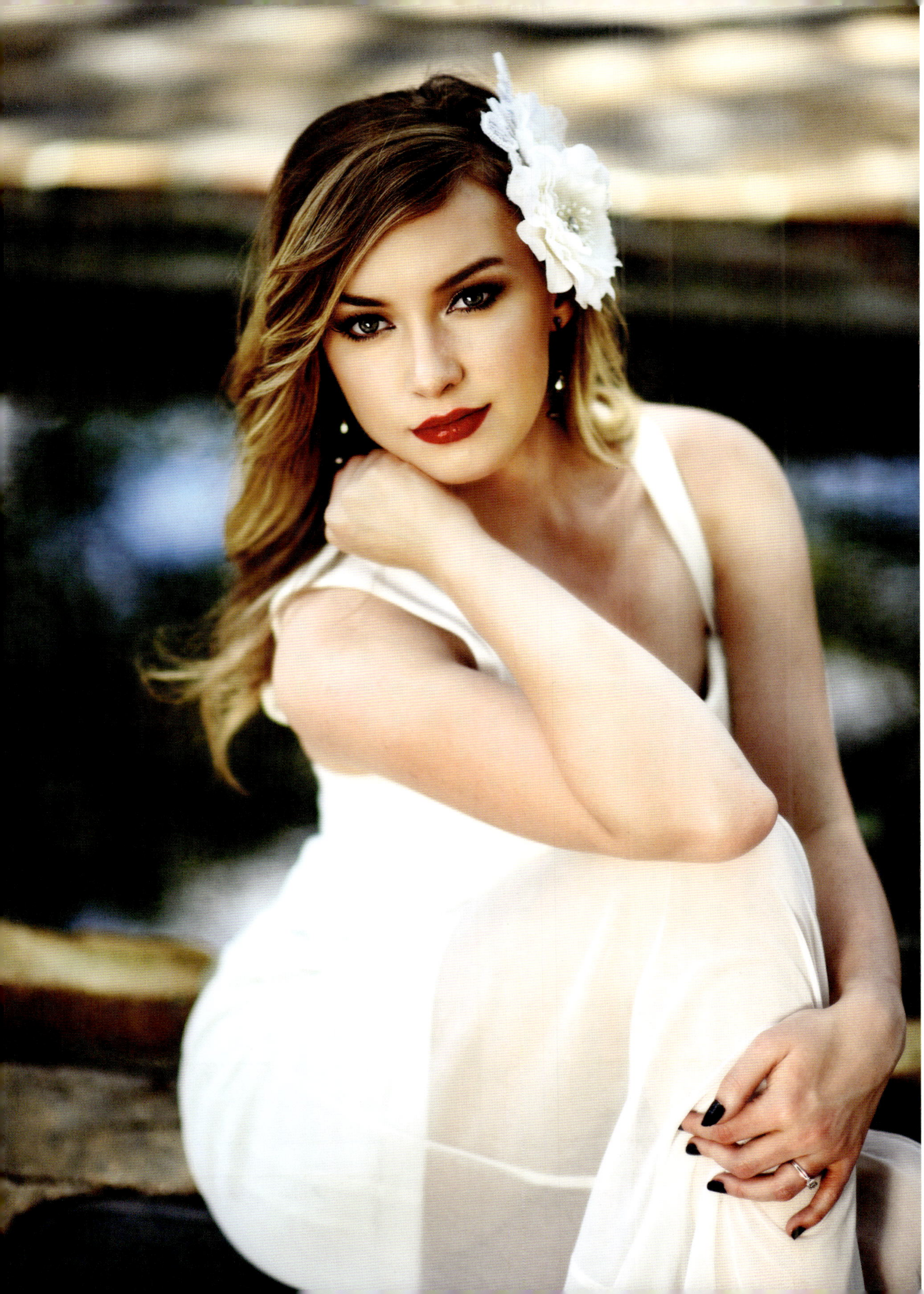

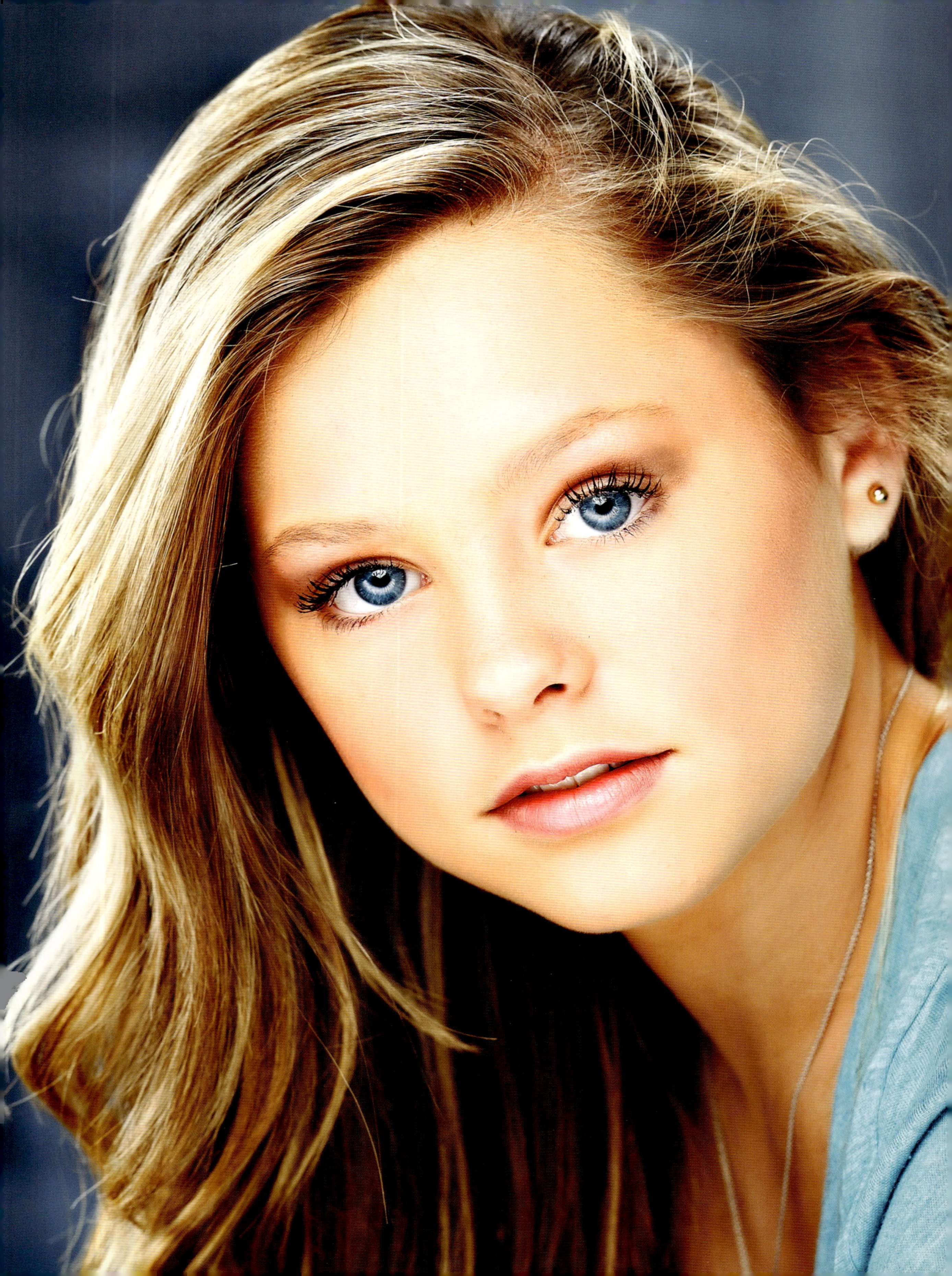

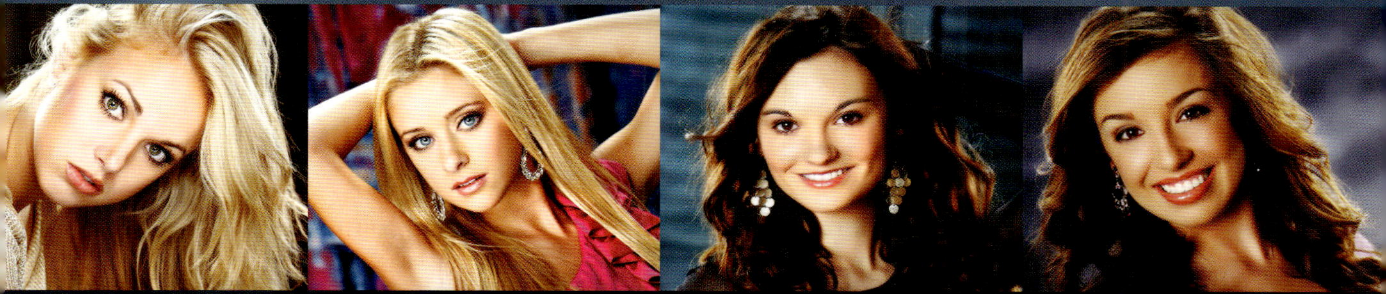

SECTION 3

Studio Photography

Make the most of the controlled studio environment for refined lighting effects and studio-only looks to make every subject look their very best.

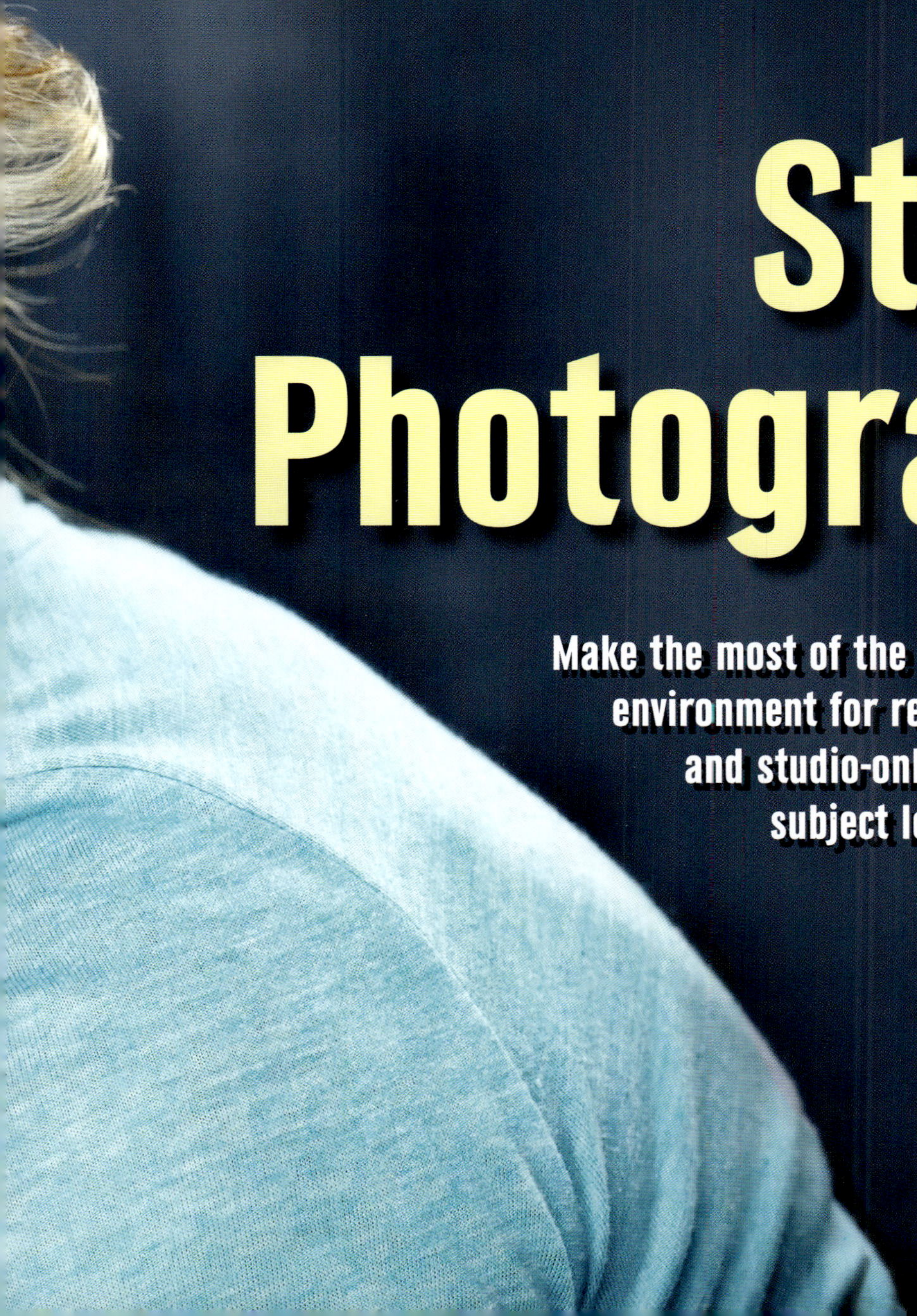

35. **Why Do Studio Photography?**

The Role of Studio Portraiture

When a new client comes to our studio, there's about a 95 percent chance they want outdoor and location portraits—that just seems to be what everybody wants today. What they don't realize, of course, is that there are a lot of advantages to doing at least some of their images in the studio environment.

There are things we can do in the studio that we simply can't do outdoors—or that are incredibly impractical to do outdoors without more time and a team of assistants. And you can't beat having a studio available in the event it rains on your session day!

Backdrops and Props

In the studio, it's easier to get lots of color in the background—and if you use gels, it can be pretty much any color you'd want to coordinate with (or contrast against) the subject's clothing. While I try not to go too crazy with props, especially anything that would make the portrait look dated, in the studio I have easy

"There are a lot of advantages to doing at least some of their images in the studio environment."

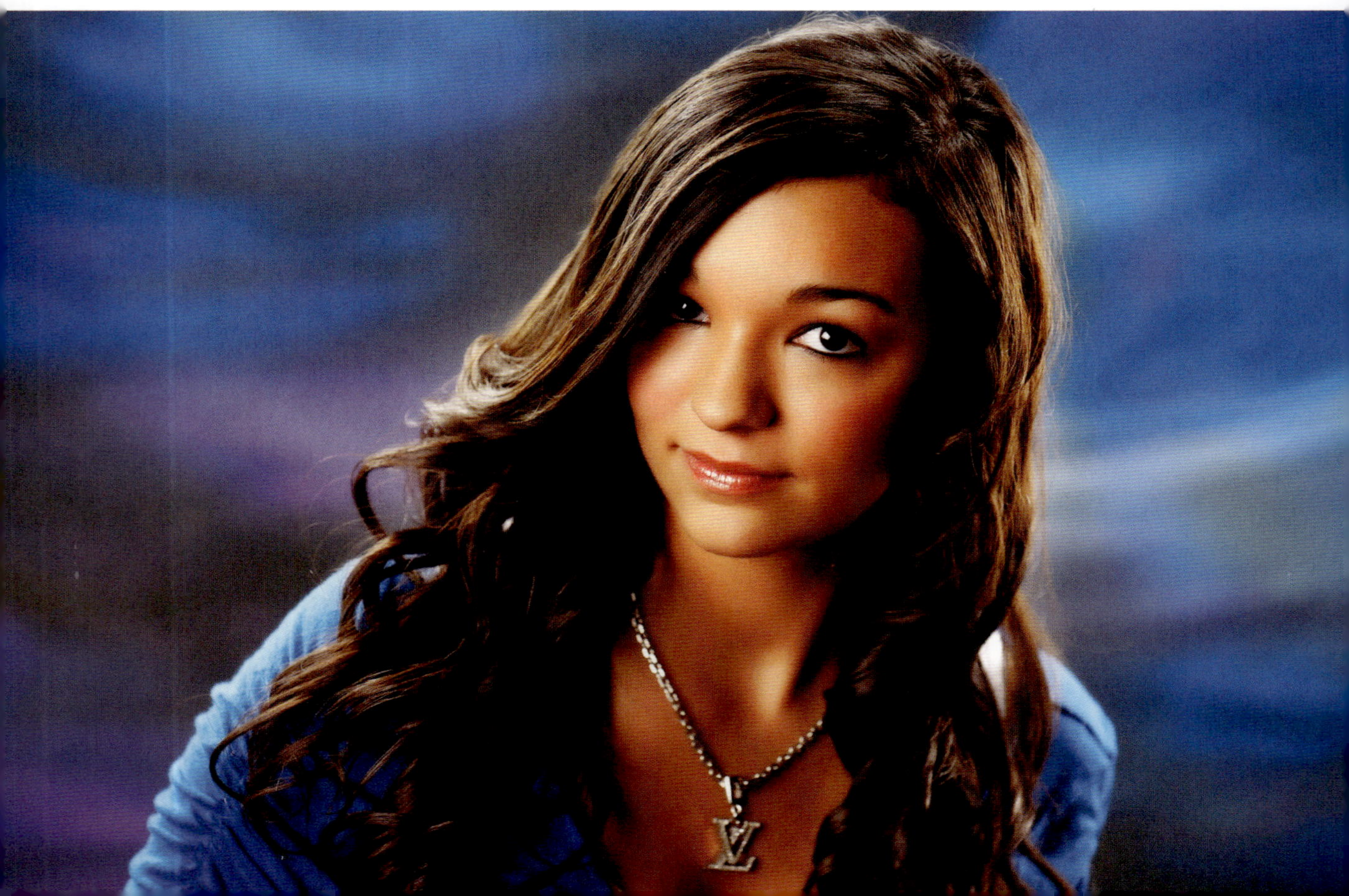

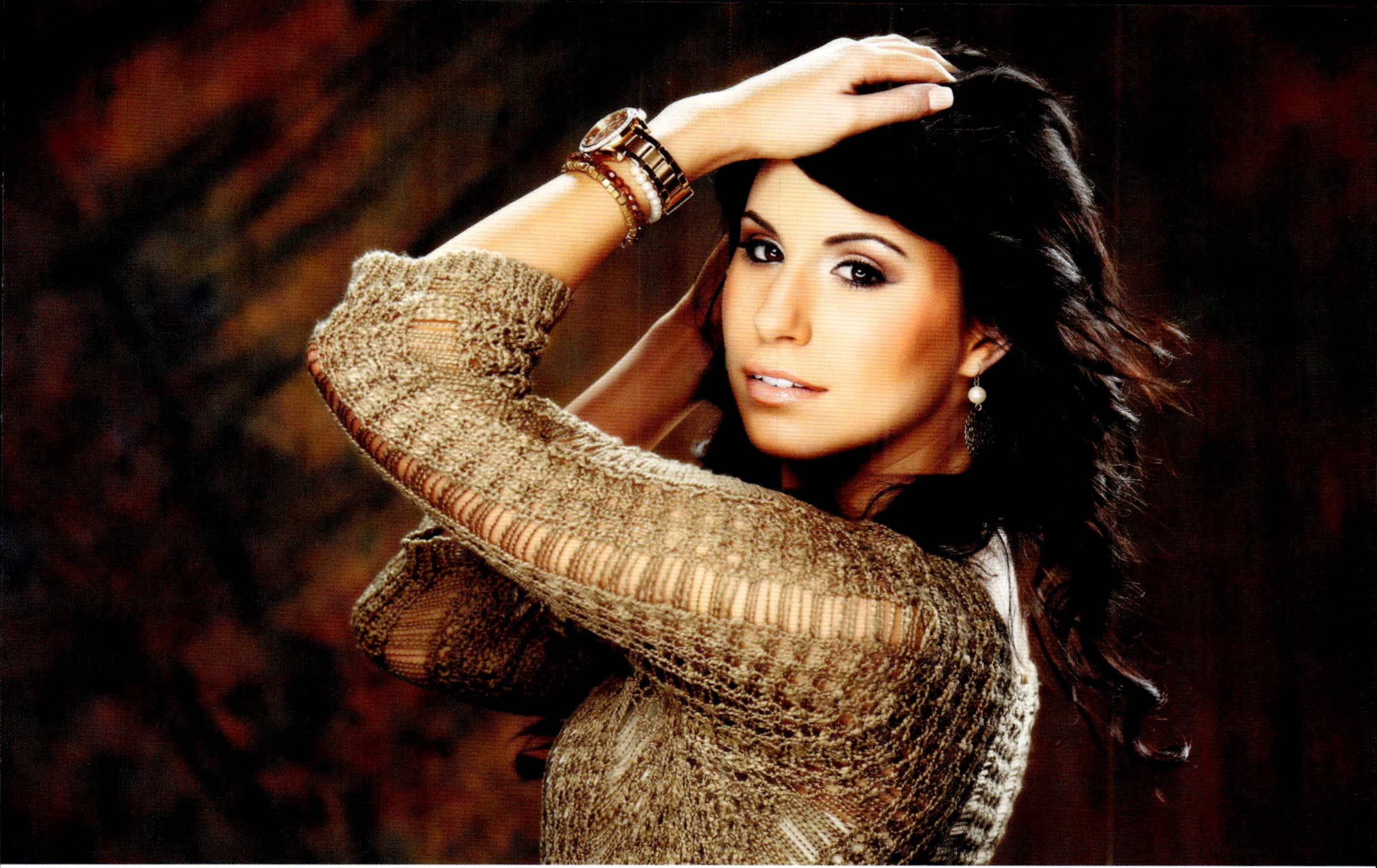

access to chairs, stools, benches, and other set elements that help make posing easier. Props can also help conceal things that subjects don't want to see in their portraits, like a not-so-flat stomach or wider hips.

A Profitable Balance

Portrait subjects love to be outside and have that experience, so I give them that; we normally do about 70 percent of the session outside. Most of our sessions then conclude with some additional studio portraits—and the images end up selling well, even to people who weren't sure they'd like the look of studio portraits. A really nice studio headshot, especially with the Westcott Eyelighter, is almost sure to sell. And, in the end, those incremental sales are why we go out of our way to do it. Adding a studio component to the session produces more images that they like, which gives us additional sales.

Work Efficiently

For each session, we set a time limit and stress the importance of arriving early. If the subject isn't traveling too far, we ask them to arrive with their first outfit already on. I tell them, "We have about two hours and I want to make the most of your time." This is the key: telling them up front. Don't spring the information on them when they arrive for their shoot. Of course, there are still times when people show up late or dawdle. In those cases, we have to gently rush them along and encourage them to change more quickly so we'll have time to photograph all their outfits.

36. Lighting: Another Studio Advantage

A Blank Canvas

In a dark studio, we start with a blank canvas when it comes to lighting. I can add light only where I want it and control the quality of the light with modifiers.

This means I can add accent lighting to make the subject's hair look pretty and kicker lighting for separation and edge lighting on their body. I can use the Westcott Eyelighter for catchlights that make the eyes look amazing. I can use huge main light sources that are incredibly soft and flattering. I can create butterfly lighting—and I can use ring lighting, which kids love for its edgy, fashion-forward look. Those are things that I *can't* do outside. If they want a totally different flavor, I can switch over to hot lights—another look that really works only in the studio. We'll look at many of these techniques in sections that appear later in this book.

Outdoors, I'm usually shooting with just two light sources (the ambient light and either a reflector or softbox). For most studio portraits, on the other hand, I use *five or more* lights to create a very refined look that can perfectly sculpt the subject.

A More Tailored Approach

I always look for directional light, but in the studio, I can use the deeper shadows to minimize problem areas and really slim people down. In an outdoor scene that is flooded with light, that's a lot harder. On a related note, I can also design my lighting and set to let me shoot from a higher angle and hide a double chin—something subjects hate to see!

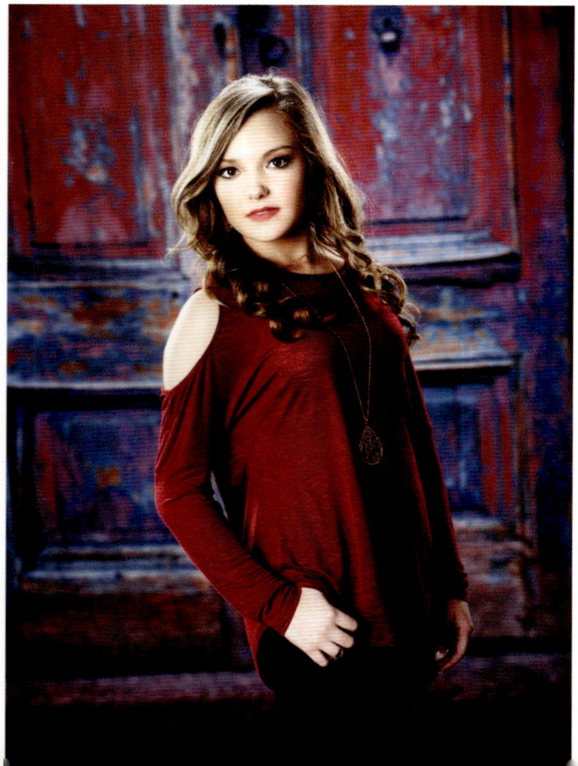

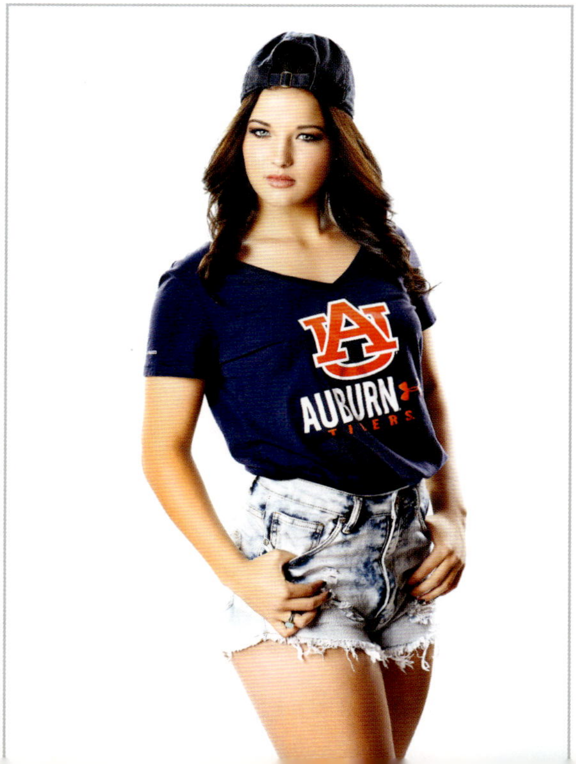

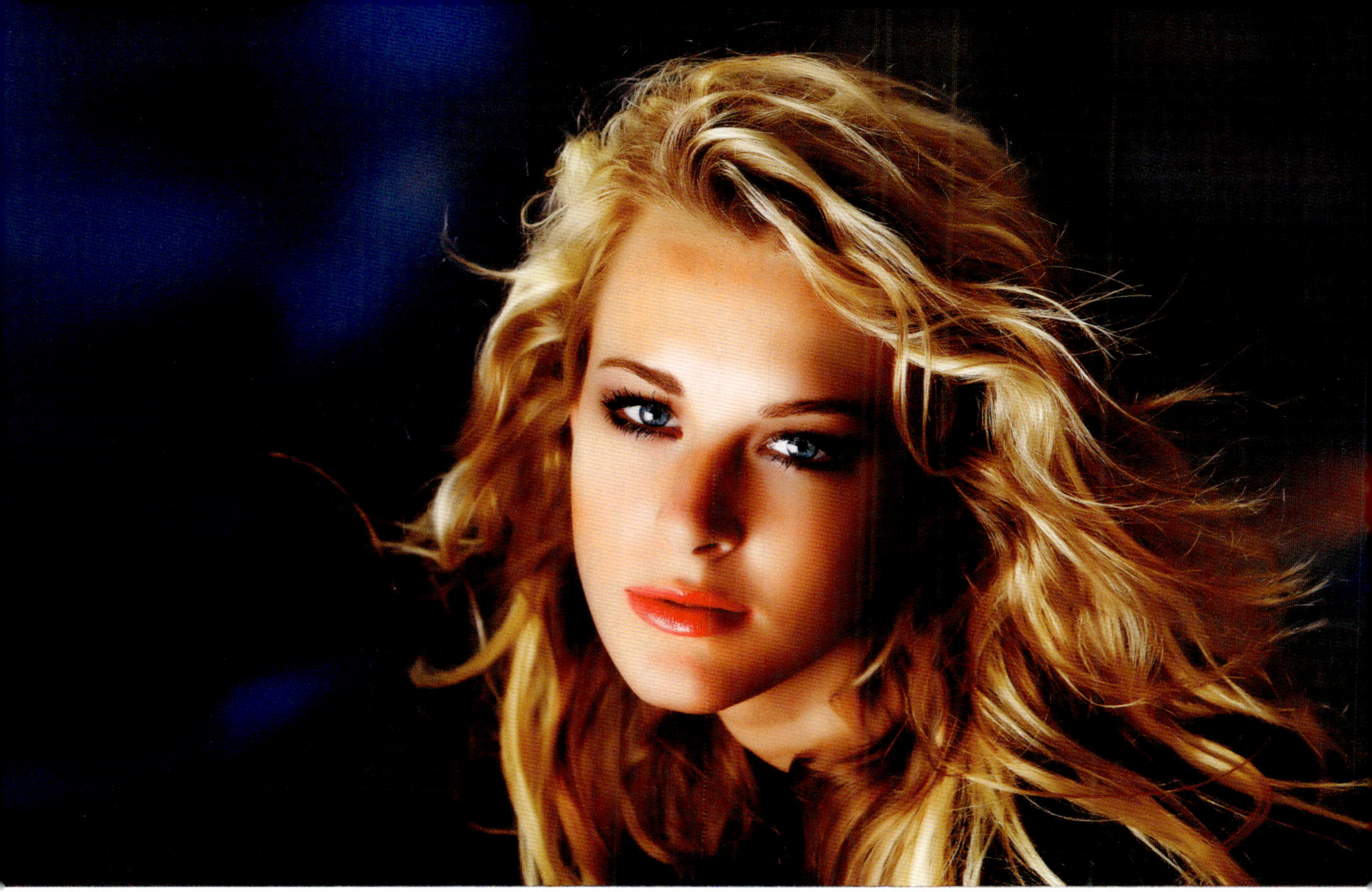

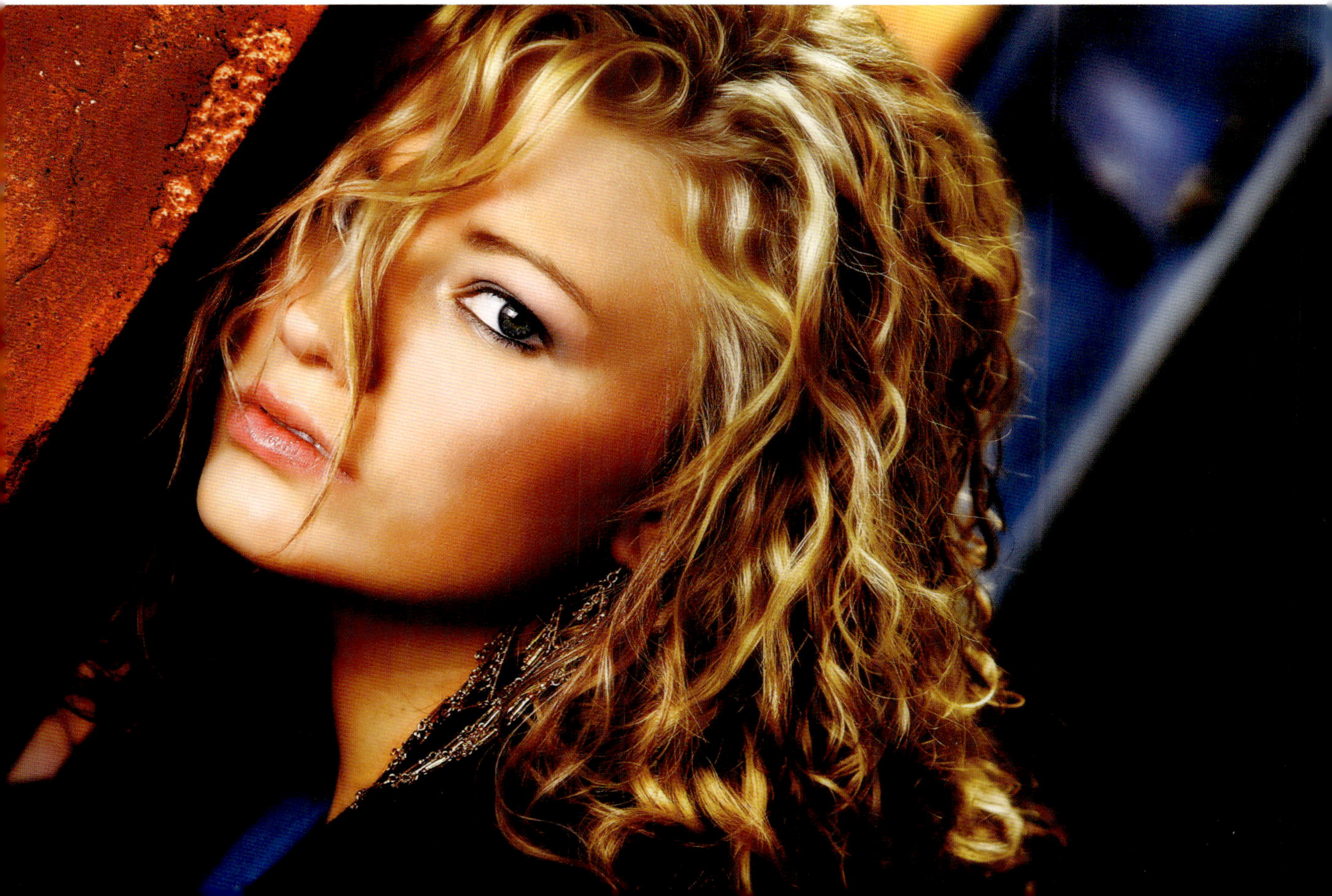

37. Backdrops and Props

Choosing the Right Backdrop

The most basic factor to consider when selecting the backdrop for a client's session is what they are wearing. Look for some kind of color harmony. This doesn't mean the colors have to match exactly; intentional contrasts can look great, too.

There should also be some logical relationship between the style of the clothing and the style of the backdrop. Just as when selecting scenes for outdoor portraits, backdrops with an industrial or rustic feel tend to make sense with relaxed outfits, while more artistic or architectural looks work well with more formal attire. For children's portraits, painted scenics are often a great choice. Backgrounds with a natural look will coordinate with many clothing styles and subject types.

Finally, be sure to take the subject's eye and hair colors into account—especially if they have blue or green eyes. For subjects with these lighter eye colors, a background with matching tones can often yield a very powerful look.

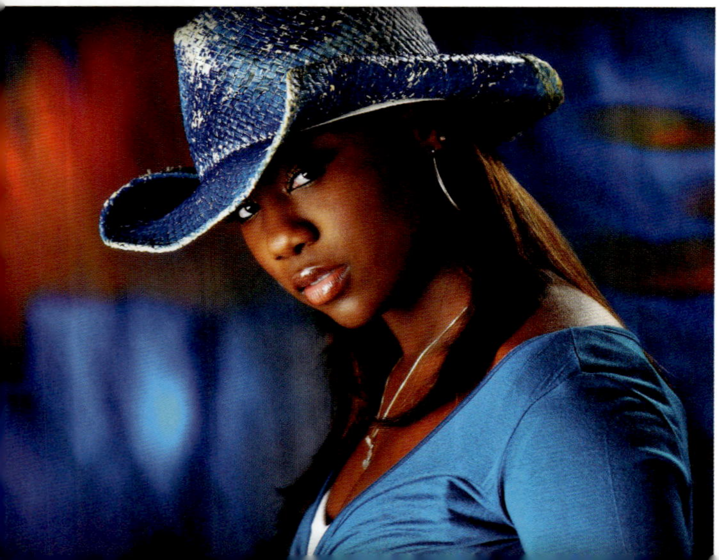

Get Input and Refine the Look

I always ask for client input on the backdrops to use for the session. I'll make suggestions and also talk to them about their ideas. If they absolutely hate a backdrop, that's fine; I didn't make the backdrops, so I don't let it hurt my feelings. In fact, I am happy to *know* they don't like it so we don't waste time shooting pictures they would never want to buy! Having a track system to move backdrops in and out easily makes this a low-effort process.

That said, sometimes showing the client an image of themselves against a backdrop they didn't initially like can totally change their minds. There's a big difference between how the whole backdrop looks and how it photographs when you only see a small part of it behind the subject. Keep in mind, too, that an "almost right" background can often be improved by adding gels to adjust the color or by using barn doors on the background light to vignette it a bit.

Trends and Traditions

While I think it's important to offer some traditional looks, it's also critical to stay on top of trends. Keep your eyes open for current colors, patterns, and styles as you peruse Facebook or Pinterest. Exploring current magazines that feature fashion and editorial photography is also useful (and, in many cases, business professionals can get free subscriptions for lobby copies). I'm lucky that my wife likes to go through *Vogue, Glamour,* and other magazines and collect images she thinks might work as inspiration for me.

In the "trends" category, digital compositing of backgrounds is something to consider. Using software like LayerCake (and other programs), you can replace or enhance your backdrops in postproduction. As with all trends, though, there's a good chance this will eventually look dated—probably sooner than later. But, selectively, it could be useful.

Adapting (Not Copying) Ideas

If I like a concept from a magazine, on-line, or even a sample image a client has brought to my attention, I'll put it in my idea file and start thinking about how to make that idea my own. I don't try to copy things directly. Honestly, it's rare to find something that is totally unique—but I always put the elements together in my own way.

Additionally, I try not to look into what other people in my market are doing (except to check for outdoor shooting locations I might have overlooked). Why? Well, it's far too easy to accidentally copy an idea.

I once ran into a young fellow photographer at a restaurant and she told me the story of an image she'd created with a very distinctive pose and set of props. When her mom saw the photo, she said, "Oh, Tim Schooler has one like that." The young photographer said she was initially flattered, thinking I had used her idea . . . until her mom pointed out that my image was taken two years earlier. At some point, the young photographer must have seen it and filed the idea away in her head. When presented with a similar subject and props, she accidentally "copied" my look (which actually appears in this book; it's the softball shot in section 47). Especially within your local market, you don't want to seem like an also-ran. If your images look like everyone else's, why should clients pick you?

Of course, clients do sometimes bring in images and ask me for those specific looks. In that case, I do my best to oblige and give them the shots they want—but I'm always looking for subtle ways to make the shots my own.

38. **Small Variations**

Backdrop

I shot this image on a Denny's Freedom Cloth. I love these backdrops; the 10x10-foot models can be crumbled up to the size of a basketball for storage, then re-hung with *no* wrinkles. They're also very realistic. It certainly looks like a real door behind this model, doesn't it? The colors in the backdrop were also well suited to her pink top and blue eyes.

Lighting

For the image on the facing page (and the bottom-right posing variation), I used a Starfish main light, but any octo modifier would work. I placed it high and angled it down for butterfly lighting. The fill was an Eyelighter on a light stand, right under the subject—as close as I could get it to her. The double catchlight this produces (like a sun and a crescent moon) makes the subject's eyes look great. A 12x36-inch stripbox mounted on the ceiling and directed down at a 45 degree angle from behind the subject lit her hair (a gobo on this prevented flare). Finally, vertical strip boxes to either side of the subject added accent light on her arms and torso.

Finishing the Look

I added a Makita cordless leaf blower to move the model's hair. Typically, I let the moms control this—and they *love* it. I want them to gently blow the hair away from the eyes and make it look fuller. It's more of a fashion look and kids love the motion and life it provides.

Another Look

At the end of the session, she asked if we could do a look with scrunched-up wet hair. I was happy to oblige and

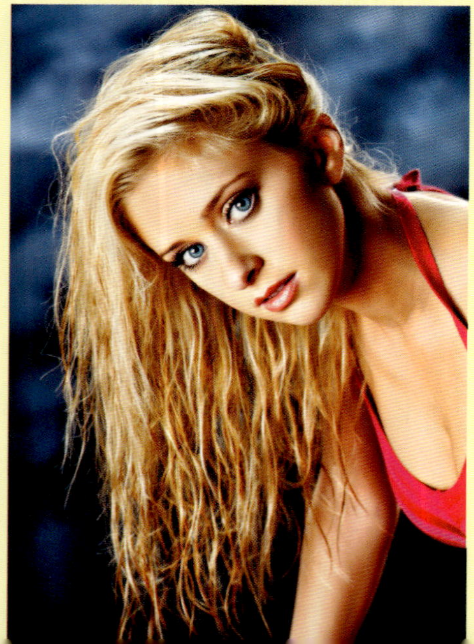

had her tip her head over to the side for a messy look. I switched the main light to a shallow 4x6 softbox with a silver interior for lighting with more of an edge.

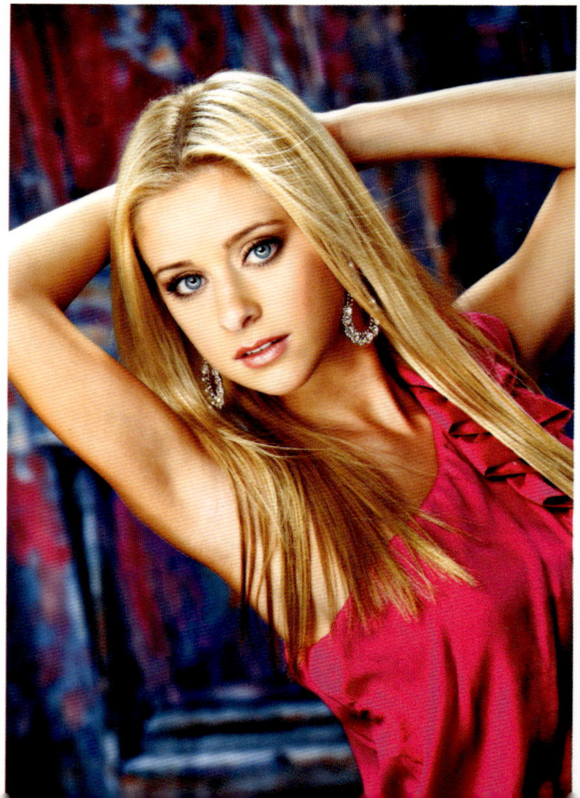

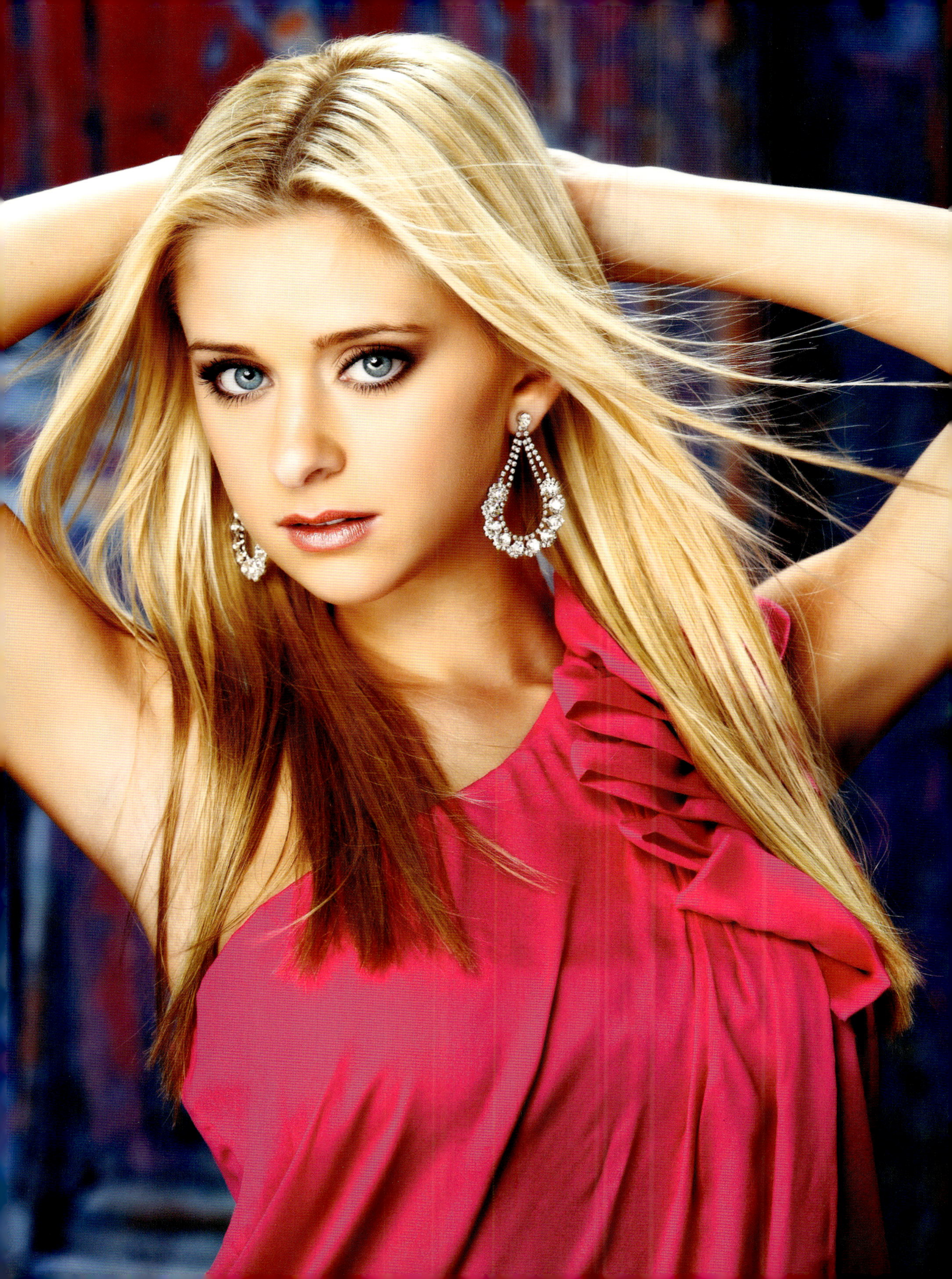

39. Same Backdrop, Different Look

Transformation

Like many seniors, when this young lady came in for her consultation, she was in casual street attire. For her session, she arrived with her makeup done, her hair styled, and wearing a sleek outfit. A lovely transformation! And I'm sure her friends thought the same thing when they saw her gorgeous images.

Versatility

Don't think a backdrop can be used only one way. If you look carefully, you'll see that this is the same backdrop as the one I used in the previous section. Here, there's much less light on it, so it coordinates well with the subject's blue jeans and black top. Her warm skin tones and blond hair really pop out from this cooler, darker set. For the full-length version on the facing page, I added a brick floor that carried the same colors and made sense with the door behind her.

Lighting

For the image on the facing page, I placed the main light (a 4x6-foot softbox) to camera right because her hair was pulled to that side. The hair light above her also put a nice highlight on her bare shoulders, helping them pop out.

Another Look

Here, I used a rubber background that is stapled to the wall and stays there all the time. It's textured, so you can light it to perfectly match the direction of light on your subject.

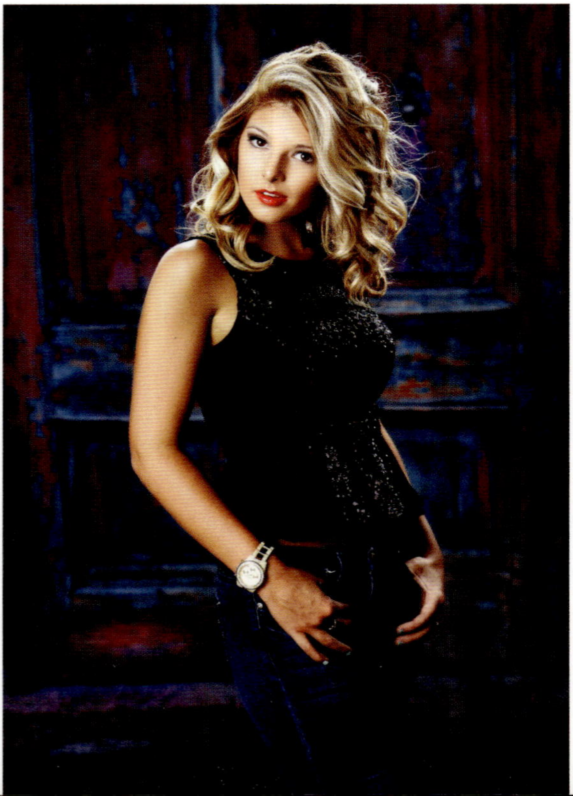

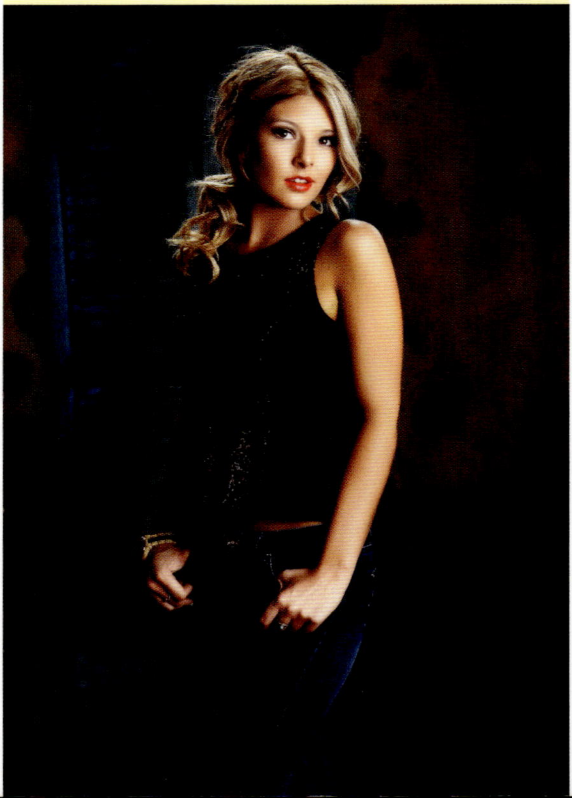

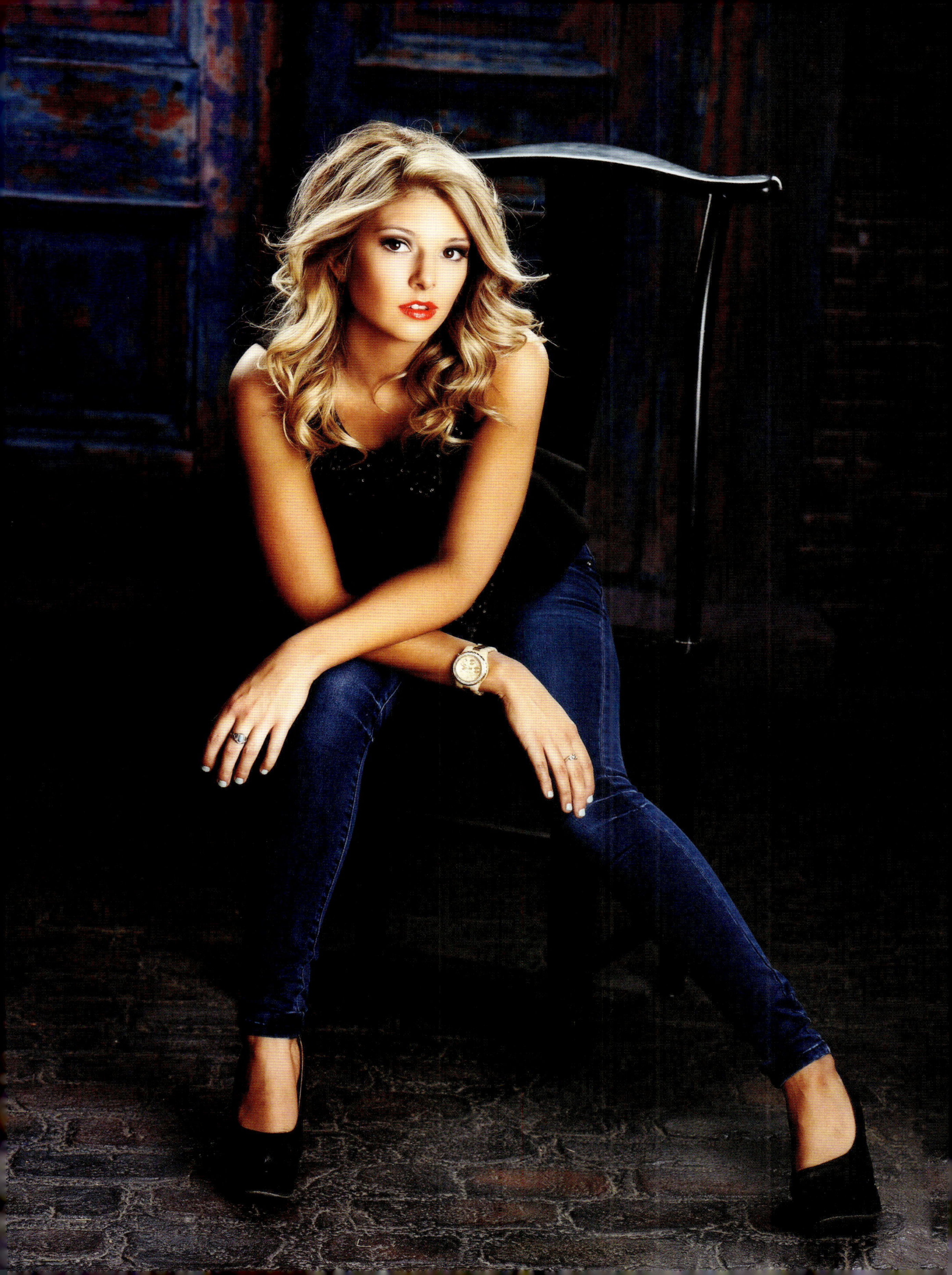

40. Highlighting Long Hair

A Popular Idea

Sometimes an idea catches on like wildfire. I create a "long hair" image with this lighting and pose for one a client during her session—but as soon as she started showing off the images around school, I got many more requests for images with the same look. As you can see, I tailored the portrait for each subject's coloration and attire, so every girl gets "her" version of the look she wants.

Pose

Ladies with long, thick hair spend a lot of time and money keeping it looking great—so when you see a client with this kind of hair (especially in combination with striking eyes), you want to highlight it. Don't crop it out!

Lighting

For the image on the facing page, I had the subject flip her hair forward and then positioned the Starfish main light for butterfly lighting on her face. I used an Eyelighter from below for fill and brought in accent lights to highlight her hair. For the bottom left image, I used a very similar setup—but the accent lights on either side had to be moved in very close to light her dark hair. If I need to move them *into* the frame, I know I can use the Content Aware Fill in Photoshop to remove them, so I don't mind doing that to get the light right.

Backdrop

Again, notice the backdrop coordination—especially the red backdrop and red lipstick!

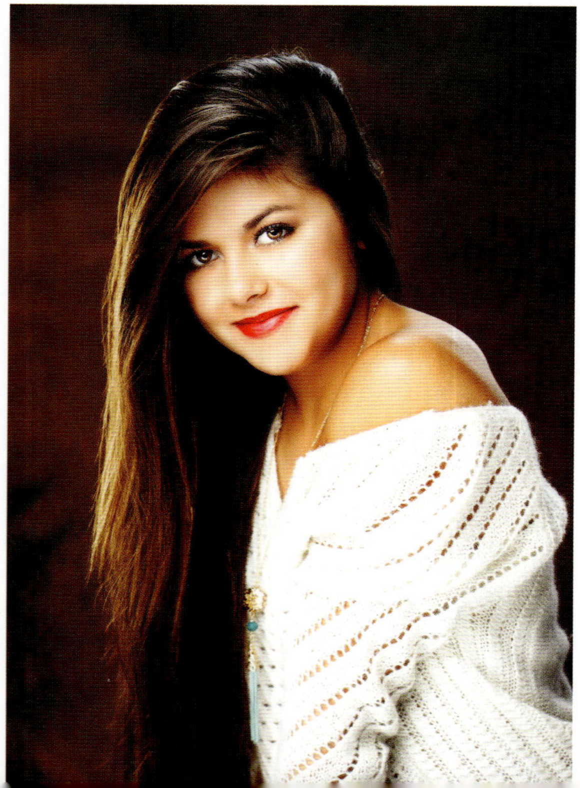

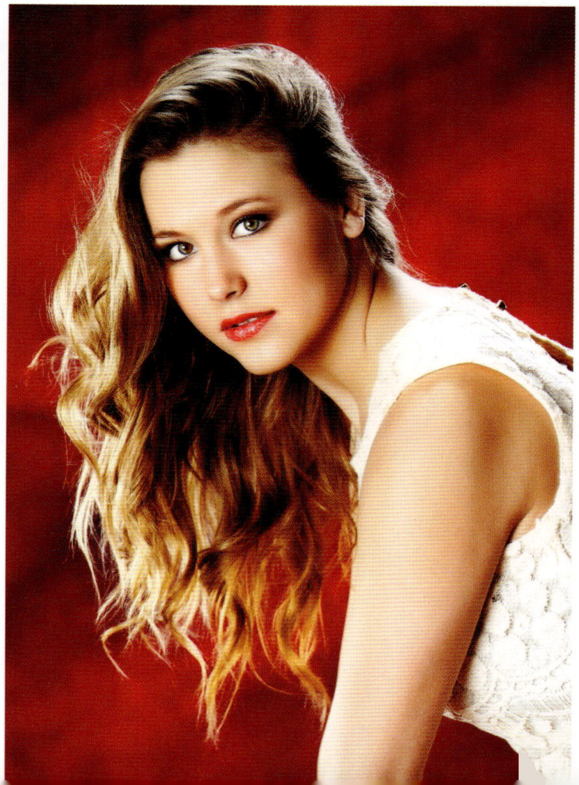

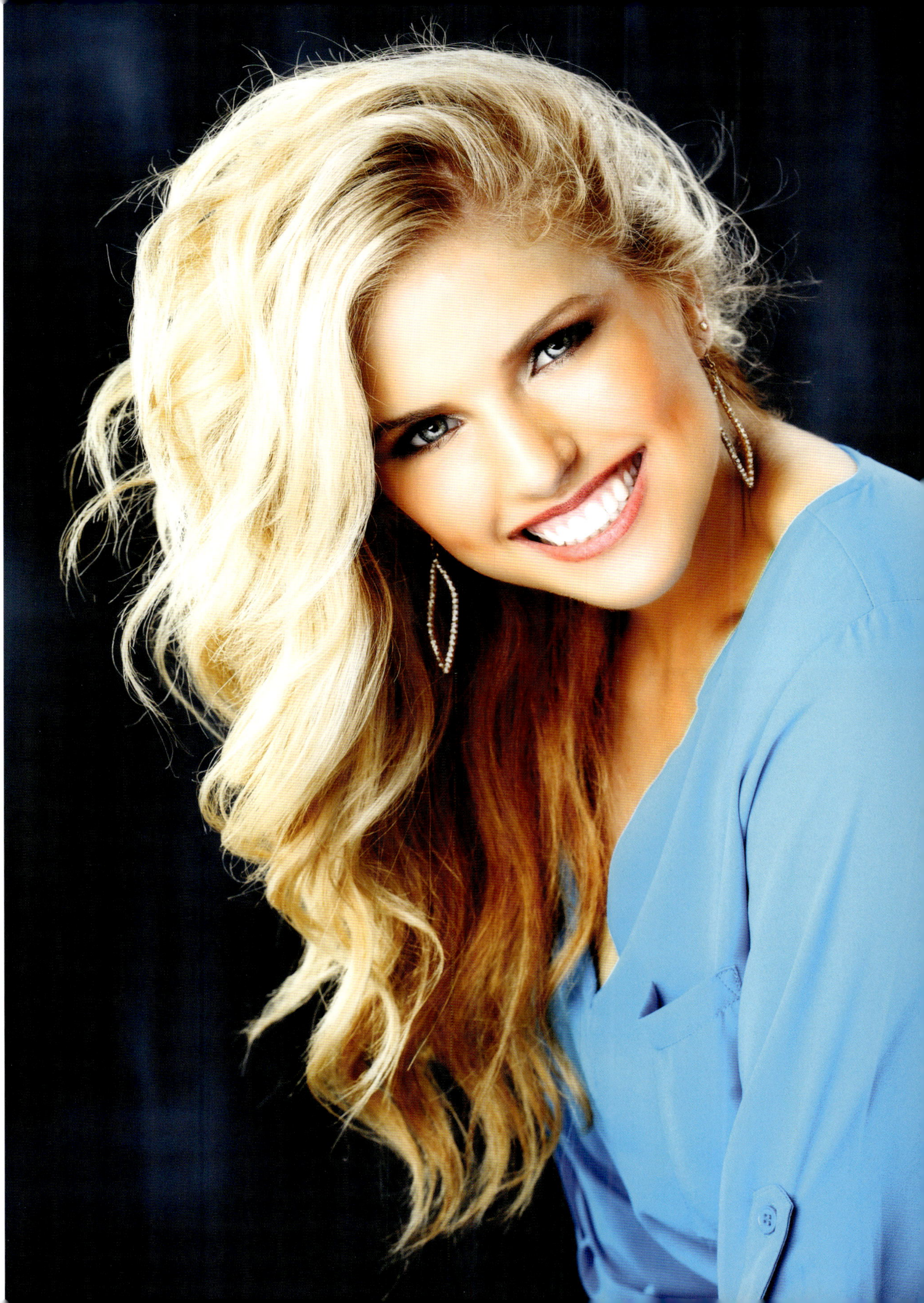

41. Lighting with a Fashion Flair

Backdrops

I had some new David Maheu backgrounds I wanted to try out—and this senior was interested in modeling, so it seemed like a good opportunity to explore a edgy, fashion-inspired look in her session.

Lighting

The same lighting setup was used for both the head-and-shoulders look below and the full-length seated portraits on the facing page.

In most of my portraits, you see much more wrap-around lighting than I used in these images. Here, I wanted a high-contrast, very directional look to the lighting. The main light was a 4x6-foot softbox—the same as I use in most of my portraits—but this time it was placed at more of an angle to give me plenty of shadowing on the far side of her face.

To keep her hair from going dark, I flanked my subject with two 12x36-inch strip lights. These were placed behind her at 45 degree angles (crisscrossing their beams) and pulled in close. Notice how the camera-right light brightened her hair but didn't fall on the shadow side of her face. This is because it was blocked by her hair. On a subject with short hair, this light would likely have caught the

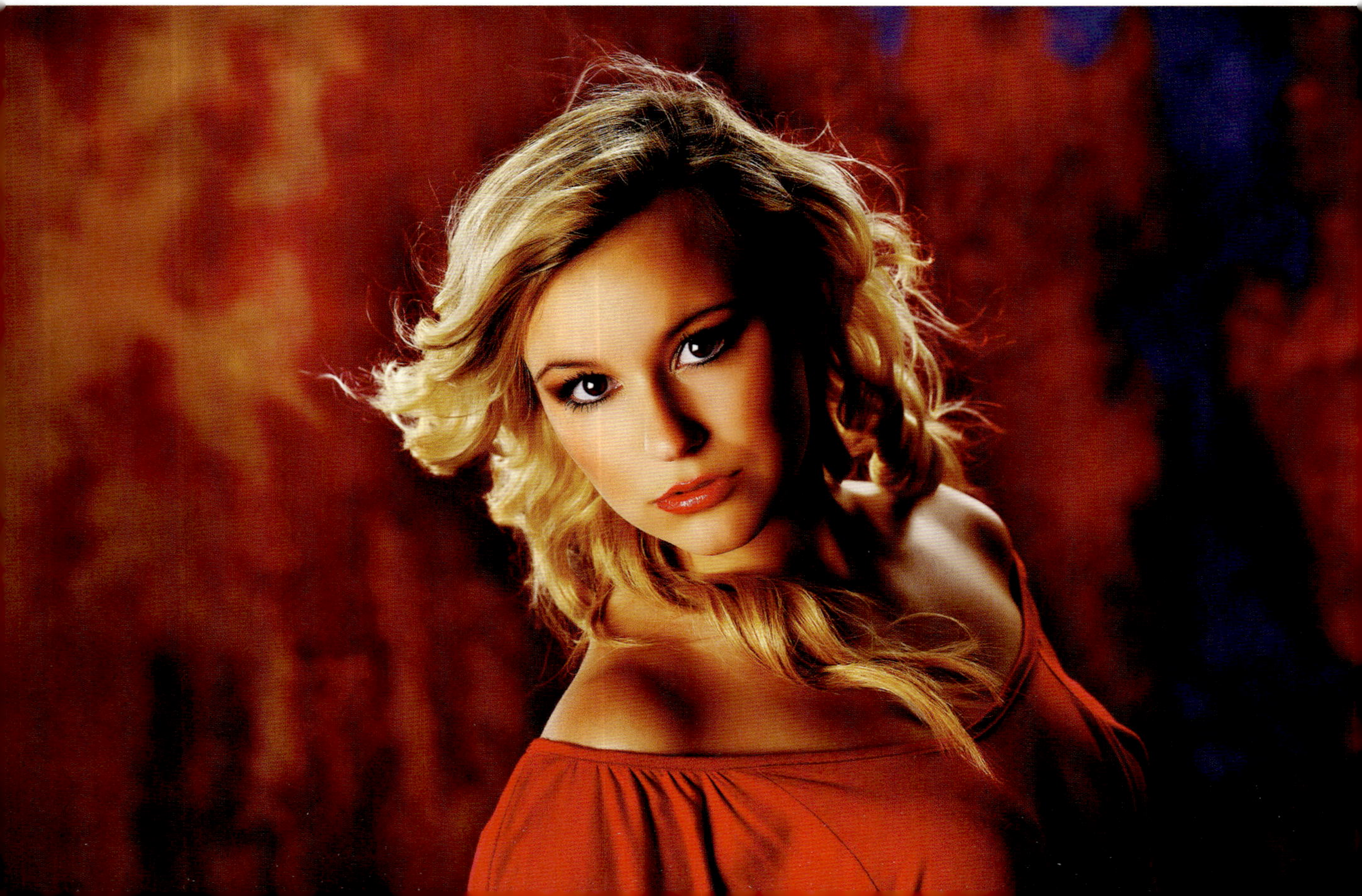

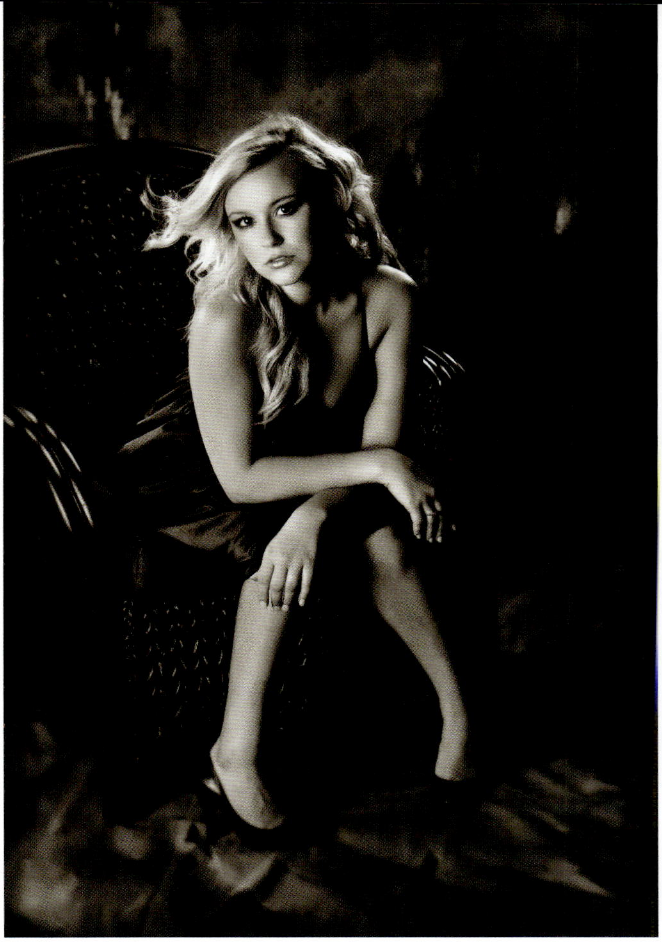

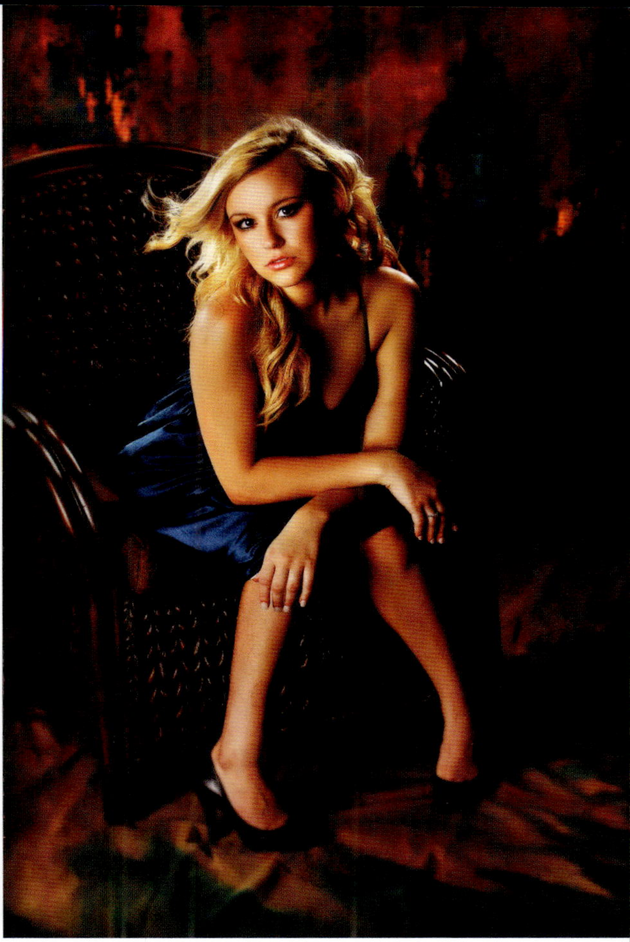

jawline and created an additional highlight on that area. Some photographers like that look in portraits of men, but it wasn't what I was going for in this image.

There was also a hair light hanging from the ceiling. This was a 12x36-inch softbox, aimed forward at a 45 degree angle to skim across the top of her head. Since this light points toward the camera, there's the potential for it to cause flare. Therefore, I have a black cloth hanging from the ceiling to gobo the light and prevent stray light from spilling into the camera.

Black & White

Black & white images are a perennial favorite among my clients. In this case, you can see how the conversion totally changes the look of the background and gives the shot more of a vintage look. It's a simple way to give the client some additional options.

When creating client previews, I often select a few images I think will look good in black & white, then add them to the presentation. They stand out, and clients usually like them—or ask to see other images in black & white, too.

Currently, I use a Kevin Kubota action that lets me quickly convert images to black & white. Therefore, my studio doesn't charge an additional fee for this service. Other studios do bill this as an upgrade, but it's up to you to decide what's right for *your* business.

42. **Edge Lighting and Separation**

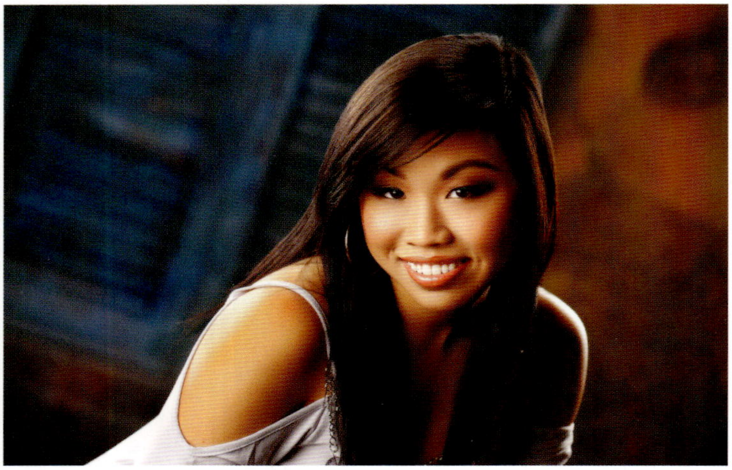

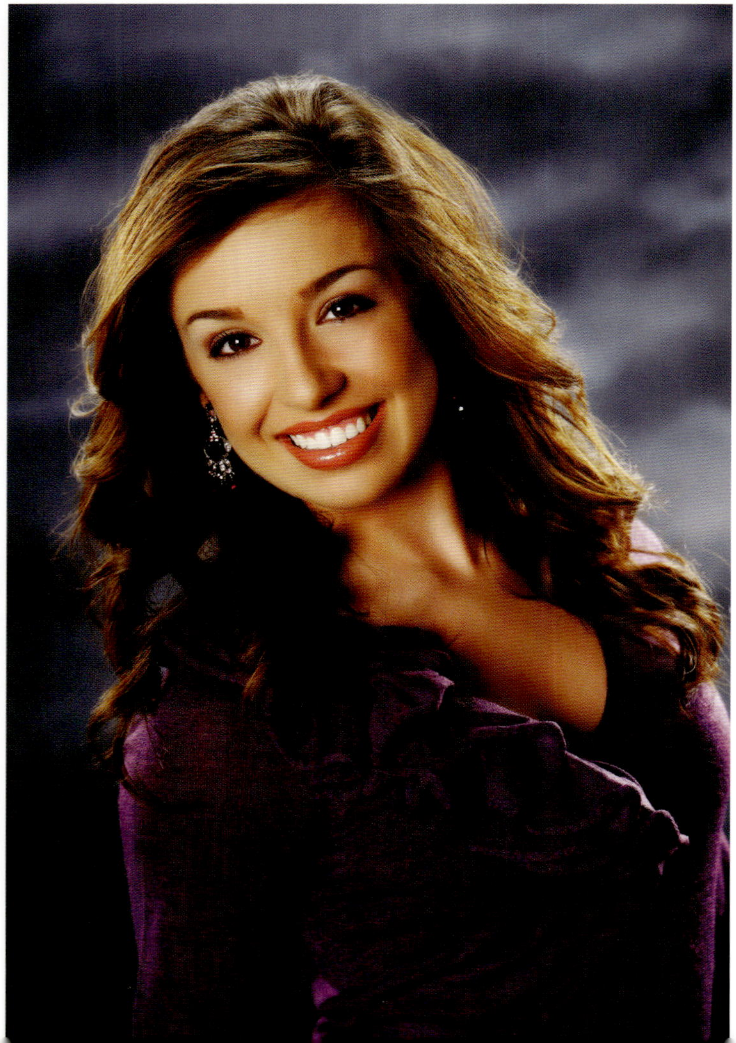

Depth and Definition

For a portrait to have depth—the illusion of a third dimension—it helps to create tonal separation between the subject and the background. Particularly with dark-haired subjects on darker backgrounds, adding edge lighting (a bright highlight outlining their form) enhances the image. It prevents unappealing tonal mergers, where the subject seems to blend into the background, and often helps to bring out the richer colors in their hair.

But edge lighting is not something I reserve for dark-haired subjects. It's a nice way to add more of a fashion edge to portraits with subjects of any hair color. I use it with all my subjects. When photographing a blond, I simply dial down the settings on these accent lights to avoid blowing out the highlight detail. With brunettes, I turn the setting up higher for plenty of bright, shiny highlights on their hair.

The Goal

If you compare these images with many of the shots in the outdoor section of this book, you'll see that what I'm really doing here is emulating the look of sunlight. The hair lights and accent lights I use to create edge lighting on my subject

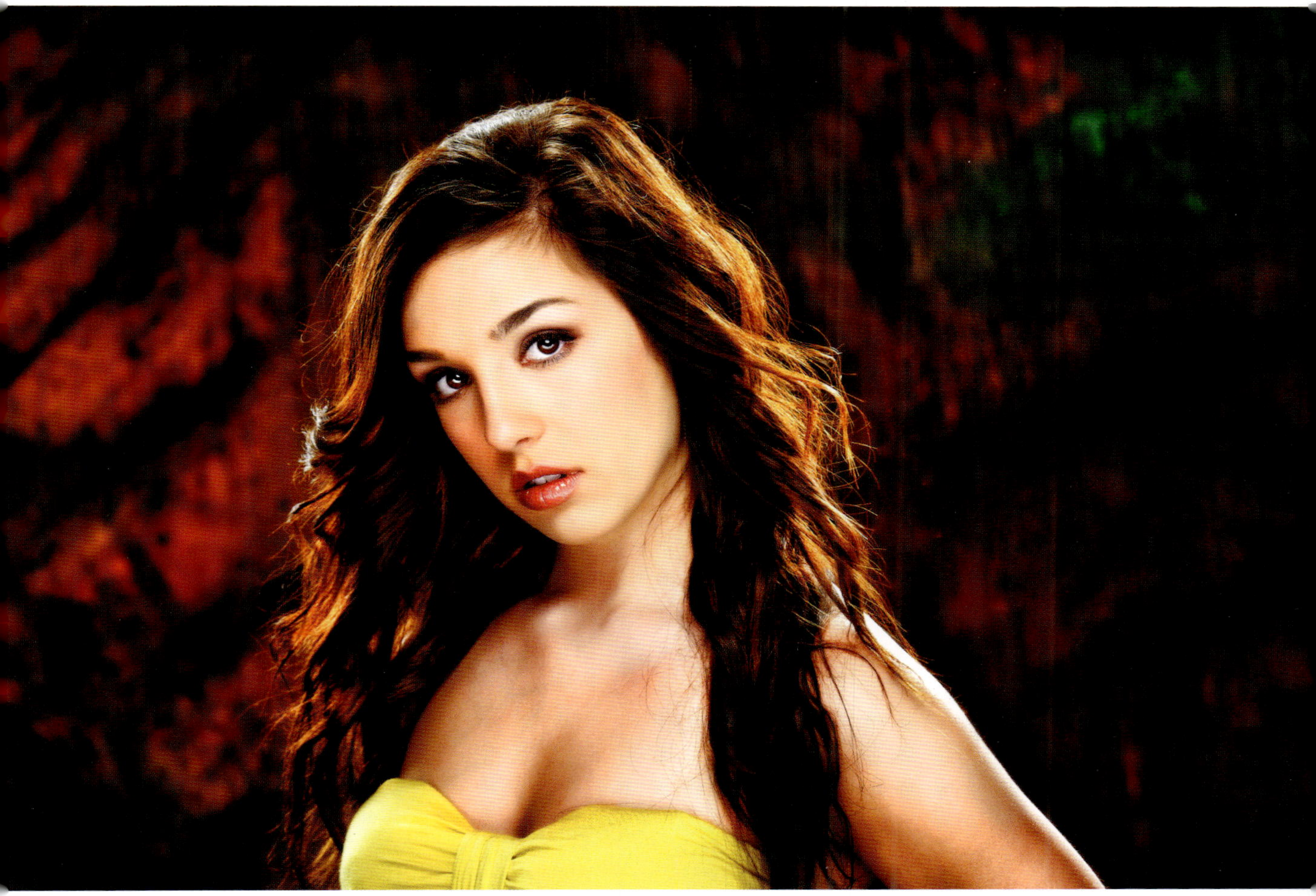

produce almost the same effect as placing them so that the bright sunlight is backlighting them.

About the Images

For the top image on the facing page, we were just looking to create a youthful, fun headshot. I turned the edge light down to produce just a a kiss of light on her hair.

For the bottom image on the facing page, there's a bit more edge lighting on her hair, but it's still a fairly traditional look. The image above, which features the same model, has much more dramatic edge lighting that suits the fashion feel of that look. In addition to the intensified edge lighting, here I switched from a softbox main light at camera left to a Larson Starfish above the camera. This was paired with a Westcott Eyelighter (a curved reflector) placed at chest level below the camera.

Another Benefit

In addition to lighting the hair, notice how the edge lighting helps to define each of these young ladies' figures. Showing these soft curves is important for creating flattering portraits of women.

43. Ring Light Portraits

What the Ring Light Does

Ring lights are a specialized light sources that completely encircle the lens. This produces a characteristic donut-shaped catchlight (as seen in the model's eyes here), along with very flat, even lighting that makes the skin look flawless. It's a common modifier for fashion and beauty photography, so seniors tend to like the look.

How I Use It

Large ring flashes can be very expensive, but I've opted for an affordable, 24-inch hot-light version that gets the job done. I pair it with a 200mm lens (to get all the way through the light) and zoom in on my subject.

I also move in close (3 to 4 feet from the model); if you're too far away, you'll find you lose some of the special effect of the ring light.

I love the ability of the ring light to really highlight the eyes—especially if the subject has green or blue eyes. I also pair it with my normal hair and edge lighting to complete the fashion look. Sometimes, I crank up the ISO and shoot with just the modeling lights, which are easy to balance with the continuous light from the ring light.

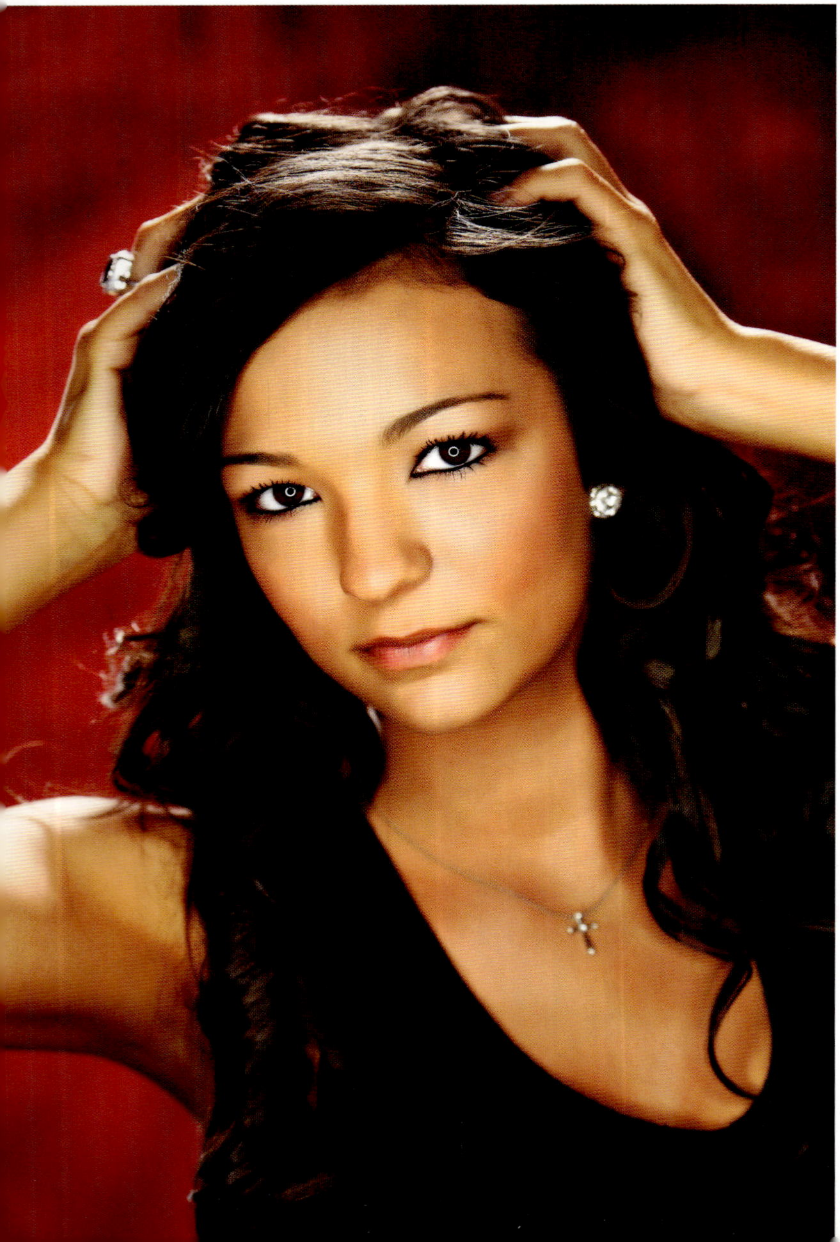

"If you're too far away, you'll find you lose some of the special effect of the ring light."

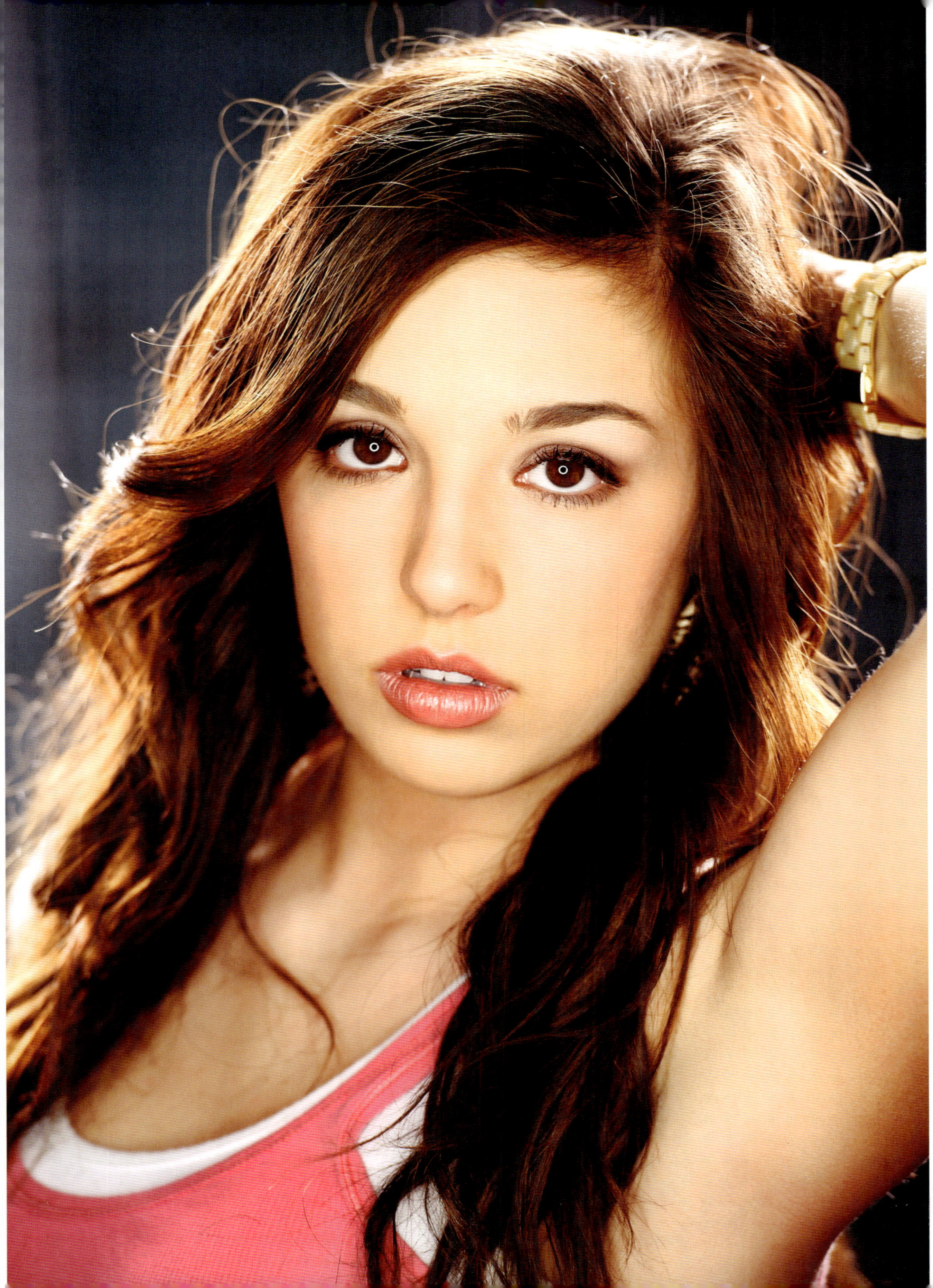

44. **Hot Light Portraits**

Make It Work

Our high school seniors love outdoor and location images, but sometimes the weather doesn't cooperate. That was the case on this senior's portrait date (*facing page and bottom left*); the rain made it impossible to shoot outdoors, as we had planned. Rather than rescheduling the session, we decided to move into the studio and create some looks with muted, pastel backgrounds—scenes that gave her as much of an "outdoor" look as possible.

Lighting and Shooting

Part of the recipe here was shooting at a very wide aperture (f/1.4) to keep the backdrops as soft as possible—leaving the setting a little more to your imagination.

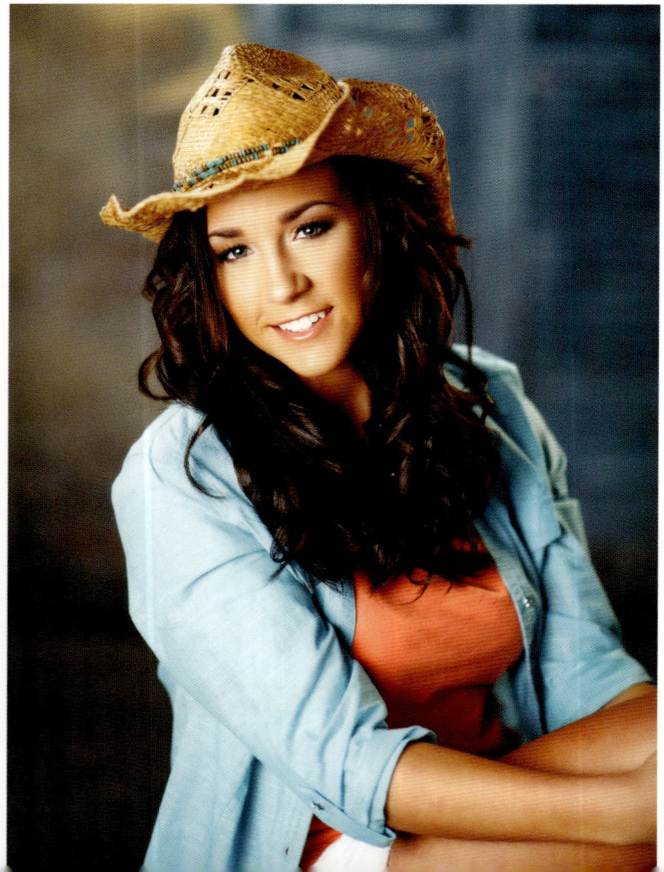

Shooting wide open with the bright light from a high-powered studio strobe is a bit challenging, so I opted for a lower-intensity hot light. In fact, I shot using just the 650W quartz modeling lights on my strobes. (*Note:* These lights are literally hot—so be careful!)

My main light was in a softbox. To compensate for the lower light level, I moved this in closer to the subject than I would normally place it. I also had two strip lights flanking her; again these were quite close—just out of the frame. The ceiling-mounted hair light was turned off, as it was too distant to register.

By increasing my ISO setting to 800, I was able to maintain a fast enough shutter speed to handhold the camera. Happily, today's digital cameras deliver nice results with very little noise, even at these higher ISO settings.

Enhancing the Eye Color

A very nice benefit of shooting with hot lights is that the brighter continuous light level allows the subject's pupils to constrict, revealing more of the colored iris—an especially nice look for those with lighter eye colors (*below*).

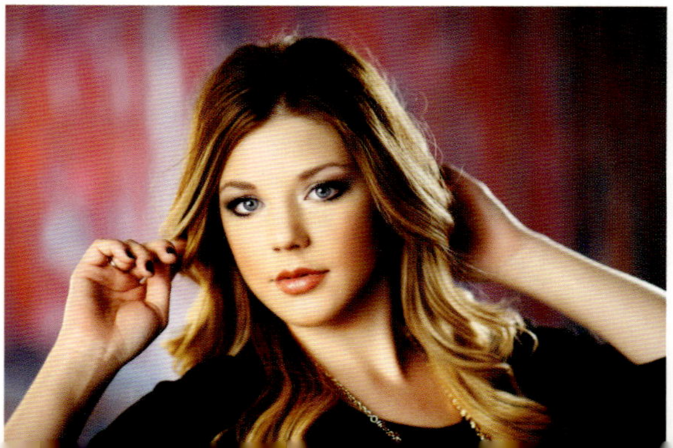

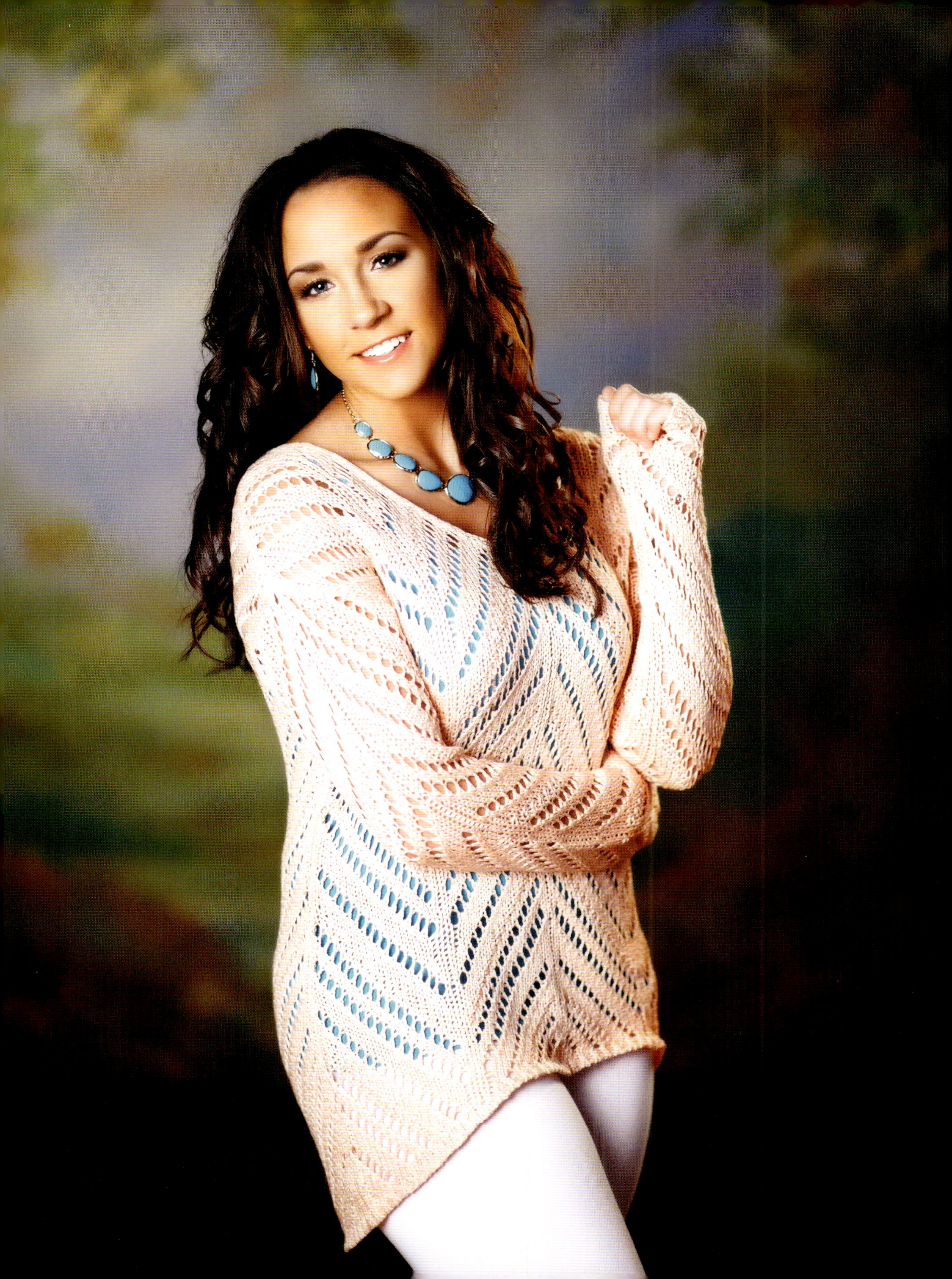

45. **High Key Portraits**

Pageant Portraits—and More

These images were created for a Miss USA contestant who needed pictures for the Miss Photogenic award and wanted more of a contemporary magazine-style look. The simplicity of a pure white background was perfect for this, since it really keeps the entire emphasis on the subject.

This is a clean, fashionable look that's also very popular among our high-school senior clients. In fact, it's a style I integrate into well over half of my sessions with women.

Lighting

For these portraits, I had a Larson Starfish right over the camera as the main light. Below the subject's face, I placed a curved Westcott Eyelighter. The Starfish nicely fills the Eyelighter, producing a crescent-shaped lower catchlight that adds a nice little pop to the eyes. This is a classic butterfly lighting setup, for smooth, even lighting. When the subject turns her face (as on the facing page), we get slightly more shadowing and contouring.

A hair light above the subject and strip lights flanking her continue the light and airy feel, adding bright highlights. For an even wash of light on the white background, I used three Novatron heads (with socks for a little diffusion) mounted on a ceiling rail. In a setup like this, there will be lots of light bouncing back from background. Watch to make sure it doesn't start washing out your subject!

"This is a clean, fashionable look that's also very popular among our high-school senior clients."

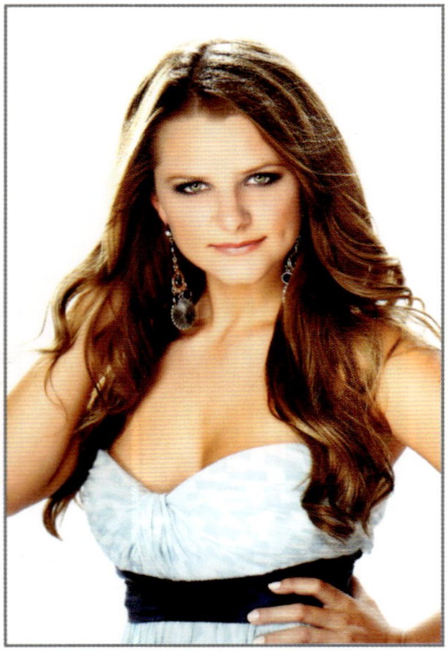

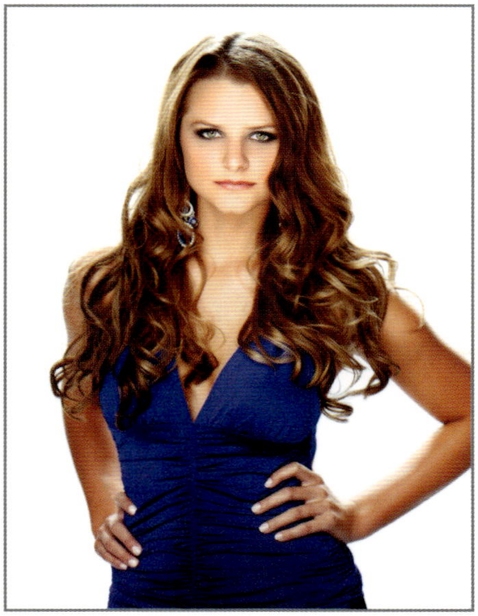

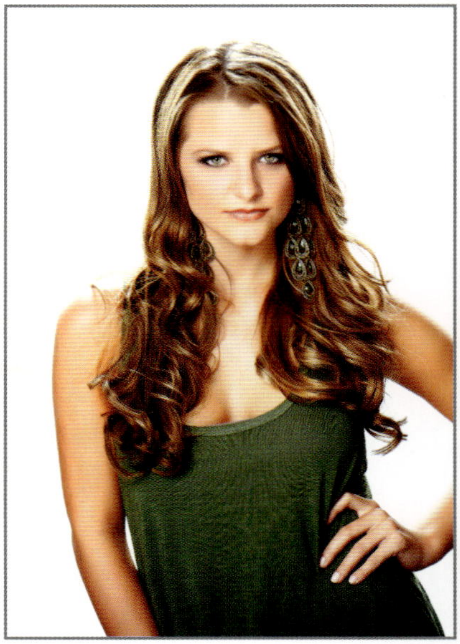

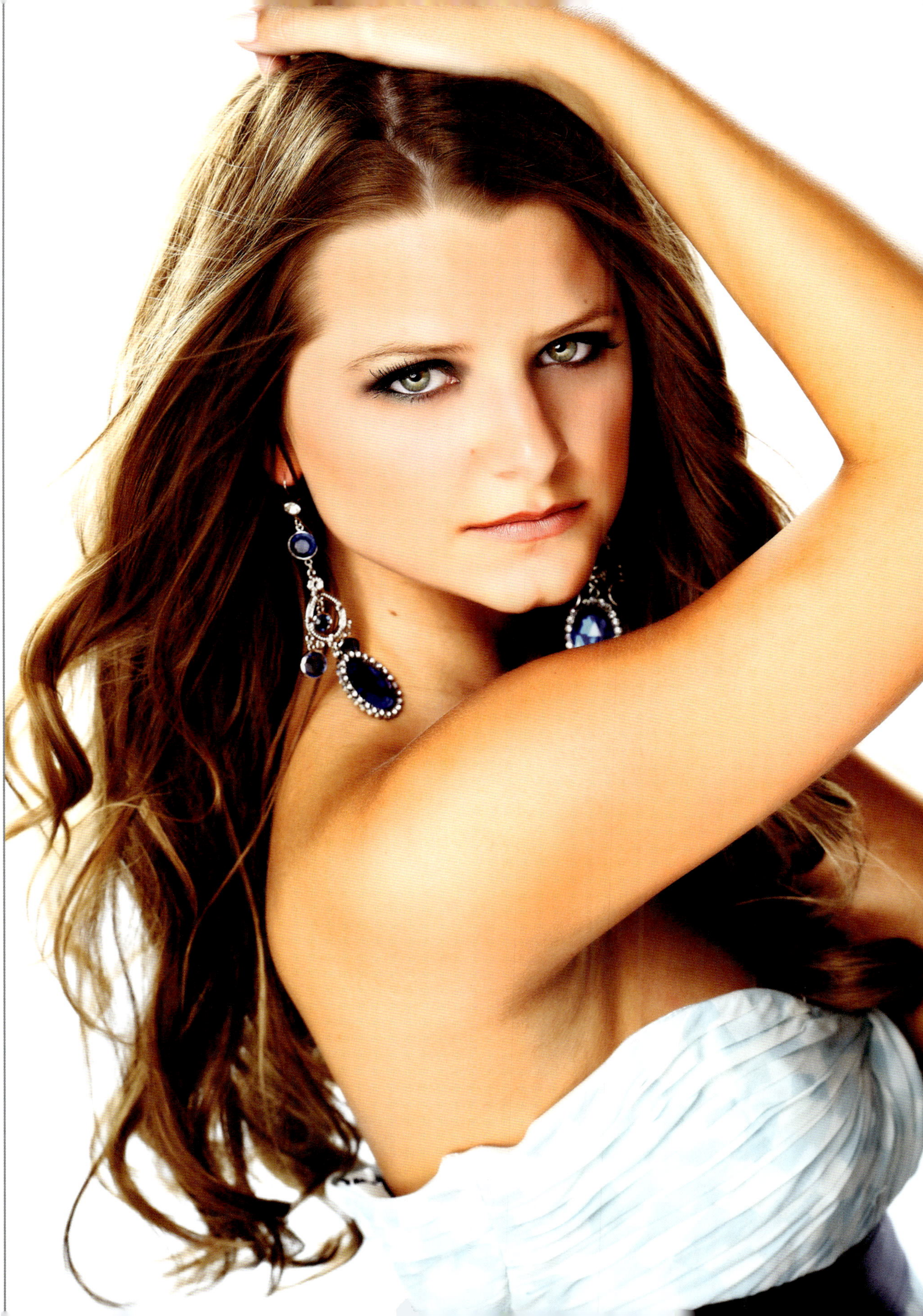

46. High-Key Clothing and Props

Clothing

While a classic high-key look usually involves light or pale clothing, I also like to shoot it with other colors. I sometimes even do it with black clothes for a very high-impact look with a little bit of that classic old-Hollywood, Katherine Hepburn style (*below* and *facing page*).

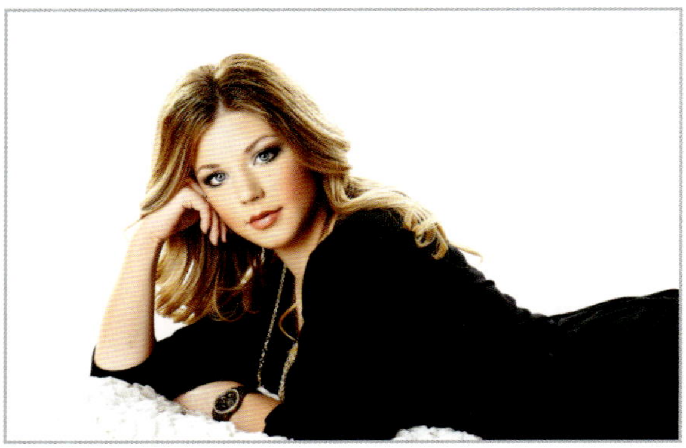

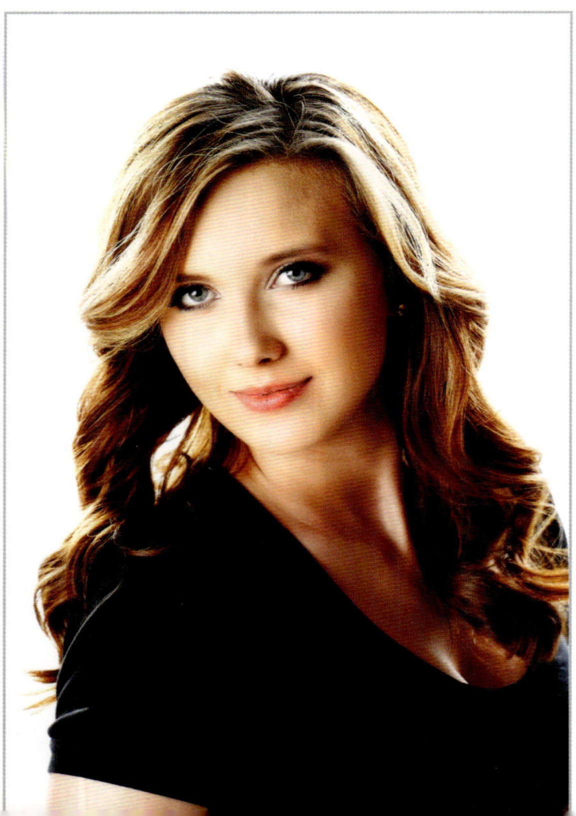

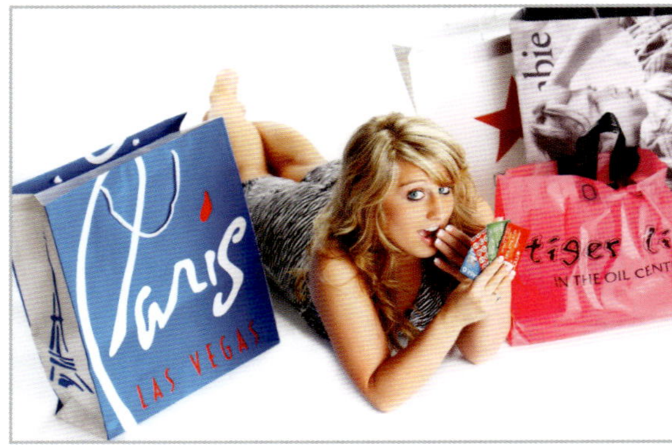

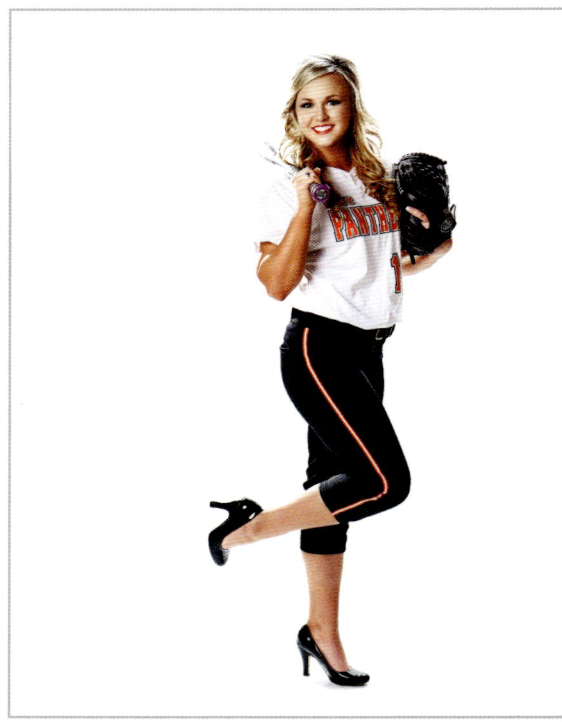

Props

From sports gear to shopping bags, props that can add a pop of color or personality to your high-key senior portraits (*above*).

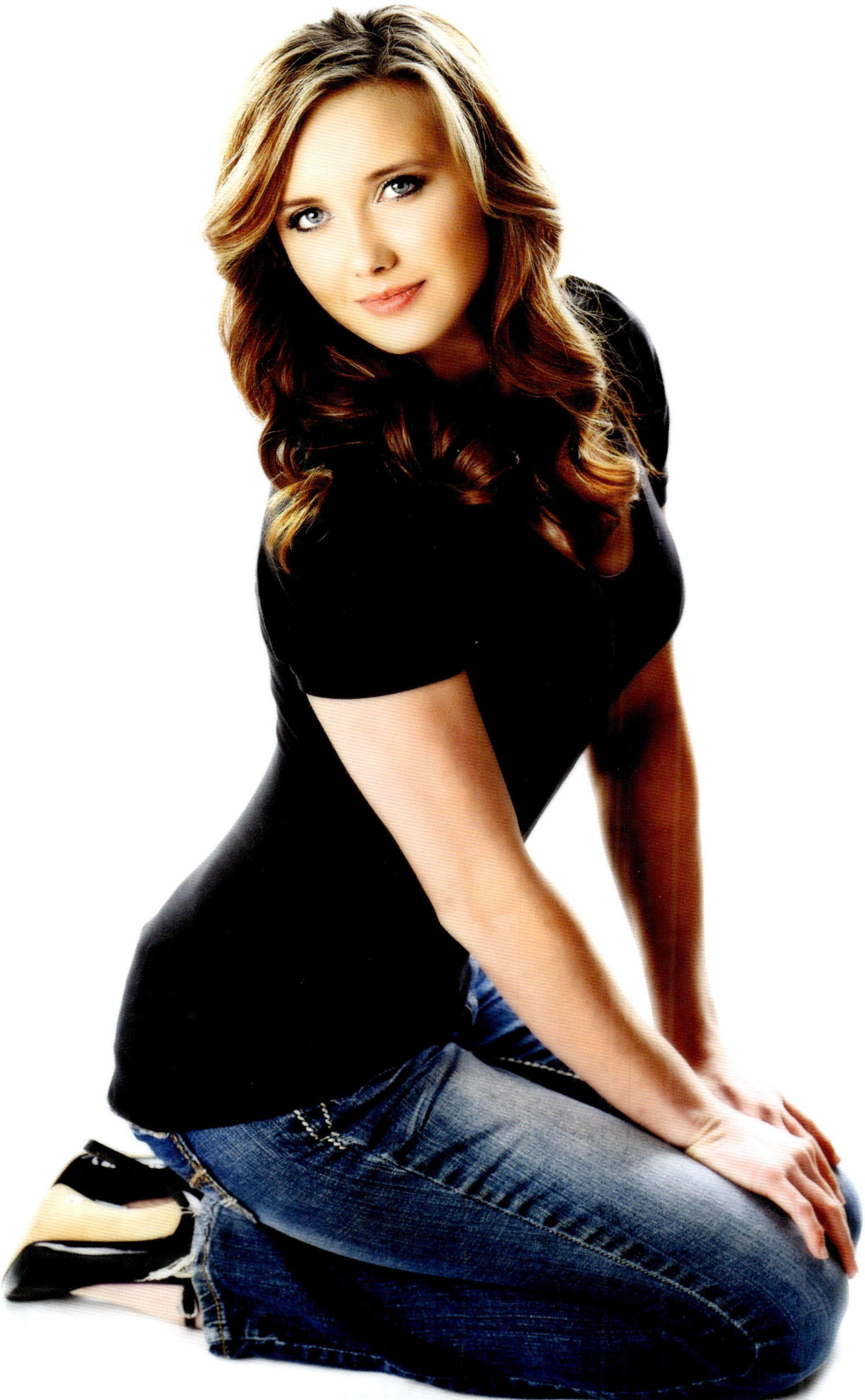

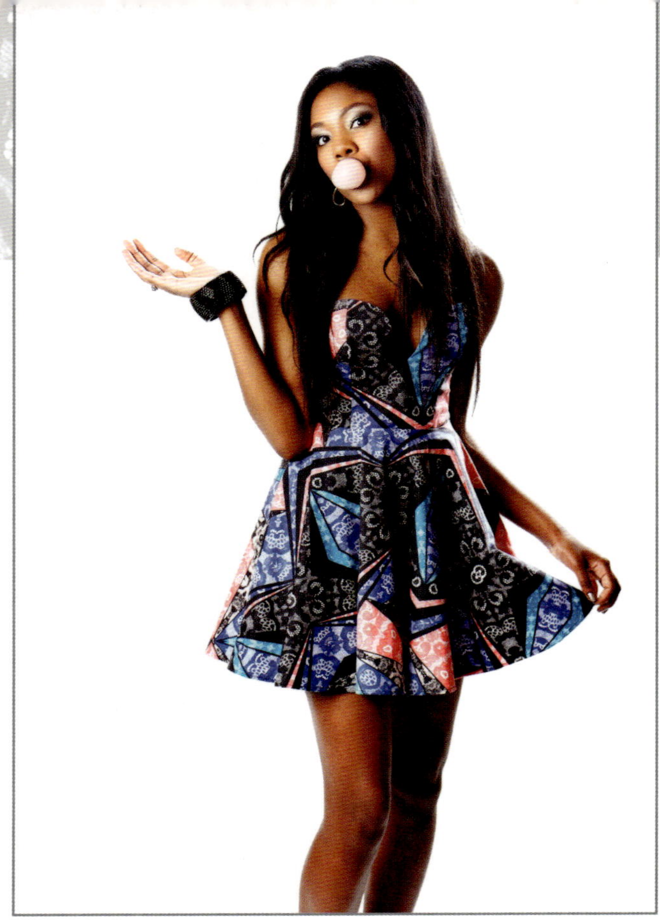

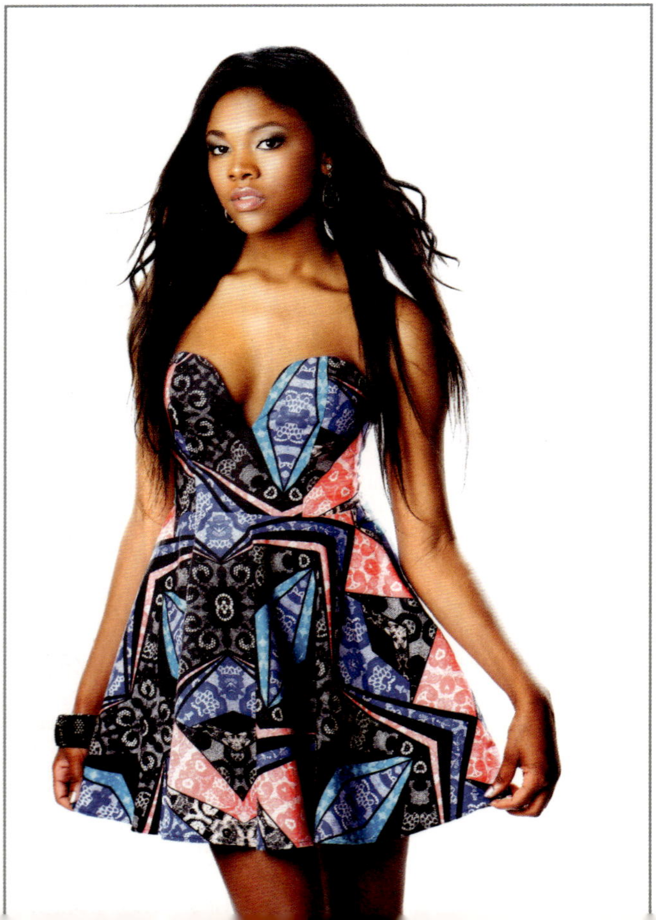

47. Bubble Gum

Juxtaposition

Part of what makes senior portraits so special and meaningful is that our subjects are at a crossroads in their life's journey; they are adults, but still sort of kids. That's probably why these bubble-gum shots have been popular with our senior girls. They capture that juxtaposition rather perfectly.

In the facing-page image, there are some additional juxtapositions that have made it a favorite. There's the girly-girl aspect of the bubble, but also the sophisticated style of the red high heels, and the sportiness of her outfit and props. In my mind, she might be saying, "I'm a woman *and* I play sports—try to keep up!" My own daughters were athletes but also girly, so I especially appreciate this juxtaposition of feminine style with a competitive, sporty side.

Posing the Hands

If she's blowing a bubble, what do you do with the hands? Have her grab her sports gear—or her dress and kick up her other hand like you'd see in *Teen Vogue*. The posing options are limitless!

The Main Light Placement

Sometimes people have a "favorite" side. If that's the case, I'll move the light there and keep the emphasis on the aspect of their face they prefer. Otherwise, I tend to put the main light to the left of the camera. Having a go-to setup is a good baseline—but you should always be prepared to adapt it to whatever best suits your subject.

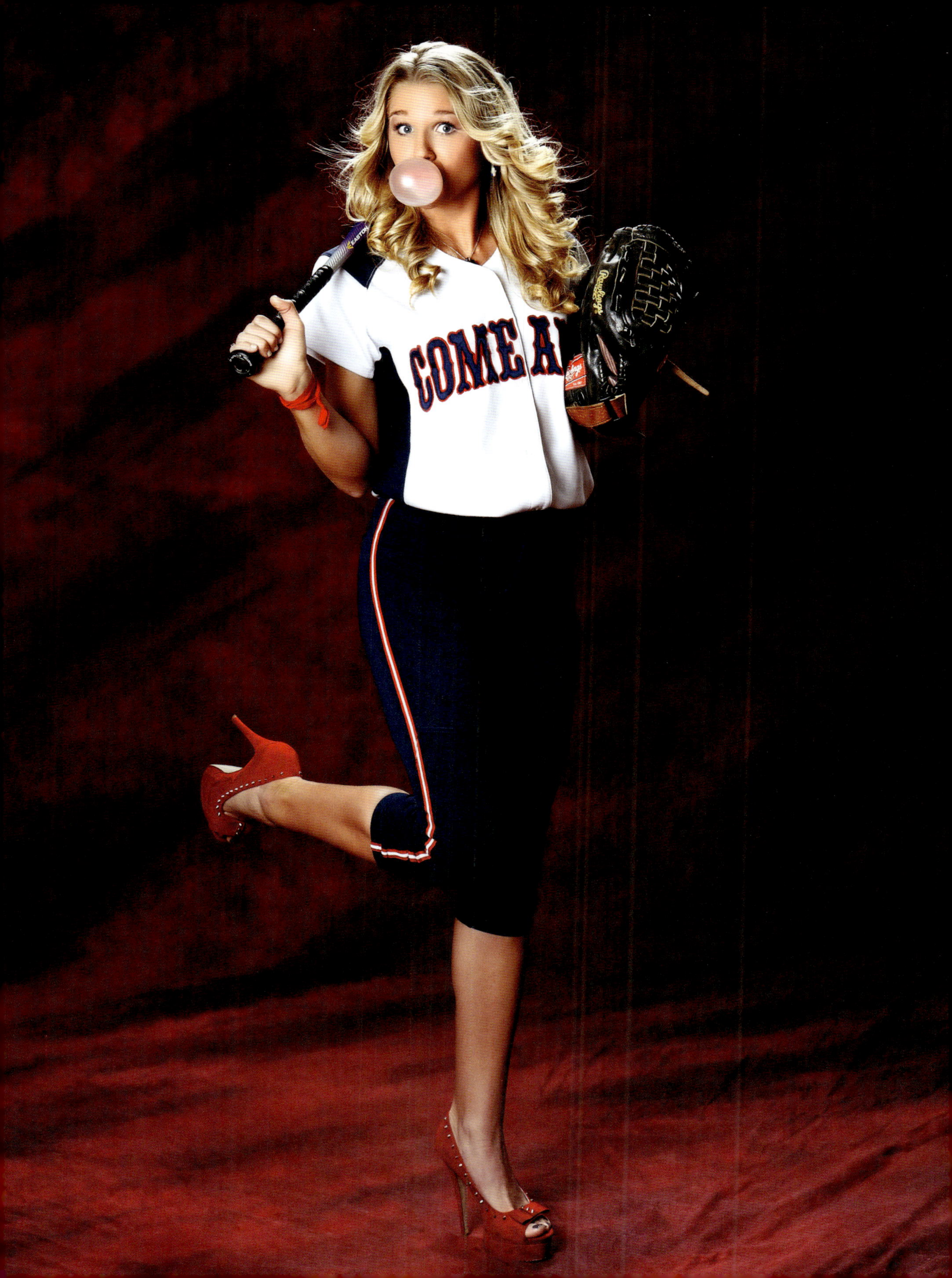
COME AL

48. Lighting the Eyes

Catchlights

In a portrait, the eyes are almost always the focal point of the image. Making sure they have nice catchlights will bring them to life. To show the eye color, especially with lighter eyes, you want the overall light levels in the studio to be high enough (leading up to the exposure) that their pupils remain contracted and reveal more of the iris.

Lighting

For the image below, I created a fairly traditional look with a single catchlight from the 4x6-foot softbox main light brought in quite close to the subject. Strip lights to either side of her added highlights on her arms and hair.

For the image at the top of the facing page, I placed a Larson Starfish in the 2 o'clock position and Westcott Eyelighter below. In addition to nice modeling on her face, check out the unique catchlights that kick up the lighter color in her eyes.

The image at the bottom of the facing page actually features an eighth grader who was looking for pageant images. A similar Starfish/ Eyelighter combo was used—this time, on-axis with the camera. Look how it accentuates her gorgeous blue eyes!

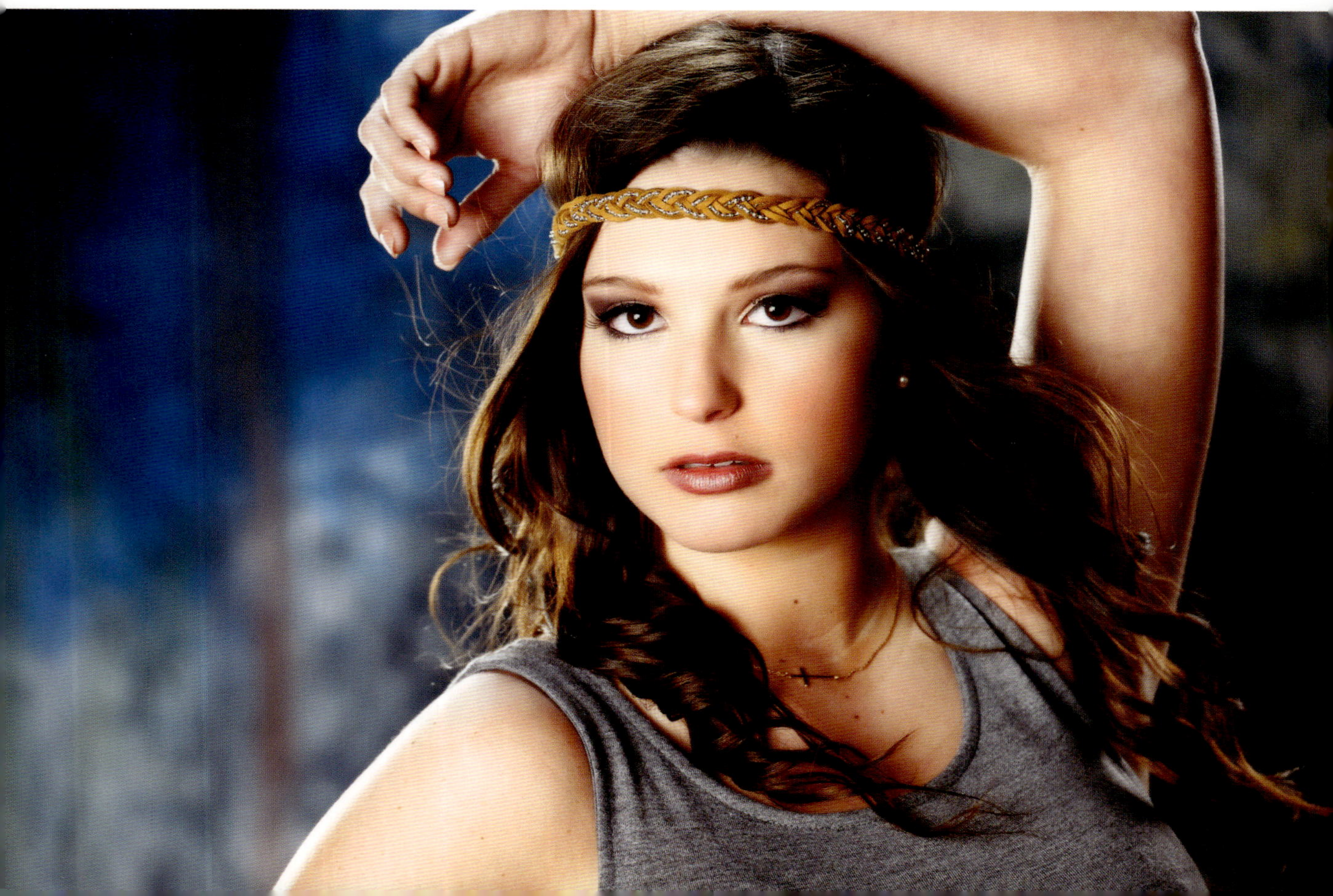

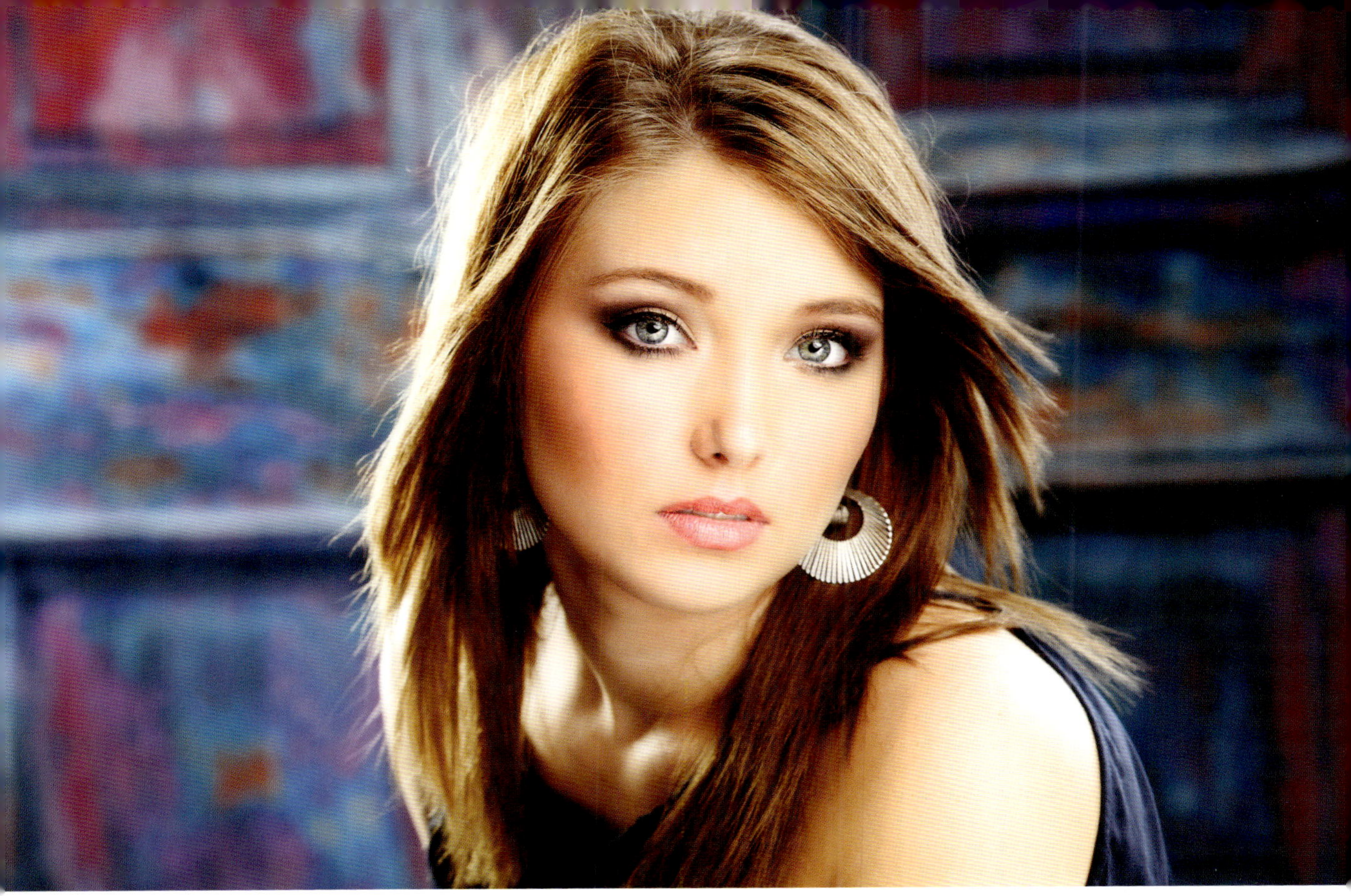

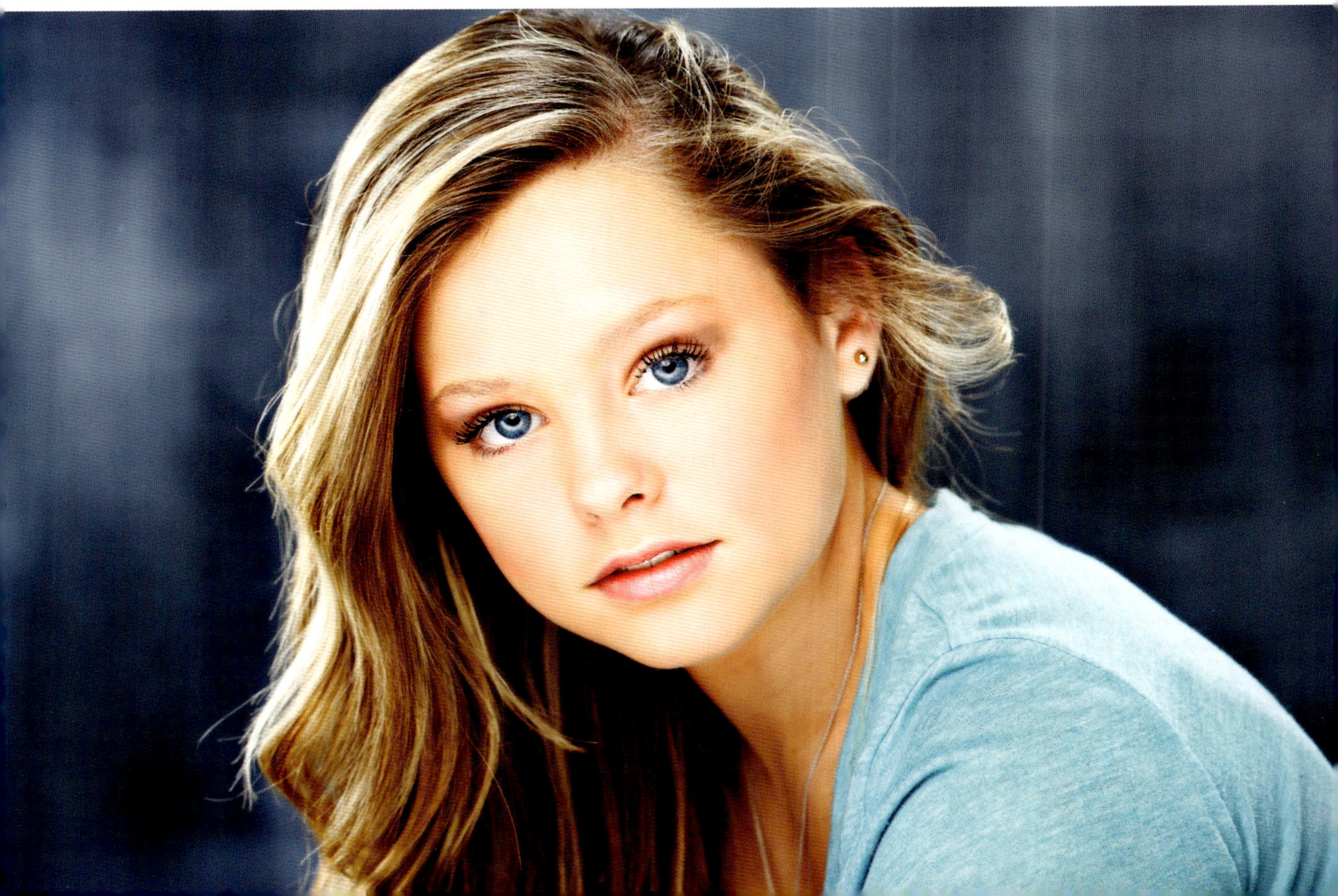

49. An Edgy Feel

What Seniors Want

For those of us who are parents (especially the parents of daughters), it's hard not to see our senior clients as kids. Our subjects, however, often feel quite grown up and want images designed to reflect this new phase of their life. Young ladies, especially, like images that show them stepping out of their teenage years. They want to look more adult and sophisticated.

Seeking Balance

For seniors, getting the right look requires a bit of a balancing act. In general, as long as the subject is dressed appropriately, an edgier pose and/or expression is fine—I'm just careful never to let it get too edgy. I always want to keep it tasteful.

> "While some elements take the look a little edgier, the clothing and cropping keep the overall style in balance with good taste for a senior image."

In the images here, notice that we have "hands up" poses (which tend to read more

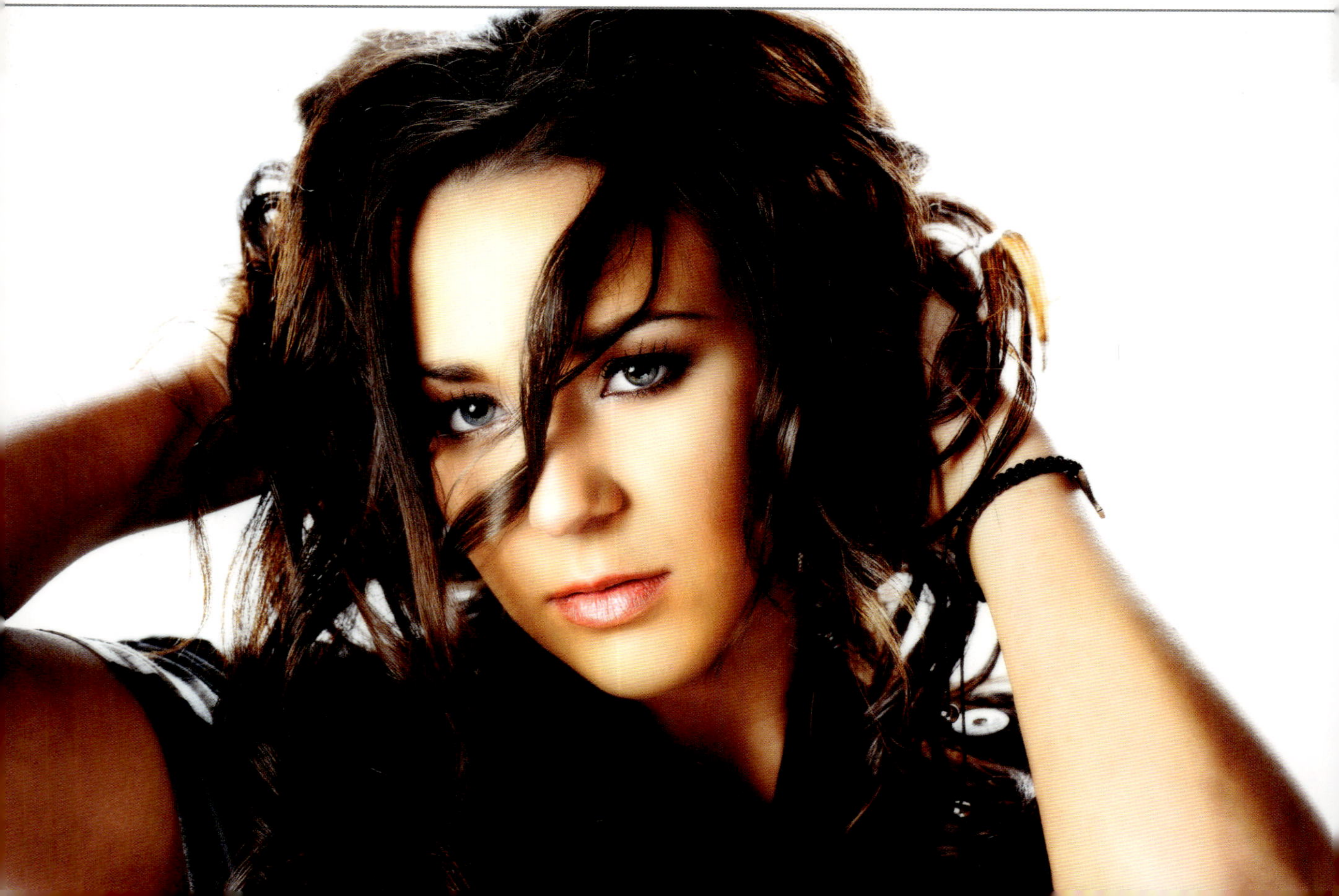

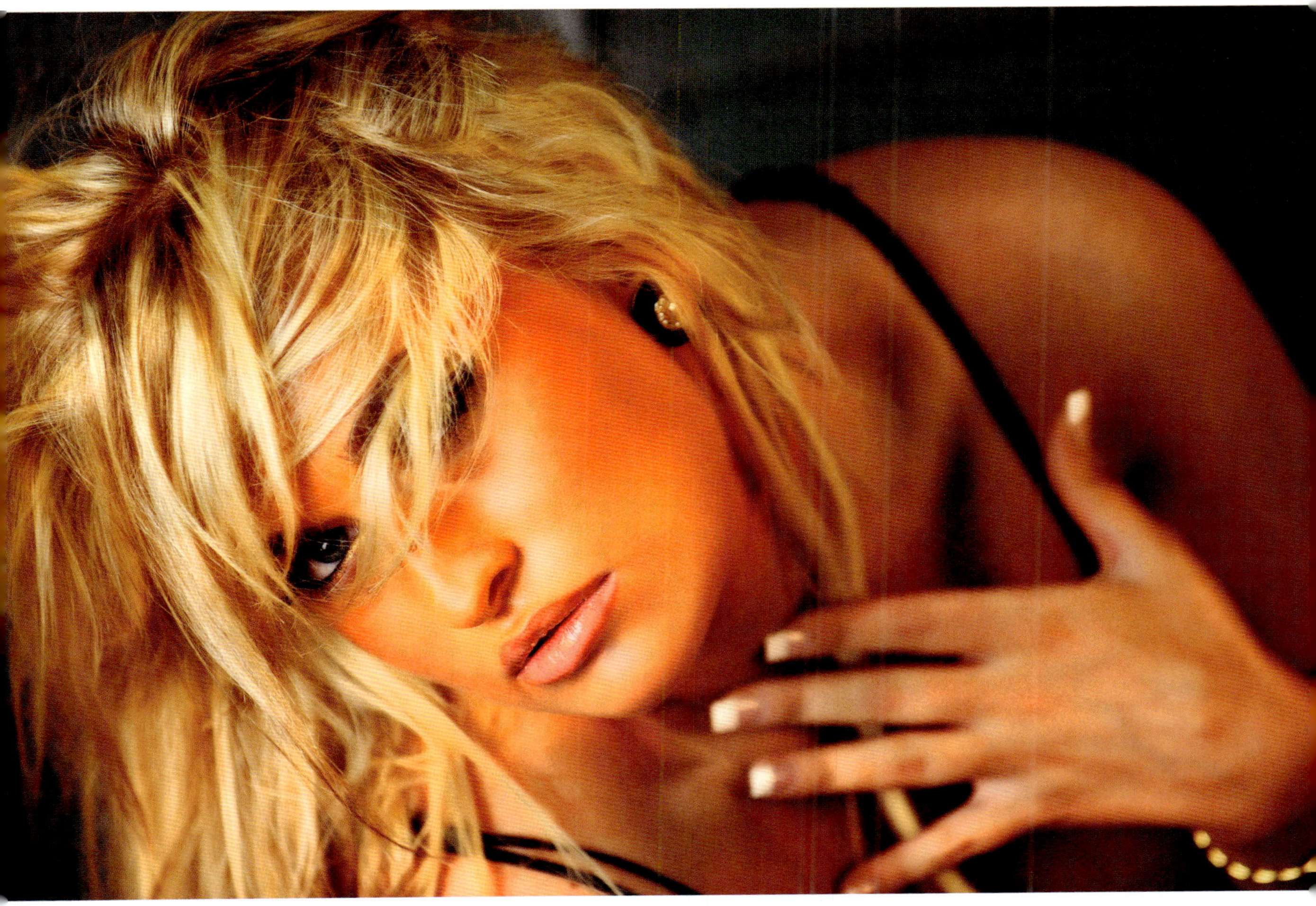

mature and less childlike), intense expressions, and tousled hair. What we *don't* have is cleavage. While some elements take the look a little edgier, the clothing and cropping keep the overall style in balance with good taste for a senior image.

Talking with Seniors

When working with seniors, especially those who express an interest in edgier looks or naturally tend to strike poses with more of a mature feel, I am always sure to be gentle with my words—after all, they're still kids. I never want to make it seem like I'm judging them for being interested in these styles. Instead, I just try to dial it back and make small adjustments that tone down the images and keep the look tasteful for the parents. I take the same approach for seniors who show up with very risqué outfits.

I'm happy to say that this was more of a problem in the past than it is today. At the moment, seniors seem more interested in natural-looking images and nice smiles. Still, it doesn't hurt to be prepared to address this issue if it should arise at one of your sessions!

50. Posing, Cropping, and Expression

Variations

I always like to shoot multiple views of the same pose—especially when the pose and lighting are nice, as they are here. With the subject leaning forward on a chair back, we swept her hair forward to show its length and texture. I lit her with a Larson Starfish to camera right and a Westcott Eyelighter below her. A hair light above and flanking accent strip lights helped separate her from the background. Once everything was in place, I shot long versions (*left*) and tighter views (*facing page*).

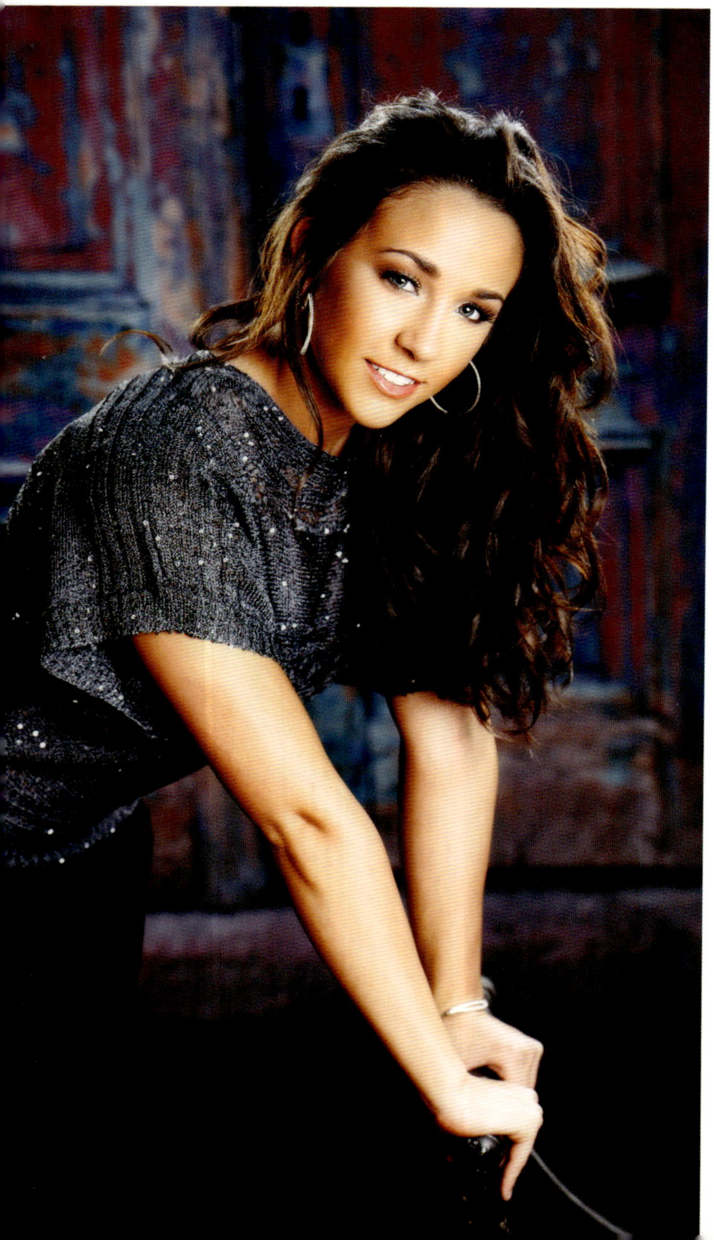

Expressions

As these photos show, I also like to provide my clients with some nice variations in expression. Moms love smiles, and they do sell somewhat better than more subdued expressions—but the most important thing is finding the best expressions for the individual.

Usually, this can be accomplished through simple direction, alternating smiles and more serious expressions. For those who are reluctant to smile, don't like their teeth, or have braces, I still try to coax a smile.

That said, some kids naturally laugh all the time and can't do serious without looking angry. If that's the case, we do all smiles; that's just who they are. Conversely, some people aren't "smiley" by nature and tend to look tense when trying to force a grin. For those seniors, we'll stick to pleasant but non-smiling expressions.

Again, the important thing is finding the right expression for the individual. Moms know when an expression doesn't look authentic, and those images will be harder to sell.

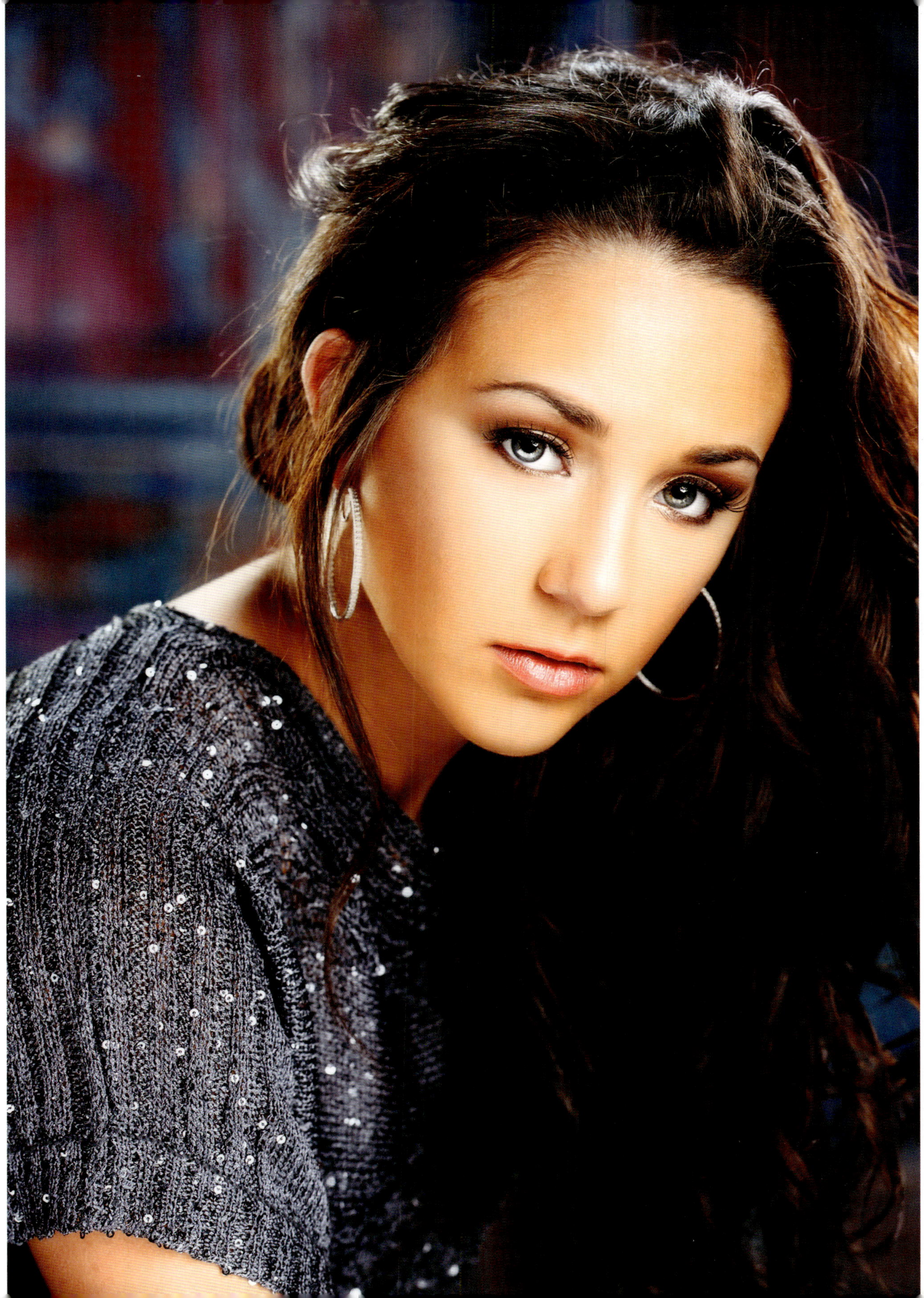

51. Fiery Drama

Subject and Style

In these images for a pageant contestant, we went for a rich, dramatic look. Her elegant dress was paired with simple jewelry, upscale styling, and a vibrant background for a series of portraits that feel rich, stylish, and just a little bit sexy.

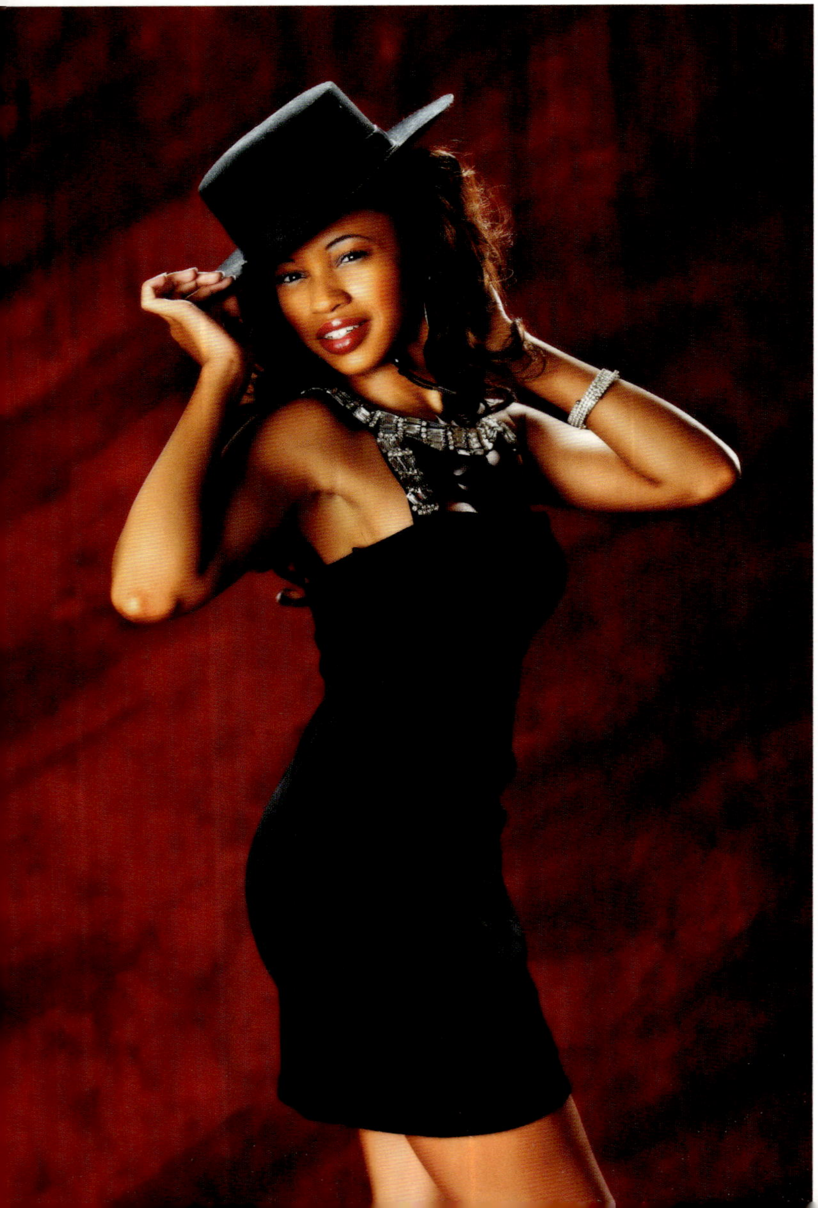

The Basic Lighting Setup

For all of the images in this sequence, I used broad lighting—a look that is appropriate for a subject with a narrow, more angular face.

A 4x6-foot Larson softbox was positioned vertically to camera left. To either side of the subject, I used vertical strip lights to accent her silhouette and long hair. An additional strip light was centered above her for highlights on the crown of her hair. Since her hair was very dark, this was set just about equal to the main light to ensure nice separation.

Adjusting the Lights

As my subject moved from standing, to kneeling, to reclining poses, I adjusted the heights of all the lights to keep them at a consistent distance and angle relative to her face and hair.

I also made other adjustments as needed. For example, in the photo where she is kneeling, I turned off the left strip light to prevent unwanted light from spilling onto her face.

For photos with hats, I often need to lower the main a little to get under the brim. I watch the catchlights to see if that's necessary. In this case (*left*), the large vertical softbox was sufficient to light her eyes nicely.

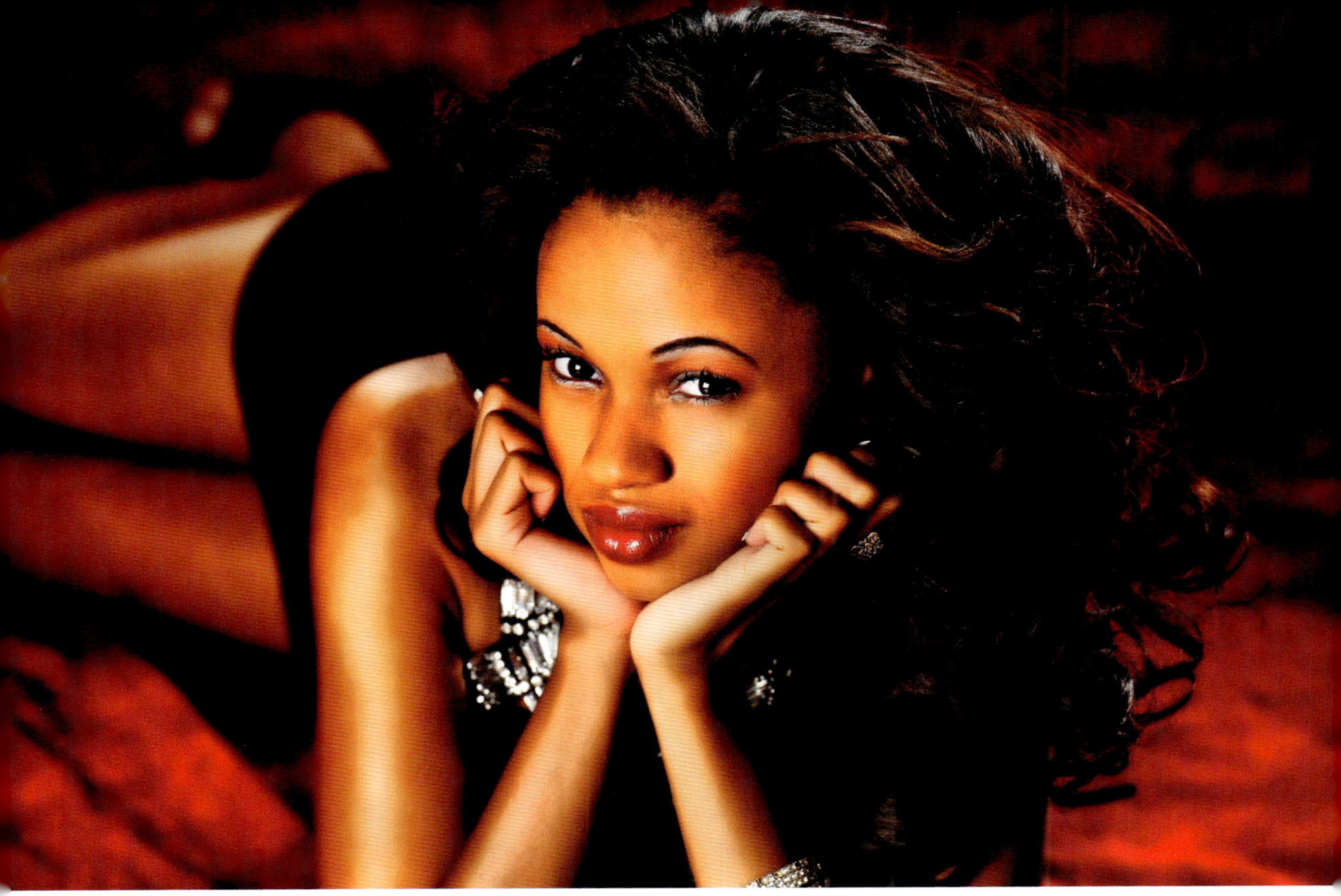

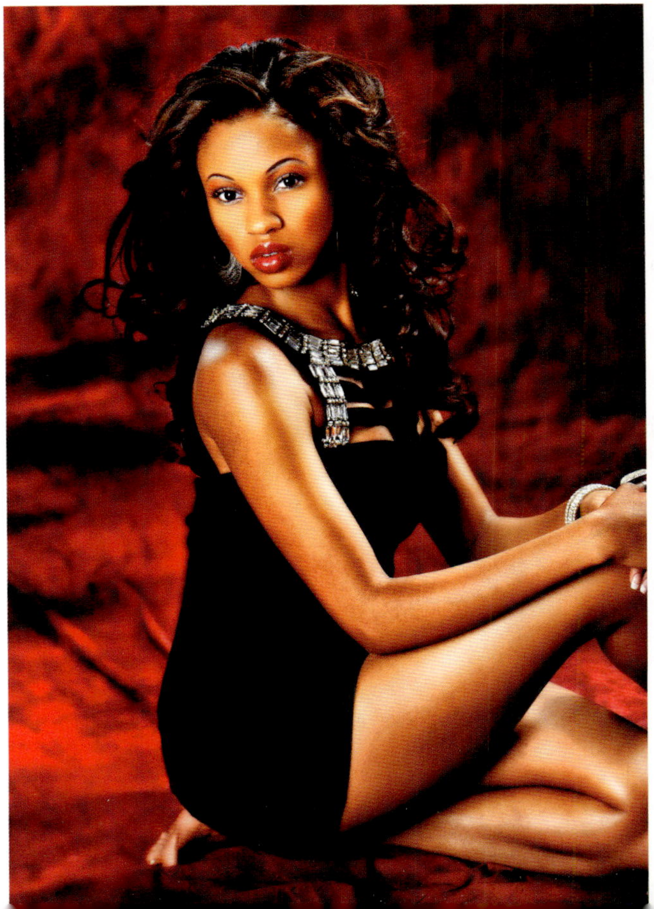

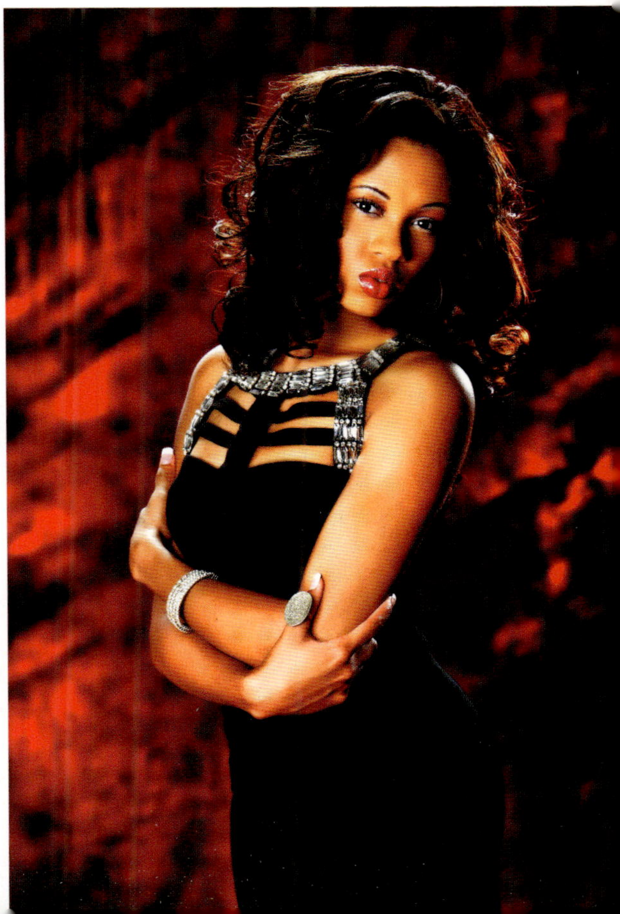

SECTION 4

After the Session

Capitalize on the success of your session with streamlined postproduction enhancements and sales-boosting techniques.

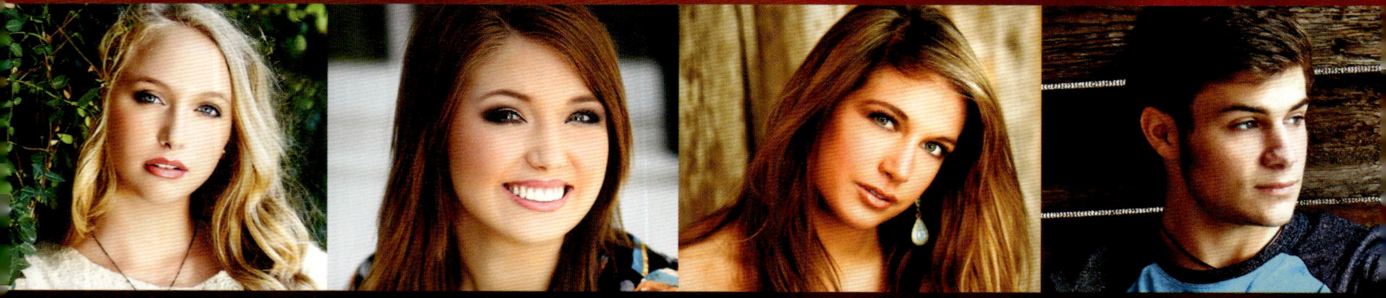

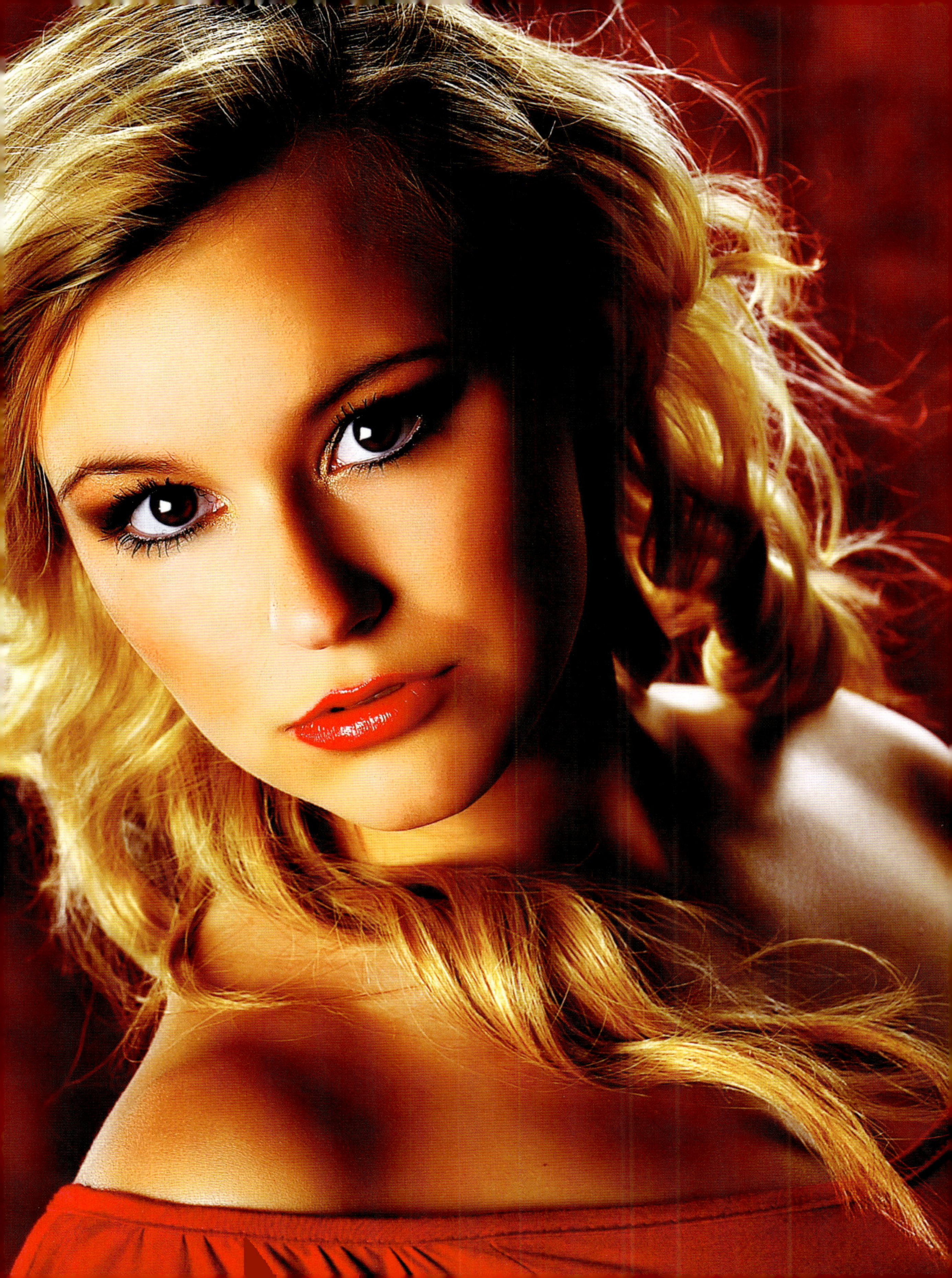

52. Retouching

Exposure Tweaks

As I have mentioned, I shoot RAW files and meter to get everything as close to final as possible in the original capture. However, I typically shoot in a wide range of color/lighting situations throughout the course of a session—and sometimes wind or clouds make for quickly shifting conditions. So, my first step in postproduction is processing the files in CaptureOne to make any little exposure or color adjustments that may be needed.

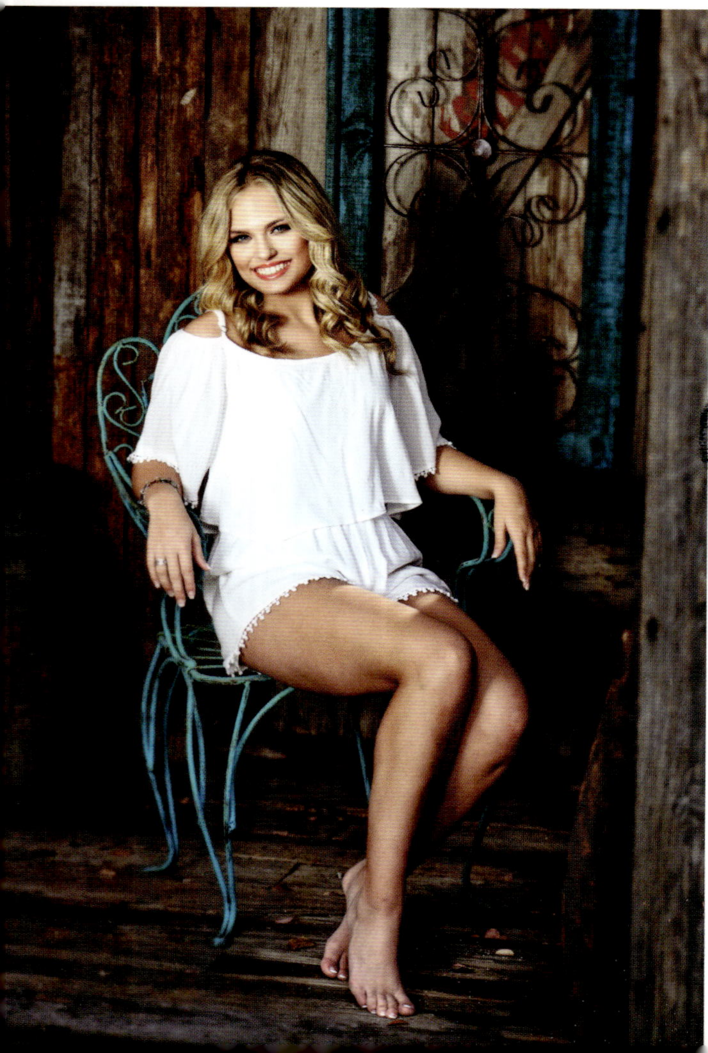

Softening, Blemish Removal, and More

From there, I export the files to JPG. Digital captures are generally very sharp—often, too sharp, especially for portraits of women. I have found that this is not good for client previews, so I run a batch process that creates a new layer, applies the Imagenomic Portraiture filter, fades back the softened layer opacity to 30 percent, then flattens the image. This results in an image that looks more like film—more natural. (Again, I do this only for women's images; for men, this look would be too soft.)

For subjects of either gender, I may then go back in with Photoshop's Healing Brush to touch out any acne or blemishes. At this point, the image is ready for the preview session.

After the client has selected their images (more on this in the next section), I will sometimes go back and do a little extra retouching work based on their requests. Most of these requests involve slimming. I try to do as much of this as possible in camera (through posing and lighting), but sometimes we do need to make a few refinements after the fact. This is almost always for female clients; guys very rarely ask for retouching.

Keep It to a Minimum

I try to keep the retouching to a minimum. After all, time spent editing is time I'm not spending behind the camera or on the many other tasks that bring money into my business!

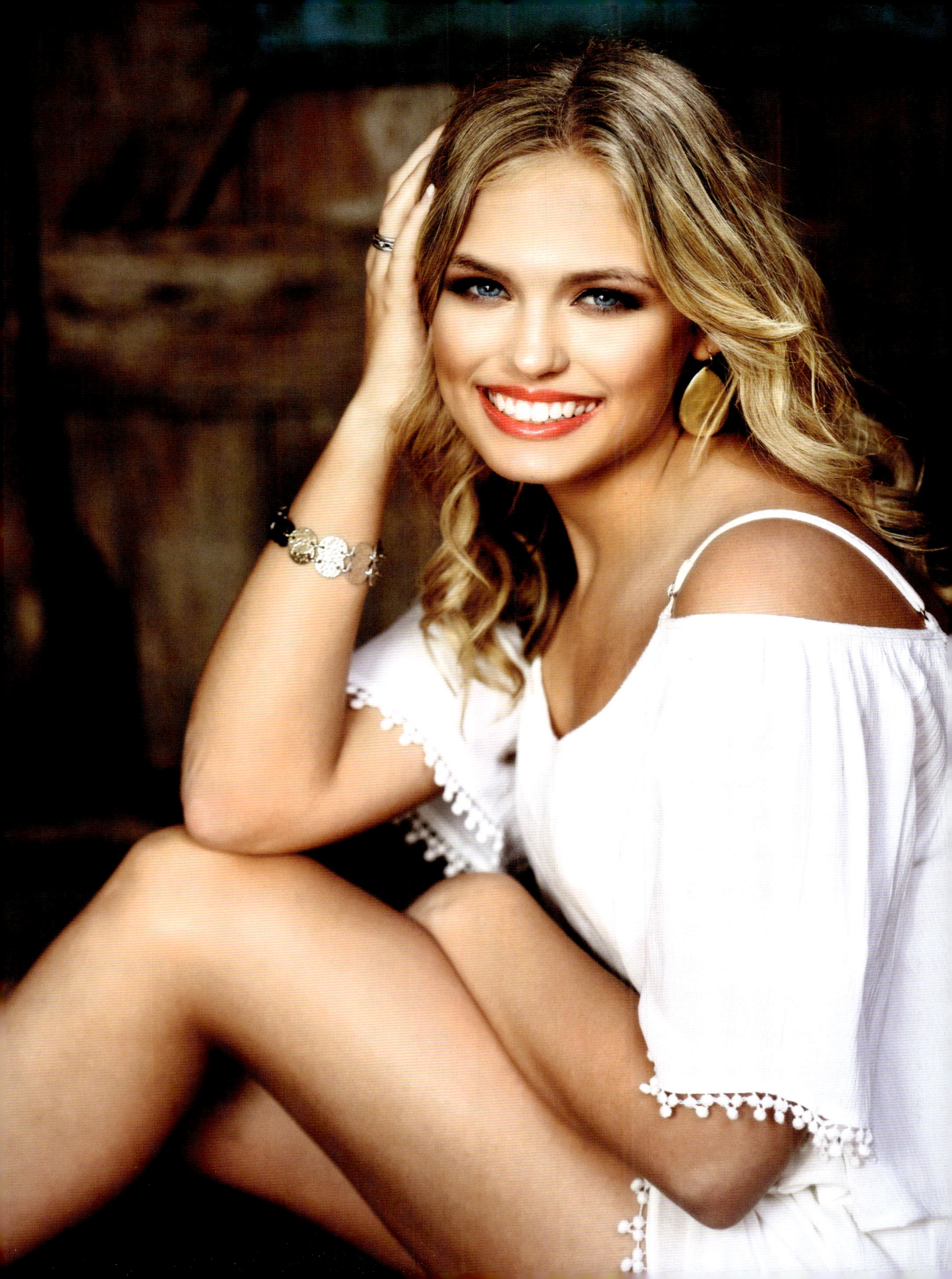

53. The Sales Session

Projection Session

Our clients initially see their images in a projection session that is designed and set to music using ProSelect software.

Proof Book

They also receive a very nice spiral-bound proof book to take home. Allowing clients to order after the image preview meeting is somewhat controversial, but it has worked well for us. Many of our clients come from far away, so they take the proof book home and show it around to friends and family. Those people love to see the *whole* session, and it often generates extra orders (from aunts and grandmas) plus referral bookings from the senior's friends.

The secret to making this work is that we offer an incentive. We give them two weeks to make their decision and get their order in. After that, the prices go up. This has the added benefit of making sure all the orders from the session come in at about the same time, which expedites production on our end.

While we do let them keep the book as a memento (this cost is covered in our session fee), we still sell a lot of wall prints, albums, and even wallets. We also provide them with photos for social media (watermarked right across the middle), minimizing the incentive to copy images from the book.

If They Don't Order?

It's extremely rare that we don't get an order from a session. If it happens, though, we have already collected a session fee and a preview book retainer fee that easily covers our time and materials. That's an important reason to have a session fee paid up front.

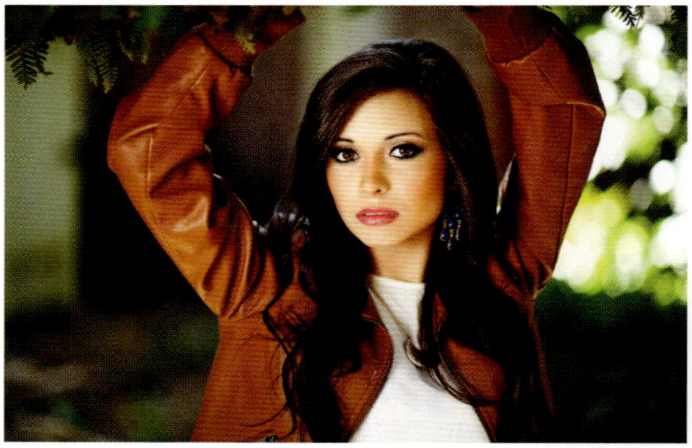

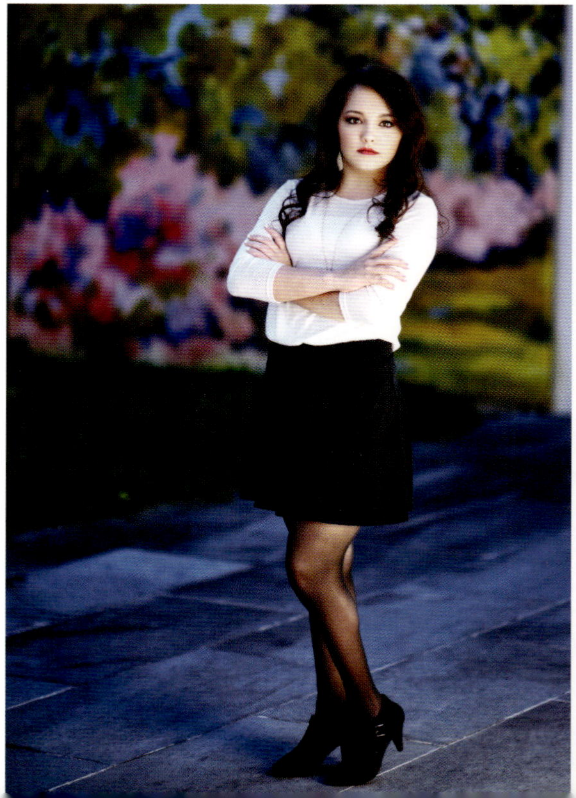

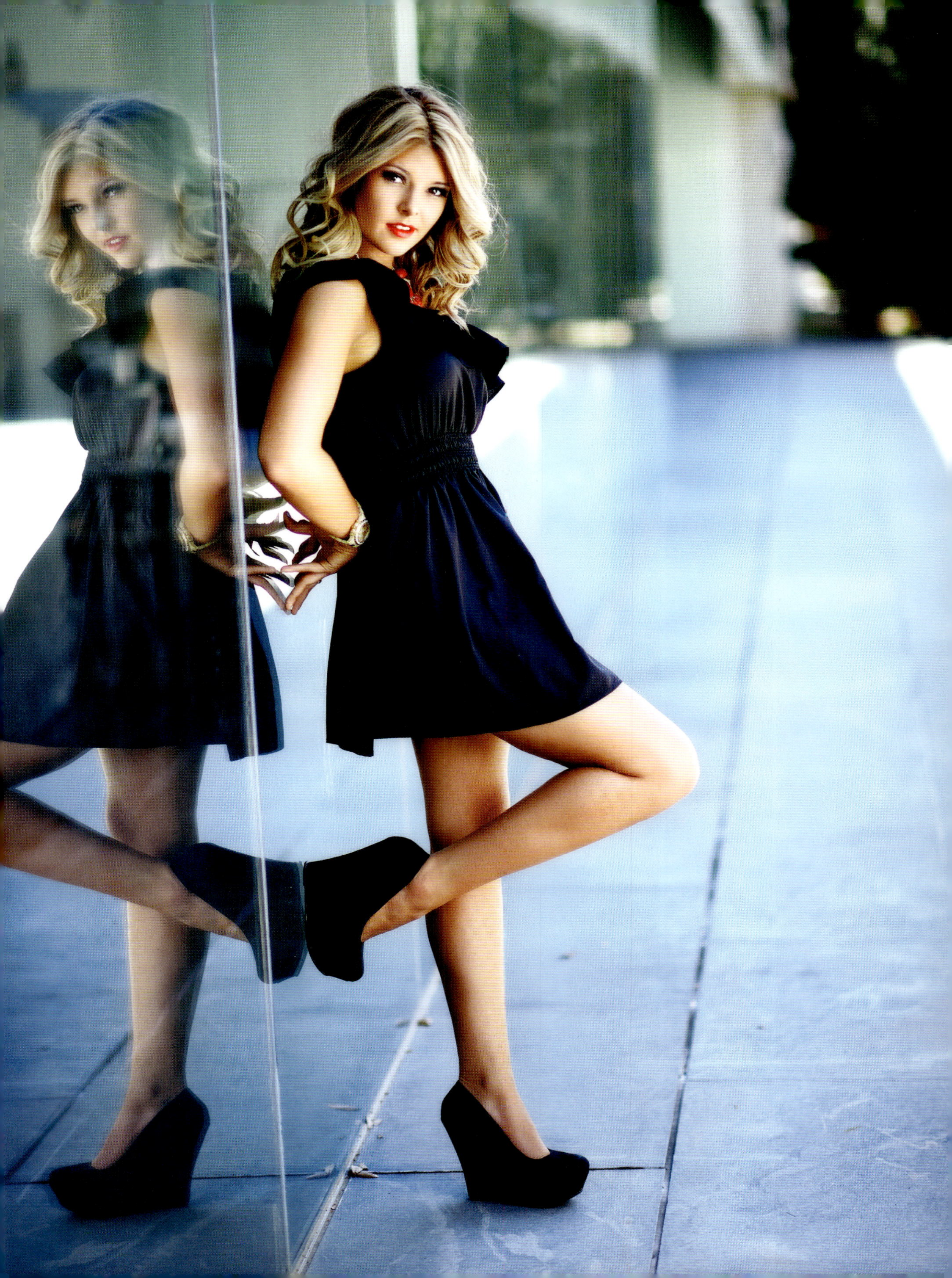

54. Time Management

Don't Try to Do It All

I used to think I could photograph everyone; I think a lot of photographers have that mindset. I was doing two sessions per day, which exhausted me physically and mentally—and meant that I couldn't give each client the time or variety as I wanted. I had to acknowledge that we were overbooked and that we needed to start turning away some prospective clients.

Lower Volume, More Service

Now, I limit the number of seniors I photograph to one session per day. Typically, I use the mornings to do my editing and place lab orders. Occasionally, I might also shoot a baby session or headshot during this time. Then, I have lunch and shoot my senior portrait session.

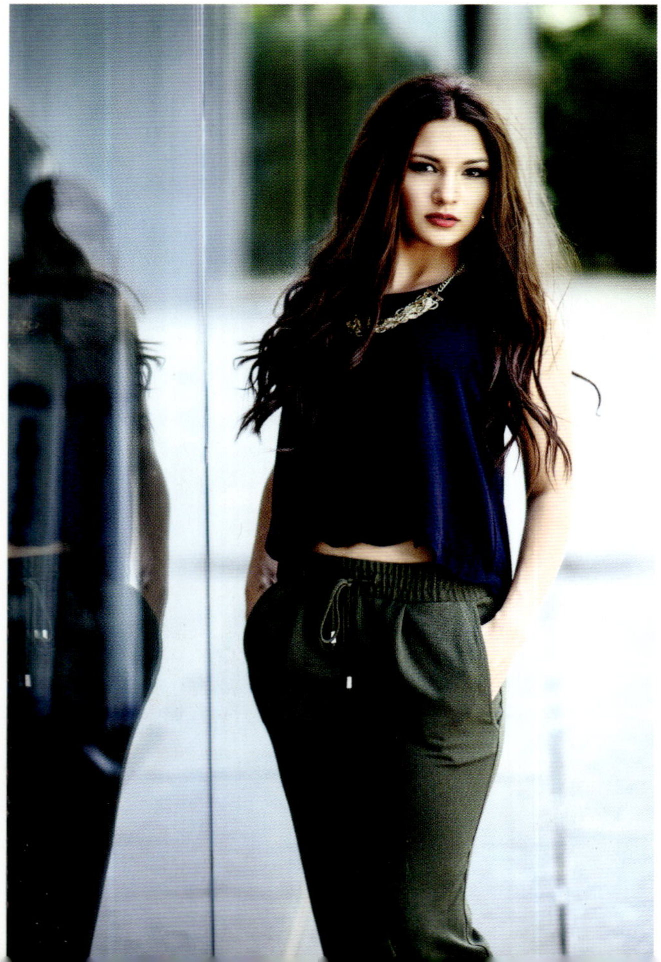

The benefits? I can now give each client my sole attention and treat them like royalty. That makes it much more likely that they will tell their friends what a great time they had—how comfortable, fun, and relaxed it was. Best of all, now I can't wait to get to work! Moving to a lower-volume system has made me more excited about my job—and more creative.

Everybody's unique, and you have to treat them that way. That's something you just can't do with a high-volume business model.

Not Overshooting

Another way that I manage my time is by not overshooting during my sessions. It may be "free" to shoot hundreds of digital captures—but there's nothing cheap about the time it takes to upload and cull them. I'm pretty conservative about shooting; I shoot digital just like I shot film, so I don't have vast numbers of images to go through. I shoot efficiently and make sure I get it right the first time.

In total, I shoot around 80–100 images at a typical senior session, depending on the number of outfits they bring. That's it. It's a manageable number of images to edit and still provides plenty of variety for the client to choose from.

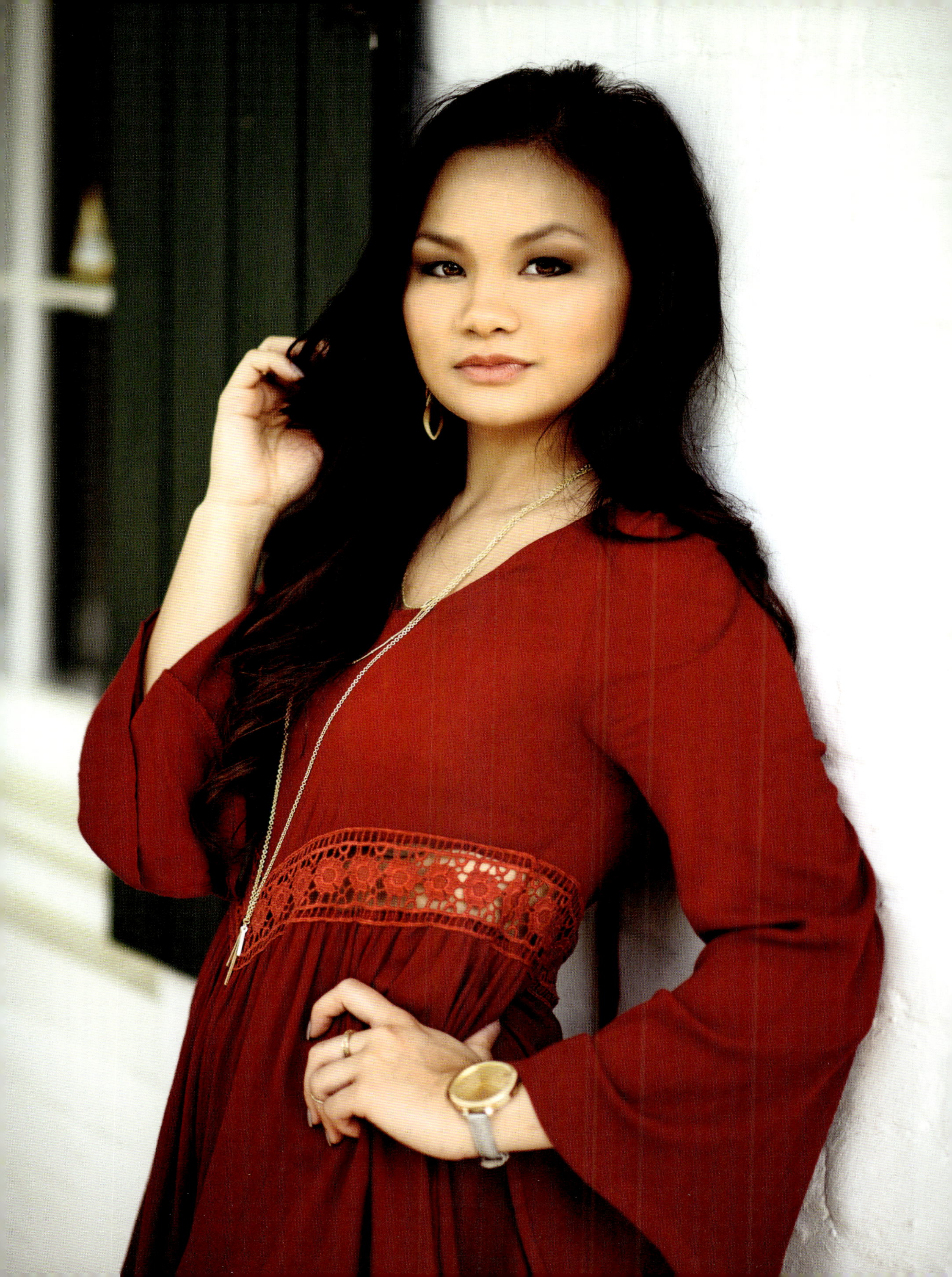

The Times Are (Still) Changing

At the start of this book, I told you about some of the ways my career in the photography industry has changed and developed over the years—and I'm going to conclude in basically the same way. The change is not over. In fact, the professional photography industry is probably changing more rapidly today than ever before.

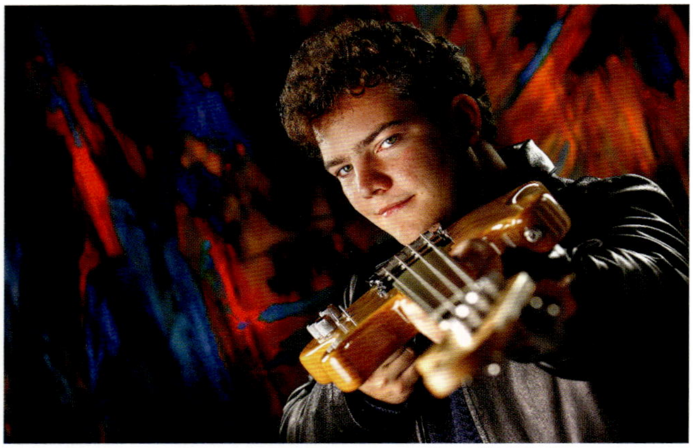

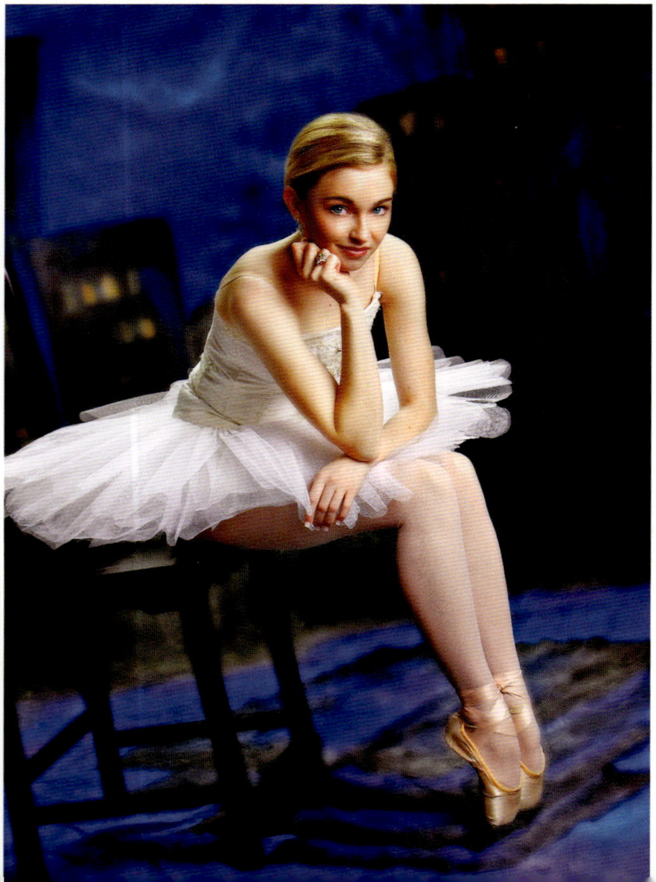

We're seeing established industry leaders struggle to attract clients to studios centered on custom services and print sales. But we're also seeing talented newcomers with file-based ("shoot and burn") delivery systems succumb to the unrelenting demands of a high-volume, low-price approach. No one seems to have the "perfect" answer.

If there's one thing I can say for sure, it's that building a career in photography will continue to require that you adapt and evolve. You can be a phenomenal photographer, but if you can't also roll with all the other changes in the industry (products, marketing, etc.) it won't be enough. In my own business, I'm continuing to actively diversify; seniors remain my focus, but I'm also shooting more families, bridal portraits, maternity images, and other types of sessions. I'm also working harder than ever to find the right marketing niche and keep my name in front of prospective clients.

And I'm happy to say that I still see exuberance and excitement from the people I photograph. As you move forward with your portrait photography, I hope that will be your experience, too!

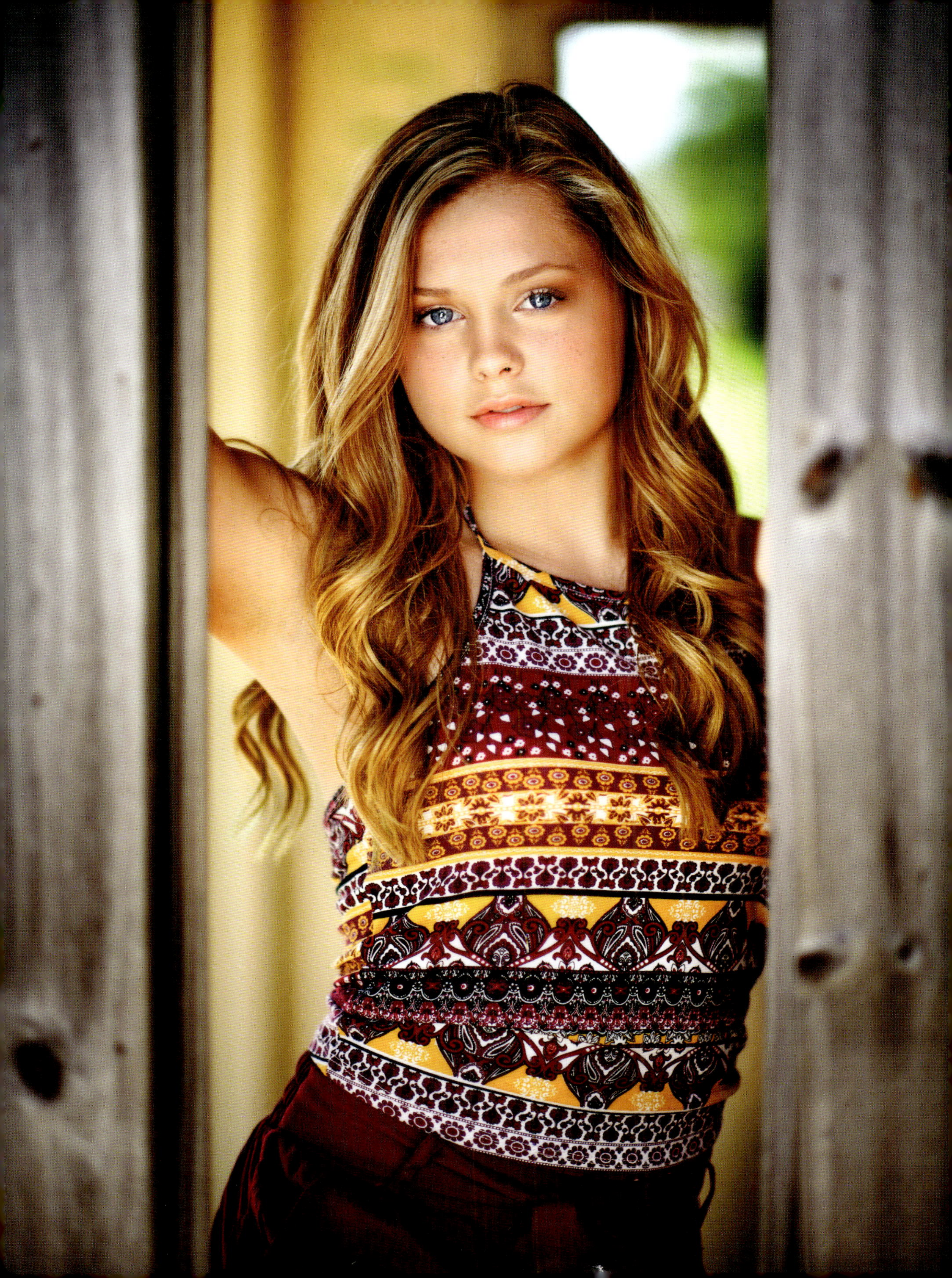

Index

Get smarter from a book!

AmherstMedia.com

- *New books every month*
- *Books on all photography subjects and specialties*
- *Learn from leading experts in every field*
- *Buy with Amazon, Barnes & Noble, and Indiebound links*

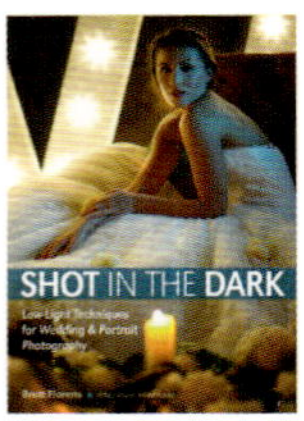

Shot in the Dark

Brett Florens tackles low light photography, showing you how to create amazing portrait and wedding images in challenging conditions. *$37.95 list, 7x10, 128p, 180 color images, index, order no. 2086.*

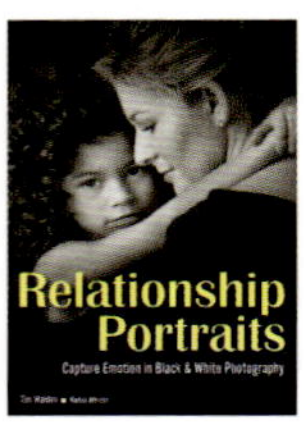

Relationship Portraits

Tim Walden shows you how he infuses his black & white portraits with narrative and emotion, for breath-taking results that will stand the test of time. *$37.95 list, 7x10, 128p, 180 color images, index, order no. 2091.*

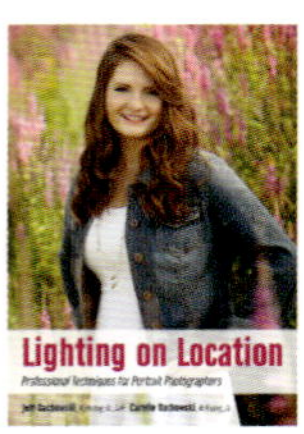

Lighting on Location

Jeff and Carolle Dachowski show you how to find or create beautiful lighting when shooting portraits on location. A practical approach to a tricky subject! *$37.95 list, 7x10, 128p, 220 color images, index, order no. 2082.*

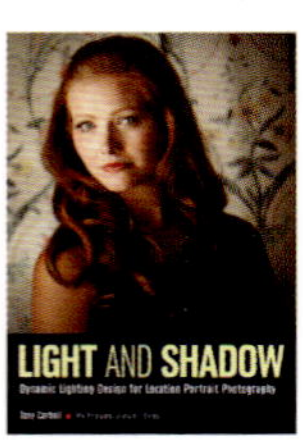

Light and Shadow LIGHTING DESIGN FOR LOCATION PHOTOGRAPHY

Acclaimed photo-educator Tony Corbell shows you the secrets of designing dynamic portrait lighting on location. *$37.95 list, 7x10, 128p, 220 color images, index, order no. 2083.*

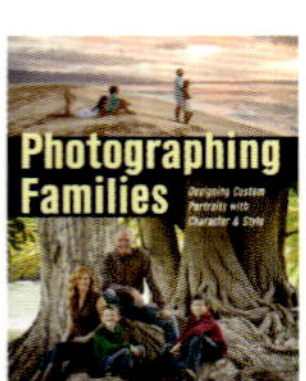

Photographing Families

Elizabeth and Trey Homan are known for their stylish family portraits. In this book, they share the techniques they use to create them. *$34.95 list, 7x10, 128p, 180 color images, order no. 2070.*

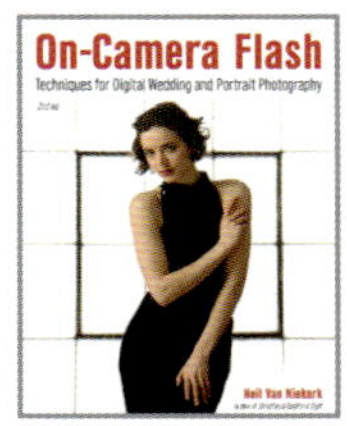

On-Camera Flash FOR WEDDING AND PORTRAIT PHOTOGRAPHY, 2ND ED.

Neil van Niekerk's new edition includes updated ideas for great on-camera flash lighting—anywhere. *$34.95 list, 8.5x11, 128p, 220 color images, index, order no. 2071.*

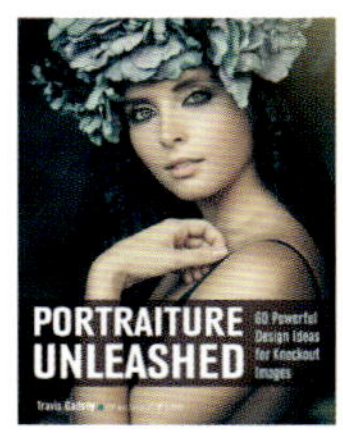

Portraiture Unleashed

Travis Gadsby pushes portraiture in exciting new directions with design concepts that are sure to thrill viewers—and clients! *$34.95 list, 7.5x10, 128p, 200 color images, order no. 2065.*

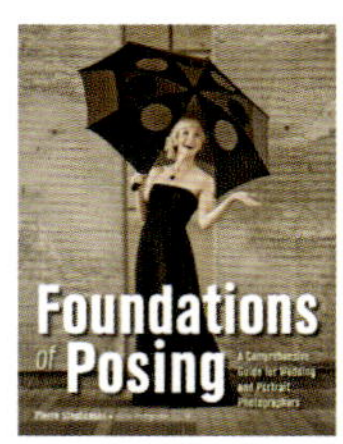

Foundations of Posing

Pierre Stephenson delves into one of the hardest-to-master aspects of photography: designing flattering, visually compelling poses. *$34.95 list, 7x10, 128p, 200 color images, order no. 2068.*

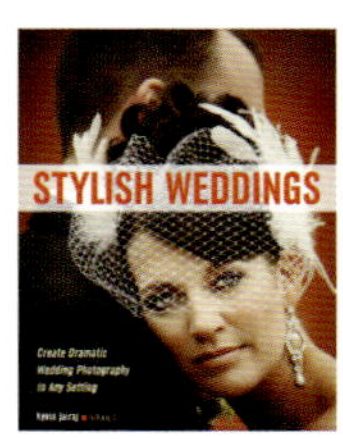

Stylish Weddings

Kevin Jairaj shows you how to create dramatic wedding images in any setting—shots that look like they were ripped from the pages of a magazine! *$34.95 list, 7x10, 128p, 180 color images, index, order no. 2073.*

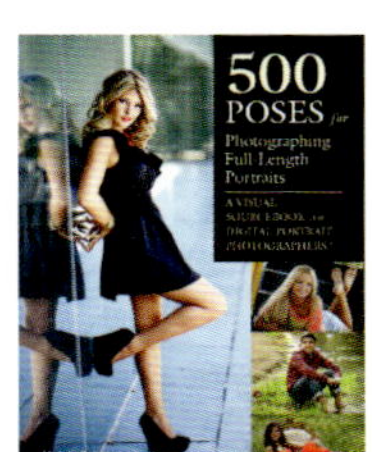

500 Poses for Photographing Full-Length Portraits

Michelle Perkins shares inspiring images to help you conceptualize and deliver the perfect full-body poses. *$34.95 list, 8.5x11, 128p, 500 color images, order no. 2059.*